The Book of
GENESIS

The Book of
GENESIS

Kevin Swanson

ISBN: 978-0-9801910-8-0

Published by
Generations
19039 Plaza Dr., Ste. 210
Parker, Colorado, 80134
www.generations.org

For more information on this and
other titles from Generations,
visit www.generations.org or call 888-389-9080.

CONTENTS

Introduction

. . . .

The Core Curriculum

"And thou shalt teach [my words] diligently unto thy children, and shalt talk of them when thou sittest in thine house, and when thou walkest by the way, and when thou liest down, and when thou risest up."

-Deuteronomy 6:7

The other day I was sitting with my family in the living room enjoying a time of family worship. I glanced at my watch and gasped, "I can't believe we've been sitting around talking about God's Word for an hour and a half! What is the State Department of Education going to say if they find out we spent our day in family devotions and didn't make up the four 'academic contact hours' of homeschooling required by state law?"

Then and there, I had to check my own reaction to what we were doing. What is this thing called "education," anyway? How have we come to think of a father teaching God's Word to his family in an age-integrated context as ineffectual for a legitimate "academic contact hour?" How did we get to the point where discipleship in faith and character was so radically separated from education in "academic" subjects? This is the way most of us have been taught to think about education. The roots of this thinking go very deep—back to the 1100s. It was the scholastics, men like Thomas Aquinas and Duns Scotus who first drew a hard and fast separation between reason and faith, and between "sacred knowledge" and "philosophical knowledge." They submitted some areas of study to faith, and other areas entirely to human reason. Effectively, they held that there were some areas of life on which the Word of God could not speak. Secular education would take care of secular subjects like science, history, and math; and the Bible would address the "spiritual" subjects such as the doctrine of the Trinity and redemption. This thinking worked strongly and effectively to undermine a biblical worldview in the modern world and precipitated the downfall of Christianity in the west.

For this reason, the Book of Genesis was of little use in the science class or the history class. Even though Proverbs is God's textbook on the paideia of a child, it was hardly considered an authoritative source on the subject of education by the colleges that trained teachers, even those colleges that bore a Christian name. Moreover, the fear of God was considered of little use for those studying scientific propositions concerning the existence of God. I know this may be hard to believe, but these truly are the depths to which Christians have gone in their attempts to separate knowledge and faith. They have ignored the basic Biblical principle that every person must fear God before trying to prove His existence. Gaining any knowledge or wisdom in the area of science also requires the fear of God. Without the fear of God, these endeavors will fail. The fear of God is the very beginning of knowledge (Prov. 1:7).

My thesis is this: The Word of God is more than just a constituent of the education of a child. It is the very core of it.

Why Is Reading Important?

When my daughter Abigail turned five years old, she announced to the family that she had two goals for the year—she wanted to learn to ride a bike and to read "God's wood." On December 31st of the same year, I sat down beside her and listened as she read John 1:1, and she did it! For the first time, she read "God's wood"!

So why do we teach our children to read? I would guess that the average parent seeks a good education so as to guarantee their child a good salary and a respectable net worth later in life. But this reason is not important enough for me. Historically, Christians and Jews have had a special commitment to education for one simple reason—God prescribes reading and writing in Deuteronomy 6:7–9! Christians teach their children to read because God insists upon His people reading His Word.

"And you shall teach [my words] diligently unto your children, and shall talk of them when you sit in your house, and when you walk by the way, and when

you lie down, and when you rise up… And you shall write them upon the posts of your house, and on your gates."

–Deuteronomy 6:7–9

Our children need to know the reason for their academics, even when they are learning the basic elements of reading and phonics. As they begin their studies in kindergarten or first grade, we tell them, "We want you to be able to read someday so that you can read the Bible!" Then, as soon as they are able to read, they read the Bible with the rest of us in our daily family devotions. There is no more important or more practical application for the academic exercise of reading for our families, than reading and teaching the Bible.

Martin Luther could see the tragic course that western education systems would take when he wrote, "I am afraid that schools will prove the very gates of hell unless they diligently labor in explaining the Holy Scriptures." And, I am afraid that this is how Harvard, Yale, and Princeton, along with most of K–12 education, became the "very gates of hell" for hundreds of millions of people in the modern world. Most education today simply fails to teach the Bible as the core of its curriculum.

Sadly, even Christians have taken on this bifurcated view of education. A recent study conducted by George Barna found that only three out of ten born-again parents included the salvation of their children in their list of critical parental emphases. And the parents who included a "good education" in their emphases out-numbered those who included "having a meaningful relationship with Jesus Christ" by almost two to one. When asked at a recent homeschooling leadership symposium whether Christian parents have family devotions with their children, Barna answered, "Only one in ten has ever tried it."

It is instructive that the command to teach our children God's Word in Deuteronomy 6 follows the *shema*—the call to love God with all our heart, soul, mind, and strength. When parents do not consider their faith worth conveying to their children, I wonder if these parents possess any faith at all. Parents not willing to teach their children to love God either do not love God themselves, or they do not love their children enough. Loving our children has a lot to do with loving God, and loving God must involve sharing God with our children.

If we provide our children excellent academic instruction in mathematics, science, Latin, and grammar, but neglect to teach them the Psalms, Proverbs, and the book of Genesis with equal diligence and thoroughness, then we have failed in the education of our children.

Certainly, our children should know the themes of most of the Psalms by heart. They should know every Proverb as they know their multiplication and addition tables. By the time they graduate from high school, they should be instantly familiar with every Bible story and illustration—from Jacob's striped sticks in the drinking water to Jephthah's vow in Judges. They should seriously grapple with complex ethical questions, bringing biblical principles to bear on issues such as courtship, debt, fractional reserve banking systems, self defense, education, art, and music. They should have carefully considered some of the most difficult paradoxes in scriptural doctrine (and of course, they should have been duly humbled in the process). These difficult doctrines include the One and the Three of the Trinity, human responsibility and the predestinating sovereignty of God, and the relationship of faith and works. But most importantly, our children should know what it is to cry out the Psalms to God in their prayers, live the Proverbs in their lives, and embrace Jesus Christ as their wonderful Redeemer and King!

This sort of education program comes through thousands of hours of patient, loving discipleship in the Word of God on the part of fathers and mothers as they sit in the house, as they walk by the way, as they rise up, and as they lie down. When families teach their children the Bible using these *Family Bible Study Guides*, they should consider this the core curriculum in their children's education program. Even if a family misses their math, grammar, or science lessons on any given day, they must be careful not to neglect the Deuteronomy 6:7 mandate provided by God Himself, who happens to hold a position higher than the National Secretary of Education.

A careful study of Deuteronomy 6:7–9 would identify several specific directions concerning this discipleship program.

- It must be thorough, covering ALL the commandments (Deut. 6:2; 2 Tim. 3:16, 17).
- It must be daily, diligent, and consistent (Heb. 3:13).
- It is primarily a parental responsibility (Deut. 6:7; Eph. 6:4; 1 Thess. 2:11; Ex. 10:2; and the entire book of Proverbs).
- It must be pervasive and carefully integrated into every area of life (Deut. 6:7,8).
- It includes both prepared lessons (written on the posts of the house) and extemporaneous lessons that are integrated into the everyday experiences of walking by the way or driving in the car (Deut. 6:7,8).
- It is personal, direct, and includes two-way communication. (Deut. 6:20–22).

Daily Family Bible Study

During our family's daily Bible study, I will typically read a chapter of the Bible, explain what it means, and draw an application for the family. We like to include three to six verses from the Proverbs, and then work as a family on memorizing a Psalm or a chapter somewhere in the Bible.

Occasionally, the practice of daily family worship might become overly rigorous, regimented, or rote. This should not happen if the Deuteronomy 6:7-9 principle is thoroughly integrated into the warp and woof of life. It should be part of the life of faith. While it does include some regular, formal discipline of reading the Word, that is not all of it. There is no specific level of formality laid out here. Although there are other Scriptures that encourage regularity. The book of Hebrews, for example, issues a number of warnings to those who neglect these regular disciplines. Hebrews 10:25 warns us against neglecting the assembling of ourselves together as a church body in order to avoid falling into willful sin and thereby subjecting ourselves to the judgment of God. But Hebrews 3:13 calls for daily exhortation, "lest any of you be hardened through the deceitfulness of sin." It may seem a little hard to believe that one of us might be hardened with the deceitfulness of sin within 24 hours of an exhortation, but I can testify that this is possible from personal experience. If we neglect our family worship for only a day or two, our children's hearts begin the calcification process and are less likely to be receptive to godly correction. For most of us, it is inconvenient to schedule a daily Bible study and exhortation with the elders or pastors or deacons of the church. But if we consider our children as part of the body, and if we are living in community with them, it is quite appropriate to exhort them in the familial context every day.

If families placed Deuteronomy 6:7 and Hebrews 3:13 together, I think they would find that the best application of these principles is a daily exhortation within the context of the home. Exhortation literally means "a call to obedience." What we obey is the Word of God. Therefore, a daily exhortation should include some particular truth from the Word of God together with a practical, direct application or encouragement to obedience for those listening. The lessons in this study manual are based on this biblical model.

Implicit in the biblical mandate to exhort is the principle of *life integration.* Without application of the Word in the lives of our children, the truths we teach them will be incomplete. Doing the Word is the capstone, or the completion, of knowledge (Jam. 1:28). If, for example, a father sets out to teach his children Proverbs 6:6–9, he may first explain the text: "Go to the ant, you sluggard!" by describing how the ant needs no supervisor to remind him to do his chores, to study his math, or to weed the garden. The ant is self-motivated, which is an important part of diligence. After this exposition of the text, the father is not done yet. He must still apply the text to his little flock.

"Yesterday," he says, "the wastebasket in the kitchen was overflowing. There were banana peels hanging over the edge and dropping onto the floor. During the course of an hour, I saw three children pass by the garbage can without applying a little self-motivation and diligence to take the trash out of the house." He stops and slowly turns to each little face looking up at him. Then, he says, "I think we have a problem with diligence in this family."

Now, you see, the father has applied the text to his own family. He has revealed the sword of the Word by explaining the text, and then he buries the sword in the hearts of his family members by way of application. He has taken it as far as he can take it for now, but the teaching is not complete until the application takes form in the lives of the family members, which hopefully will include the emptying of a trash can from time to time.

No one is more equipped to apply the Word to their children than the father and mother who know them best and live with them from day to day. Indeed, the most powerful form of evangelism, or discipleship, is God's recommended form. There is no more effective form of discipleship than that which involves a father taking the hand of his son or daughter, and saying, "Let me show you Jesus. Let me show you how to walk in the ways of the Lord by my daily words and living example."

Covenantal faithfulness from generation to generation is God's intended design for His people (Gen. 17:10–12; Deut. 6:7–9, 7:9; Ps. 78:4–6; the book of Proverbs; Is. 59:20–21; Ezek. 37:24–27; Mal. 2:15; Acts 2:38–39; 1 Thess. 2:11; Eph. 6:4). Rebellion should be the exception, not the rule. Sadly, apostasy is the norm in present-day Europe, Canada, and America. As we see by the studies conducted in conservative, evangelical denominations in our country, 80% of Christians' children are leaving the faith. Could it be that we have neglected God's appointed means by which children will carry on the faith of their fathers? Our abandonment of God's designed means, and our displacement of it with other programs devised by men, will in the end produce meager results. Maximize on the means that God has designed and we will be truly blessed. Ignore these means, and the faith will languish over the generations. May God bring about a true reformation that represents a fulfillment of Isaiah's prophecy in our own generation!

"My Spirit which is upon you, and My words which I have put in your mouth, shall not depart from your mouth, nor from the mouth of your offspring, nor from the mouth of your offspring's offspring, says the Lord from now and forever."

–Is. 59:20, 21

Amen.

Using the Study Guide

The basic presupposition used for this study guide is that the book of Genesis is actually the inspired Word of God; and if God speaks to man, He cannot but speak with absolute authority. We take God's Word as truth, and assume the unity of Scripture throughout. Therefore, the primary interpretive tool used in studying the Word is the principle that Scripture interprets Scripture. Moses is the best interpreter of Moses, and our understanding of Moses will help us to understand Paul, and vice versa.

Genesis is the book of beginnings. For those families seeking to give their children an education rooted in the fear of God, here is where they will find: History 101, Economics 101, Ethics 101, Government 101, Worship 101, Marriage 101, and Redemption 101. Without a firm understanding of Genesis, one will find it hard to understand the rest of the Bible, even the ideas and actions of Jesus and the Apostles contained in the New Testament books. To take the New Testament without a foundational knowledge of the Old Testament is somewhat like purchasing the 2012 software updates for a computer program (like Microsoft Office or Quickbooks Accounting program) without first purchasing the basic program. Genesis is foundational.

The book of Genesis is primarily a historical account, containing over one third of the history of the world. Since many world events that would seem important to those who are enamored by the empires of men have been intentionally excluded from the book, we must conclude that these events are not important from God's perspective. What is contained in this book is "the basic info." All of this, of course, assumes that Moses wrote this holy book by the inspiration of the Holy Spirit of God (2 Pet. 1:21).

The following guidelines are suggested for the benefit of the families using this study manual.

1. Obtain a copy of the study guide for each child who can read. Encourage the children to write their own notes in the manual. Children under eight or nine years of age may have a hard time understanding the material contained in these lessons. Younger children are able to comprehend the Bible stories, but sometimes they have a hard time understanding the teaching behind it. Of course, it is never harmful for younger children to be present when material exceeding their ability to understand is being taught. You

never know what children hear and what they will understand. Always aim high in your family worship. By aiming high, you encourage a maturity in the knowledge and discernment of each of the children. Nevertheless, do not neglect the little ones. In our worship, our family includes at least one Bible story written for little ones from the time they are one year old up to six or seven years old.

2. In order that our children learn the major themes and the general flow of the first book of the Bible, each chapter has been assigned a two-word summary. I suggest that the family learn these summaries together. As Dad or Mom asks the question, *"What are the themes of Genesis Chapters 1 through 10?"* The family will together recite the themes from memory:

    "Chapter 1. . . The Creation"
    "Chapter 2. . . The Garden"
    "Chapter 3. . . Man's Fall"
    And so on. . .

    By the end of this study, the whole family should have learned the general overview of the book of Genesis.

3. Establish a regular order to your worship time. I would suggest something like the following—this is the pattern that our family has found most edifying.

    Singing. Open with the singing of hymns, psalms, and simple choruses. This is a good way to call everybody together and get them involved from the outset.

    Scripture. Read the Scripture together. Have each child that can read participate by reading several verses or one verse at a time. We find that if each person reads one verse at a time around the circle, the children are more likely to pay attention for the length of the chapter (or there will be a long pause as it comes around to their turn to read!). You may wish to split the chapter in two, as well as the exposition. Also, since the book of Proverbs is God's basic book for the instruction of a child, I recommend visiting the book of Proverbs for a few verses after the discussion in the book of Genesis.

Memory Work. Have the children recite memory verses or catechism answers they have been learning.

Bible Story. You might take a few moments and have one of the older children read a Bible story to the younger children.

Extra Reading. If you have extra time, I also suggest reading an additional devotional book like *Pilgrim's Progress*, Foxe's *Book of Martyrs*, or another book on church history.

Prayer. Close in Prayer. Tie in aspects of the exhortation in the prayer. You might include confession of family sin, as well as the other elements of the Lord's Prayer. Your church's prayer request list may be put to good use at this time.

4. As much as possible, I recommend that you conduct family worship at least once per day, six times per week. This is the Hebrews 3:13 principle. If you have never to this point established the discipline of a regular family worship time, begin with a small, manageable chunk. Consistency is the priority. If you can maintain a consistent five minute worship time per day, that would be better than thirty minutes, three times per week. At the very least, make sure you have enough time to read the Word, develop at least one application, and pray.

5. Endeavor to retain an enthusiasm for God and a rich enjoyment for the deep truths of His Word during this time. If those leading the worship are not into it, you can bet the others will follow suit. Make this a matter of fervent prayer. It is easy to fall into the trap of losing a sense of the importance of this time in the Word. May God help you to remember that this is your family's life blood. It is as important as bread and water for your physical life. A true disciple of Jesus Christ will come back to Him again and again, crying out, "Where else would we go? Only you have the words of eternal life!"

As we hear God's Word, we must realize that this is God speaking directly to us! This is God speaking to our family. Our relationship with Christ grows as we receive this personal communication from Him. The more personal we take the message, the application, and our prayers, the more intimate our relationship will be with our God.

CHAPTER 1

The Creation

In the beginning God created the heaven and the earth. Gen. 1:1

Summary of Events:

1. God creates the heaven and the earth.
2. While the earth is without form, the Spirit of God moves over the face of the waters.
3. God creates light, the firmament, the seas, the plants, the sea creatures and birds, the land animals, and man in six days.

What does this passage teach us?

Verse 1. The Bible gives us a worldview perspective concerning all of reality, truth, and ethics. From the very first verse in the Bible, we know right away what to believe about reality. What is real? God is real. He was the very first reality. Before anything else came into existence, God was there. Immediately, this raises a strong contradiction to the theory of reality taught by "secular" schools today: that God is *not* a factor in science and history. By summarily ignoring Him, they demonstrate their rejection of God as the first and most important reality. Christians, on the other hand, consider God as the first reality, because that is what they read in the very first verse of the Bible.

At the beginning, there was no space, no time, and no material creation—no sun, moon, and stars. There was nothing but God. Then, God made the universe and filled it with three-dimensional space and raw material. This raw material was ready for what God would do with it in the next few days. God was the One who created the raw materials at the beginning. We know that man makes his houses out of wood and nails, but it is God who made the trees that men form into lumber, and the iron ore from which nails are made.

As human beings set out to learn about their reality, they see this material world and enquire about its origins. But enquire no further! The first verse of the Bible answers this question. God is the source of all things. Look around you. God made all that is material—all that can be seen, felt, smelled, heard, and tasted. He made all things in heaven and in earth, that which is material and immaterial, including angels, human minds and souls, gravity, electrical forces, and magnetism.

Verse 2. After creating the universe by laying out space and matter, we are told that everything was still without form. These raw materials had yet to be shaped into the sun, moon, trees, animals, and man. Apparently, the material creation at this point existed in a liquid mass, described in verse two as water.

Another personality is introduced to us in the second verse. The Holy Spirit moved over the face of the liquid mass. Immediately, we discover that God Who is One consists of multiple Persons. The word "Persons" is a word we can all understand. Persons are those who relate to each other and speak to each other. It is impossible to miss this element of the Godhead in Scripture from the very first chapter to the last. God the Father, God the Son, and God the Spirit relate to each other as distinct Persons. Thus, the mystery of the Christian Trinity appears at the very beginning of divine revelation! In John 1:1-4, the Son of God appears in the Creation story as well. John writes, "All things were made by Him, and without Him was not anything made that was made." Putting this data together, we conclude that the Father, the Son, and the Holy Spirit were all present at the Creation.

Verses 3–25. Beginning in verse three, Moses describes the formation of our world in detail. God began with the creation of light and time on the first day, and then proceeded with the rest of creation over a six day interval. On each day, God did something else to form this mass into a universe appropriate for His highest creation—man. Here is a simple summary of those six days.

Day 1 – Light

Day 2 – Separation of Firmament of Waters Below and Above

Day 3 – Seas, Dry Land, and Plants

Day 4 – Sun, Moon, and Stars

Day 5 – Birds and Fish

Day 6 – Animals and Man

On Day One, God created light. We do not know precisely the source of this light, but we do know that light is a product of chemical reactions like fire, and it is produced by the excitation of electrons in the atom. Prior to the creation of light, the material mass must have been static or without the excitation of these electrons. After the fourth day, the sun became the major light source, but with the first day came the motion of electrons, producing light.

Immediately, God decreed a light period and a dark period of the day. Remember, God was primarily creating this world of time and space for man. Before creating man, capable of work and sleep, He made a day for man to work and sleep in, dividing a period of light from a period of darkness. We recognize these periods to be about twelve hours in length. God called them "day" and "night." To this day, most people refer to them as "day" and "night" as well. While there is some debate among Christians today over the length of the Creation days, the most natural interpretation is a standard twenty-four hour day. The day was made for man, even as the Sabbath was made for man. In any given 24-hour day, we work during a light period of the day, and we sleep during the dark period. God called these periods "evening" and "morning" on the first day of creation, and that is what we call them today! Also, Exodus 20:18 compares our week of seven twenty-four hour days to God's week of Creation, and it would be hard to maintain this comparison without equivocating on the word "day" in that passage.

On Day Two, God put a firmament of water in the atmosphere above the earth, and also left some water on the face of the earth. At this point, water covered the whole earth.

Then, on Day Three, God established the dry land and the ocean(s). This prepared the earth for plants and trees, which He also created on the third day. Some have wondered how these plants and trees could have survived a day without the benefit of the sun, which was created on the next day. Of course, they could have survived a full twenty-four-hour period without a problem, just as plants survive throughout the night without the benefit of the sun. But God could have also provided an ulterior light source for the initial days of Creation.

On Day Four, God put the sun, moon, and stars above the earth, and by His wise, creative power assured that the light from these far-off bodies was visible on the earth, as He prepared the world for His highest creation— man.

On Day Five, He created the birds and the fish, and then on Day Six, He made the rest of the animals. If we reflect that God created sea and air animals inside of a 24-hour period, we must realize that this does not leave room for an evolutionary mechanism. According to humanist evolutionary theories, birds evolved from theropod dinosaurs, which are land animals. But from the biblical record we understand that these dinosaurs did not exist until after the creation of birds and fish, so it is not possible for birds to have evolved from land dinosaurs. While many Christians have worked hard to synthesize Genesis 1 with these evolutionary theories, their efforts have proven futile and even harmful, since they create doubt concerning the veracity and historicity of Scripture.

Verses 26–31. In these final verses, mention is made of the creation of man. Unlike the animals, man is a special creature of God, created in the image of God. This does not mean that a human is exactly like God, but that there are striking similarities. For example, we are created such that we may have a special relationship with God. As God's creatures, and as those adopted back into His family, we are accounted as children of our heavenly Father. Goldfish, dogs, and cats do not enjoy this kind of relationship.

Another reference to the Trinity is found in verse 26: "Let us make man in Our image." Curious clues such as these pull the curtain back a little from this mysterious doctrine that touches on the nature of God the Creator. If it is true that God is One (as He is presented in Scripture), then this use of the first-person, plural pronoun must be a reference to the three Persons of the Godhead.

From this very first chapter in the Bible, we learn the basics of a biblical worldview. As the Creator of all things, God is the source of reality. But He is more than that. In these last few verses, we learn that God is also the source of ethics and law. Immediately after creating man, God initiates an ethical mandate (verses 28-29). When God tells man to do something, He makes an ethical mandate. If God is God indeed, then He must be absolutely authoritative in the area of morality and ethics. To this day, these first commands are binding on mankind. He still wants us to bear children and subdue the earth. Many unbelievers are concerned that the earth is over-crowded, and that God did not make the world large enough to accommodate His command. This manifests a lack of faith in God's wisdom, creativity, and power. Because God commanded it, we have to believe that God made an earth large enough to handle a good number of people and to produce sufficient crops and animals to sustain these people. It is our job to populate the earth by the womb, and to rule over the earth by making good use of the animals, plants, and minerals that God has created. This includes the right ordering of self government, family government, church government, and civil government according to God's laws.

Upon providing these primitive orders for man, God assigned a diet of vegetables to sustain him. Both man and animal were created to be vegetarians. So man was not to eat of the animal kingdom before the fall, for there was no death before the fall.

How does this passage teach us to walk with God in faith and obedience?

1. Each time God created something, He called the creation "good." This is another basic lesson in "ethics" from biblical revelation. If God says that giraffes, maple trees, and oceans are good, then we must agree, because God is the highest authority on what is good and what is evil. It may not come naturally for us to discern what is good and to enjoy it as God's good gift. But we must learn to think God's thoughts after Him, and enjoy the

things He enjoys for the same reasons that He enjoys them. How much do we enjoy God's creation?

2. If God created us, then it is natural that we should obey Him. In fact, it would be ridiculous to rebel against Him! Let us always keep in mind that God is our Creator. This will help us to listen to His Word, believe what He says, and obey Him.

3. We have a responsibility to take care of this world. We do this in different ways. We take care of our bodies by eating good food, or by taking good vitamins and medicine when we need it. We take care of our souls by participating in church and family worship. We take care of the property and the animals God gives us. We also protect property and people from robbers and murderers who destroy. Property is protected when good and righteous civil governments enforce good laws—those laws defined by God Himself.

If we are to be good stewards of God's creation, let's be careful not to waste these resources. Before man fell into sin, God expected men to work and take dominion of the earth. This is no less important today. By faith, we continue to follow God's creation mandate, and we teach our children to do work for the Lord in their generation. We also manage our herds and flocks, such that these animals procreate and produce more food for the years ahead.

Questions:

1. What is the theme of Chapter 1? (Respond out loud as a family. See Appendix A for answers.)
2. What did God create on each of the six days?
3. Why did God create a day?
4. What did God say (towards the end of the chapter) that provides a hint of the doctrine of the Trinity?
5. How did God create man different from the animals?
6. What were the two ethical directives God gave man at the beginning?

7. What did the first men and animals eat?

Family Discussion Questions:

1. What are some of the ways our family engages the dominion mandate? Does our family have a vision for multiplying and filling the earth?

2. When we look at the world around us or when we look at our pets, do we think about the Creator who brought this all about? What does the Creation say about God?

CHAPTER 2

Man Created

And the LORD God formed man of the dust of the ground, and breathed into his nostrils the breath of life; and man became a living soul. Gen. 2:7

Summary of Events:

1. God rests on the seventh day.
2. More specific information is given about the creation of man on the sixth day.
3. God plants the garden of Eden and places Adam in the garden.
4. God gives Adam instructions.
5. God creates Eve from the rib of Adam.

What does this passage teach us?

Verses 1–3. After creating the universe, God rested on the seventh day from His labors. According to the Fourth Commandment (Ex. 20:8ff), God's pattern of work and rest is an example for man, and it remains an example to this day. He sanctified the day and set it apart as a special day of rest. With due respect for the commandment and God's example, we should also work six days and rest the seventh day. This pattern began anew after the resurrection of Christ, in which Monday became our first day of work and Sunday became the seventh day.

Verses 4–7. Beginning in verse four, the manner in which God communicates His revelation changes abruptly, as He introduces Himself as "the Lord God." This is the personal Name for God, couched in His covenantal communication to man. If you were to visit with the President of the country, it is proper that you refer to him as "Mr. President." However, this propriety would not apply to the president's wife or close friends. Most likely, they would use his first name "George," or "Barack." In a similar way, those not in close covenant relationship with God would probably refer to Him as simply "God." Since God is a personal Being, it is appropriate that He bear a name, and His Name is Yahweh. Most modern translations follow the Septuagint (the Greek translation of the New Testament, which was also used by the Apostles) in translating Yahweh as "LORD." Nevertheless, the important thing to note is that here God began to relate to His people in a personal way, by revealing His personal Name, Yahweh, to man. As you continue to read through the Old Testament, you should keep an eye out for uses of the word "Yahweh" or "LORD." This is God relating to man in covenant.

Continuing through the rest of the chapter, Moses addresses the creation of man, the planting of the Garden of Eden, and man's relationship with God, the Creator. Because there was no man prior to the creation of Adam, God planted the garden in preparation for Adam. Up to this point, God has laid out a universe, an earth, and a garden for the benefit of man, and He has appointed man as ruler or vice-regent over His creation.

Now, God made man out of the dust of the earth and breathed into his frame the breath of life. This is the manner of the creation of man, and it stands in direct contradiction to the theory that man evolved from monkeys and amoebas. Of course human beings did not inherit the capacity of breathing from a monkey, a bird, or a fish.

This passage also provides insight into the constitution of a man, the irreducible elements that constitute a human being. At the creation of man, there was dust, and there was whatever God breathed into the man. We refer to these basic constituents as the "body" and the "soul," or that which is material and that which is non-material.

Verses 8–14. As we continue through this next section, we learn more about the character of Yahweh, the Creator of heaven and earth, and Yahweh's relationship with man. First, He planted a special garden for Adam and Eve, a clear demonstration of His love and kindness for these personal creatures that He made in His image. "Eden" means "delight" or "paradise." It was a beautiful garden stocked with everything man needed to live and flourish. Then, God placed two special trees in this garden— the tree of life and the tree of the knowledge of good and evil. They are commonly referred to as "sacramental" trees. As long as Adam continued to eat from the tree of life he would live forever. But if he ate of the tree of the knowledge of good and evil he would die.

Verses 15–20. Upon creating Adam, God connected with him right away by way of verbal communication. Adam was not left to function apart from "special revelation." From the beginning, he understood himself and the world around him through the lens of God's revealed words. Man is not meant to function apart from a relationship with God. He is not alone in the universe. He should rely on God's communication with him, and live according to God's commands. Man's relationship with God is governed by certain "expectations." These come in the form of ethical commands. Adding to the original laws given in the previous chapter, Yahweh provided several more requirements for Adam. First, He commanded Adam to work hard and take good care of the garden. Then, He told Adam to categorize the animals by naming them. And finally, He instructed Adam not to eat of the tree of the knowledge of good and evil, upon the threat or sanction of death.

Verses 21–25. In verse 18, God declared that it was not good for man to be alone. Therefore, in the following verses He proceeded to create a "helpmeet" for him, or a "helper appropriate for him." A woman completes a man when they are married. A man without a woman is like an ax head without a handle. If you have ever tried to chop trees with an ax without a handle, you know that it would take a very long time to cut through a single tree. God knew that man needed a woman to make him effective in the work he was going to do. So He put Adam to sleep and took a rib out of him and created the woman. Adam called her "woman," which means "taken out of man." From this story about Eve being created out of Adam's rib, we find a startlingly vivid picture of God's intention for marriage. God made two human beings out of the one, and then He brought them back together into one in marriage. When a man and a woman are married, they really do become one flesh. True, they are not joined together like conjoined twins: connected at the hip. But the picture is unforgettable. As Adam lost his rib and regained it in the person of another; there is a part of the man in the woman. This is why a man leaves the home of his father and mother and cleaves to his wife, and they are one flesh. If one were to try to separate the two, it would be akin to ripping a rib out of the chest of the other. In marriage, a man and a woman live together, they depend on each other, and take dominion over God's earth as a team.

Before Adam fell into sin, he had no need for clothes because there was no guilt and no sin. Since the fall, however, we are ashamed of our nakedness because it is a constant reminder of our sinful condition and our guilt. While many people are reticent to admit their guilt verbally, the very fact that most people do wear clothes while appearing in public does testify to their guilt before God.

How does this passage teach us to walk with God in faith and obedience?

1. This passage provides the first command in Scripture to work, and to this day God has not suspended this requirement. In fact, throughout the Bible, you will find many reaffirmations of this original mandate. We are warned about the sluggard and sloth in the book of Proverbs, and the Apostle Paul tells the Thessalonians that a man who does not work, should not eat.

2. After working six successive days, we are to take a seventh day as a day of rest from our labors. For twenty-four hours, we should lay aside our normal dominion work. This is also the day when we worship and fellowship with brothers and sisters in the church. Elsewhere in the Scriptures, this rest day is referred to as a "convocation," or a gathering of God's people. This convocation continues into the New Testament church (Lev. 23:3; Heb. 10:25).

3. Divorce is a terrible evil that has eroded the integrity of the family in our country and has produced great misery in the lives of millions. Of course, marriage was never designed to accommodate divorce. This was not God's optimum design for a happy and blessed life. From the beginning, a man and a woman were designed to come together as one flesh in marriage, and there was no original provision for dissolving that unity. If you were to super-glue two pieces of cardboard together, you would create one piece. If you were to try to take them apart, you could not make a clean break of it. The original intention in the action is important, because anybody who

glues two pieces of cardboard together does not intend to separate them, ever again. And that is the way God designed marriage. Divorce is the destructive consequence of sin.

4. As societies progressively descend into paganism, natives shed their clothes and lose their standards of modesty. When missionaries and Christian families appear in these societies (whether they be the South Sea Islands or California beaches), their examples of modest dress will inevitably reveal something of the shame of those who failed to cover their bodies. The purpose of clothes is to cover our bodies. Unfortunately, modern clothing designers are committed to displaying and highlighting certain parts of the body that ought to be hidden. It would be prudent to keep these things in mind when shopping for clothes.

Questions:

1. What are the themes of Chapters 1 through 2?
2. How many special trees did God create in the Garden of Eden? What were they called?
3. What special instruction did God give Adam concerning eating of the tree of the knowledge of good and evil?
4. What were the tasks God assigned to Adam in the garden?
5. What do we mean when we say that a wife is a helpmeet for her husband?
6. Why do we wear clothes?

Family Discussion Questions:

1. How is our family doing with our work ethic? Are we working six days and resting a seventh? Is this rest a joy or is it drudgery to us?
2. What are our standards of modesty? How does this compare to the world around us? Does the world have the same philosophy of clothing as we do?

CHAPTER 3

Man's Fall

And when the woman saw that the tree was good for food, and that it was pleasant to the eyes, and a tree to be desired to make one wise, she took of the fruit thereof, and did eat, and gave also unto her husband with her; and he did eat. Gen. 3:6

Events:

1. The serpent tempts the woman to sin.
2. The woman takes the forbidden fruit and gives it to her husband.
3. They adapt fig leaves for clothing and hide themselves in the garden.
4. God curses the serpent, the woman, and the man.
5. God makes clothes for them and sends them out of the garden.

What does this passage teach us?

This is the book of beginnings, which explains the name given the book. Thankfully, we are not left ignorant of our history and our roots. We need only to look into the book of Genesis for the origins of creation, the origins of sin, and the origins of the first civilizations. Here is where we learn how God relates to man by way of covenant. We also find out about God's will for our lives on earth regarding dominion, child birth, and clothing. Without these important revelations, where would we be?

The third chapter of Genesis explains how sin and evil entered the good world that God created. What makes this chapter so heartbreaking and devastating to each one of us is that Adam was acting as our representative when he sinned. According to Romans 5:1-10, sin fell on all mankind when Adam ate of the forbidden fruit. In a real sense, Adam's sin was our sin. Even as we inherit two eyes, two ears, and two legs from our first father and mother, we also inherit a sinful nature. And this is the very root of all of the evil in the world. This chapter, then, presents our family history. It is extraordinarily relevant to every single person who has been born into the human line.

Make no mistake about it; sin is disobeying God's rules. When we read about this first sin, we are provided with an understanding of what is going on in every disobedient child and evil tyrant in the world. This first sin marks the root of all murder, cruelty, sickness, pain, and death. The Bible tells us that God is not the author or source of sin, so all of the evil in the world can be traced back to sinful rebellion against God the Creator. This rebellion first appeared in Satan and the angels who revolted against God, and then it passed to mankind through Adam and Eve's sin in the garden.

Verses 1–7. The story unfolded when an evil spirit, called Satan, entered the garden and began to tempt the woman. Apparently, evil spirits can enter the physical bodies of animals, as seen later in the Bible when demons possessed some pigs in the land of the Gadarenes (Mark 5:12,13). Evidently, the Devil chose to possess a serpent because of its cunning nature. Further references to the Devil as a serpent appear throughout the Word (as in Rev. 12:9), and pagan symbols often contain the imagery of a snake.

Satan rejected God as the only true God when he offered Eve the opportunity to be a god herself. By definition, a god both knows and determines what is good and evil. Thus far, Satan was correct. Yet, he offered several misconceptions of the truth. First, there can only be one God who both determines and knows what is good and evil for all of us. Second, Satan was denying God's goodness and His ability to determine what was good for man. It is true that Eve would never have had an intimate knowledge of sin if she hadn't actually sinned against God. In a similar sense, you would never know how good (or evil) it might be to stick your hand into a whirring blender unless you were to try it. But is an intimate experience with a blender worth the pain of a mashed-up hand? The Devil was suggesting that an intimate knowledge of sin and the evil consequences of it was a higher good than avoiding sin and evil altogether. He conveniently avoided mentioning how horribly unpleasant it is to stick your hand in a blender.

Well, as it turned out, Eve bought the lie and gave in to the temptation. She assumed that God didn't know anything about blenders, and that He certainly did not know what was best for her. So she put herself in the place of God—as the one who must discern what is good and evil—and she chose to take a bite of the forbidden fruit. In essence, Satan taught Eve to mistrust the Word of God, and Eve failed to believe God. By eating of the tree of the knowledge of good and evil, Eve refused to trust God's Word, His goodness, His wisdom, and His commitment to follow through on His sanctions.

There is one more important lesson to draw from this story of man's first sin. When the Serpent approached Eve, he was turning God's order of creation on its head, for you may remember that God created man to rule over the animals. But Eve took her cues from this animal, a serpent! Then she turned around and directed her husband to eat the fruit. From the beginning, God had intended the man to be the head of the woman (1 Tim. 2:12,13).

Verses 8–13. Instantly, Adam and Eve realized they were naked, and they covered themselves with fig leaves. Then they tried to avoid God's all-seeing eye. Clearly, the loving, trusting relationship with God that had previously flourished was now destroyed. This is the basic psychological problem with every man, woman, and child. It is the problem of guilt. Man may attempt to deny his sin, but he cannot deny his guilt. Imitating the pattern of Adam and Eve in the garden, people continue to deny their guilt by trying to hide from God in a thousand different ways. Very smart men have put together complex philosophical systems and psychological explanations so as to generate doubts concerning God's existence and the reality of guilt. Sometimes men run to opiates like alcohol, drugs, and entertainment so as to avoid thinking about these things.

When God asked Adam to explain his sinful actions, Adam turned around and blamed his wife. Eve turned around and blamed the Serpent. Blame-shifting is another classic response to guilt. This explains a great deal of human behavior everywhere around us, because, by nature, man will do anything and everything to avoid facing his own guilt and sin before God.

Verses 14–19. The Lord God's response to this tragic event revealed both His justice and His mercy. Of course, He followed through on the covenant He made with man at the beginning. One day Adam would face physical death. His body would return to the dust. Interestingly, God also cursed the Serpent, sentencing him to move upon his belly, which must not have been how snakes moved about prior to man's fall. Specifically for Adam, God ordained a hard life of misery and difficulty in his daily labors, something Adam did not experience before the fall. Also, Eve was cursed with added pain in child bearing, along with the challenges she would suffer in submission to a sinful husband in a fallen world. Consequently, the lot of women has never been very good throughout the history of the world. Although humanists have attempted their own "solutions" for this problem with the birth control pill, socialist governments, and no-fault divorce, time will prove these to be false solutions. With 50% of children born out of wedlock, fathers and covenant husbands disappearing, half of marriages ending in divorce, the abortion holocaust marring the consciences of these nations, and political freedoms declining, it is hard to say that humanist solutions have improved things. The woman of the 2020s will be far worse off than her predecessors were in the 1920s. There is only one way to address the curses of the fall, and that is found in Jesus Christ (Eph. 5:20-33).

Upon man's fall into sin, the physical world changed in dramatic ways, such that it would be impossible to understand the pre-fall world based on current scientific paradigms. Environmentally, physiologically, and socially, the entire creation changed form. Completely different biological and physical laws took effect. Recently, certain fields of science such as biology, zoology, and geology have rested strongly on uniformitarian assumptions in order to interpret the past. From a biblical worldview perspective, these are the wrong presuppositions. It wasn't until after the flood that God provided a basis for uniform physical laws (Gen. 8:21, 22), which then became the basis for our scientific work. Life after the fall would be difficult—full of stress, disappointment, pain, misery, and death. Yet God is merciful in judgment, and He included one short but significant and beautiful side note in verse 15, concerning His plan of redemption! Even as He cursed man, Yahweh God pitied these miserable fallen creatures by providing them this little glimmer of hope—the possibility of salvation for those who would believe. "The woman will birth a Child," He said. The Devil would bruise the heel of the Child, but in the end the Child would crush the head of the Devil. This is what some theologians call the proto-evangelium, or the first revelation of the Gospel of Jesus Christ. In fulfillment of this great promise, the child of Eve was the child of Mary. The Lord Jesus Christ was the Son of God Himself, and He crushed the Serpent at the Cross. Some believe in God's solution and some do not, but Christ, the seed of the woman, is the only hope for fallen man.

Verses 20–24. Following God's pronouncement of the promise, Adam named his wife Eve, which means "Living." Without Eve, there would be no more human life on earth and no possibility of the redemption spoken of in verse 15. Before sending them out of the garden, God provided Adam and Eve with more adequate coverings of animal skins. Here is the first record of death in the animal world, and here also is a living picture of blood atonement for our sins. We cannot cover our own guilt by our own sacrifices and our own good works (or our pathetic fig leaves), although today many people still attempt various forms of self-atonement. We must rely on God's sacrifice. From the beginning, God provided a pattern of blood sacrifice. A completely effectual sacrifice came later at the Cross of Christ.

Finally, God sent the couple out of the garden, and placed angels as guards over the tree of life. Apparently, this mysterious tree had sustained physical life for Adam prior to the fall.

How does this passage teach us to walk with God in faith and obedience?

1. The temptation in this passage has been repeated billions of times, and men and women are still taken in by it. By nature, men want to be God. They want to be the one to make up the rules, and they do not want to submit to the definitions contained in God's laws. When our minds and wills are brought into submission by the Holy Spirit of God, we desire more and more to submit to God as our ethical authority (the One who has the right to tell us what to do.) This is why it is important to study the law of God in the Old and New Testaments. This is also why we memorize the Ten Commandments and lovingly submit to God's rule in our lives.

2. Wherever sin and evil predominate in a culture or country, we will usually find God's created order of things being unraveled. Along with Adam, men abdicate their responsibility as heads in their homes, and women rule in family, church, and state. This abdication has produced a great deal of social chaos over the last two hundred years in the western world. Also, environmentalism displaces true dominion work, and men begin to worship and serve the creature rather than the Creator.

3. Have you ever blamed your brothers and sisters for wrong things that you did? Can you honestly face your own sins, and say, "I did that, and I am guilty?" It is only when you can plainly say, "I have sinned and I am guilty before Mom and Dad, and before God," that you are ready to bring your sins to Jesus for forgiveness. If you deny your sins, you will only grow hard in them. Unless you repent and turn to Christ, you will suffer the consequences of eternal death.

4. God's great mercy was evident even as He pronounced His judgment on Adam and Eve. Eyes of faith will scan the text for God's mercy in the midst of His judgment. Do not miss this. Hold to it with everything you are worth. There in the garden, God promised to send His Son Jesus, who would crush the head of the Serpent, and provide a covering for His people through blood sacrifice. According to Colossians 2:15, He accomplished this at the cross. Let us give thanks to God for His provision of marvelous salvation when we were caught in the most desperate of circumstances.

Questions:

1. What are the themes of Chapters 1 through 3?
2. How was the created order turned upside down when man sinned in the garden?
3. What were the three curses that God placed on the serpent, the woman, and the man?
4. What was the great promise tucked away in verse fifteen?
5. What kind of clothes did God provide Adam and Eve? How is this significant?

Family Discussion Questions:

1. Do we willingly confess our sins, or is there a great deal of blame-shifting going on in our family? What does it mean when people are constantly shifting blame to somebody else?

2. Is our family careful to study God's law? Do we really know the laws of God? When was the last time that we made a moral decision based upon the principles of God's Word?

3. In what ways have we actually experienced the effects of the fall in such things as child-bearing and our dominion work?

CHAPTER 4

Cain's Line

And Cain talked with Abel his brother: and it came to pass, when they were in the field, that Cain rose up against Abel his brother, and slew him. Gen. 4:8

Events:

1. Eve gives birth to Cain and Abel.
2. Cain offers an inappropriate sacrifice to Yahweh.
3. Cain murders Abel.
4. God places a curse on Cain, and he becomes a vagabond on the earth.
5. Cain produces generations of children.
6. Eve gives birth to Seth.

What does this passage teach us?

Verses 1–8. After leaving the Garden of Eden, Eve gave birth to two sons, Cain and Abel. In time, Cain became a farmer, raising crops for food, and Abel raised sheep, presumably for wool for clothing. They both presented God with a sacrifice: Cain of his crops, and Abel of the sheep of his herd. But God outright rejected Cain's sacrifice. Cain did not acknowledge that a sinful man who wants to approach God in worship cannot do it apart from blood sacrifice. No mere offering of fruit and vegetables will do. We see that Cain minimized the issues that separate God and man when he offered his unacceptable sacrifice.

Cain took this rejection badly, betraying a strident pride in his own heart. In his angry response, he demonstrated an unwillingness to submit to God's requirements to worship Him on His terms.

It is interesting to note that at the same time as Cain was resisting God's requirements, Yahweh was taking the time to address Cain as a father would speak to a wayward son who is on the brink of total rebellion. In His challenge to Cain, God described sin as "crouching at the door." We can imagine a mountain lion about to gain the victory over an unwary soul. As long as Cain was aware of the sin (or the lion) he might take the preemptive opportunity to jump the lion and kill it. If he were to ignore the beast, it would eventually overcome him and devour him. As the story unfolds, Cain refused to face his sin and the lion consumed him.

Verses 9–15. Among the most serious sins men commit, murder stands out as particularly egregious. The Creator always takes it seriously. He cannot ignore the shedding of innocent blood, and here we witness His absolute commitment to His standard of justice.

God designated the civil magistrate to be His minister to bring vengeance upon those who do evil things (Rom. 13:4). When Cain murdered his brother, there was no civil government in place to address such a crime. Because God never intended for the family to administer the death penalty, He forbade anyone from lifting a hand against the man. It was not until after the Flood that God ordained the office of the civil magistrate and issued the first civil law requiring that all murderers be put to death (Gen. 9:6).

In this case, Yahweh placed His own curse on Cain and sentenced him to the life of a vagabond on the earth. Cain would be both rootless and fruitless. He was to forfeit relationships with family and friends, and even his labors to produce crops would be fraught with more frustration and failure. When farmers plant a field with corn seeds, it is always God who determines whether those seeds yield ten or ten thousand pounds of corn. God is in total control of the increase produced by the labors of men's hands. God made farming more difficult for Adam after the fall, but here He made it even more difficult for Cain.

Verses 16–24. These verses continue to chronicle the line of Cain by listing his sons and grandsons. His family began to build cities, herd cattle, produce music, and work with metals. What makes this chapter important is that it presents the development of the "children of men," which will stand in sharp contrast with the line of the "children of God," the line of Seth in the next chapter (Gen. 5).

As they perpetuated more rebellion against God, the line of Cain built the city of man. This project reached a climax later with the building of the tower of Babel. Both then and now, men without God are driven towards building great empires in defiance of God. Typically, they centralize power with the intent to establish a one-world-government, devoid of Christ's rule. Since Cain built his first city, this has been the passion of the men who run from God.

Consider also the further rebellion of Lamech, Cain's great, great, great grandson. Over a century after God's declaration against Cain, Lamech continued to mock and twist God's Word. Apparently, someone had injured Lamech, so Lamech took vengeance into his own hands and murdered the man who offended him. Then Lamech set himself up as a god over the Creator Himself. He went so far as to taunt God with his own declaration of vengeance, promising to avenge any that should offend him—ten times more than what God would require. This is the genesis of the tyrant, a powerful man who refuses to bind himself to the laws of God and feels no qualms about tyrannizing others by the most severe punitive measures. This is ultimate and radical rebellion against God. We see this today in tyrannical communist and socialist governments that try to take the place of God.

In a further attempt to destroy human relationships and undermine the oneness of covenant marriage, the line of Cain introduced polygamy. With the rejection of his relationships with God and his brothers, Cain built cities of anonymity, gave birth to tyrannical governments, and advocated polygamy. When a man destroys his relationship with God, he usually proceeds to destroy his own relationships as well.

Verses 25–26. After this terrible story of disobedience in Cain's line, the chapter ends with a light of hope—God gave Eve another son, whom they named Seth. It was this line of children that began to call on the name of Yahweh.

How does this passage teach us to walk with God in faith and obedience?

1. In this chapter, Cain asked the question: "Am I my brother's keeper?" He pretended that he was not responsible to love and care for his own brother. By shirking his responsibility to look out for his brother, he denied the mutual accountability and love that should exist in brotherly relationships, both in church and family. Of course, God expected Cain to be his brother's keeper. He expects us to look out for the well-being of our brothers and sisters as well.

2. The life of the vagabond, the wanderer, and the stranger is a cursed life. It is a life void of long-term relationships, accountability, and real community. It is very much the picture of life in the modern city. As men build their cities and wander from community to community and church to church, they gradually give up on maintaining close relationships and accountability. They become increasingly comfortable in their world of anonymity. But let us rather strive to live in good relationships with our families and churches. A heart that constantly seeks to gravitate away from relationship with God and relationship with brothers and sisters is not a heart we should desire.

3. Often men ignore what God requires in worship and they present their own novel forms to Him. With Cain of old, these people are more interested in worship that is pleasing to themselves, than the worship that pleases the God whom they are supposedly worshiping! We must always bring God the worship He desires. Thankfully, the entire Bible presents the will of God concerning the worship of God. The book of Psalms is particularly helpful in this.

4. Murder is a terrible crime. From elsewhere in Scripture, we learn that the shedding of blood defiles a land, and the blood of the innocents cries out to God for His interposition. That is why the civil government must

deal with this wicked crime by putting murderers to death. That is also why abortion, the killing of unborn children, is such a heinous sin in the eyes of God, who has created these little ones in His image.

Questions:

1. What are the themes of Chapters 1 through 4?

2. What was Cain's first sin in this chapter? What was his second sin?

3. Why didn't a civil government deal with Cain's criminal act of murder?

4. What was the curse that God placed on Cain?

5. Which of Cain's relatives considered himself greater than God? How did he express this?

6. Which of Adam's sons began a righteous line?

Family Discussion Questions:

1. To what extent have we lived the life of the "stranger," moving from city to city and state to state, over the years? Do we have well-established roots in our community? Do we seek out accountability, or do we try to avoid developing close relationships?

2. Are we careful to look after each other's spiritual and physical well-being in our family? For example, if you saw your brother stepping into a bear trap, would you intervene? What if your brother was falling into a sinful habit? Would you be able to approach him in a loving way and offer helpful correction? Would you ask for forgiveness and try to reconcile with your brother if you offended him?

CHAPTER 5

Seth's Line

And Adam lived an hundred and thirty years, and begat a son in his own likeness, after his image; and called his name Seth. Gen. 5:3

Events:

1. God creates Adam in His image.
2. God provides Adam another son in his image, whom he names Seth.
3. Seth's line develops through Noah.

What does this passage teach us?

Verses 1–3. This passage reminds us again that Adam did not have an earthly father, nor did he descend from an ape as the evolutionists want to believe. God created man in His own image. The text goes on to say that Adam produced a child in his image. When we look at our children, we can see the imprint of the father in the son. We speak of a little boy having his father's eyes, his father's sense of humor, or his father's sinful nature. This is not to say that the child has removed his father's eyes and put them into his own head. What is intended by such language is merely to point out that a son's eyes are a close copy of his father's. There are features in a son that remind us of his father. In a similar sense, as you look at a man, there should be something about him that reminds you of his Creator.

Verses 4–32. The remainder of the chapter lays out the genealogy of Seth's line. No further mention is made of Cain or any of the other children of Adam. According to verse four, Adam had many other children. After the flood (Genesis 6-8), deleterious environmental conditions greatly affected the human genetic make-up and the immune system, so it was very possible that men and women were enjoying an extraordinarily robust health before the flood. This robustness would have produced longer and more prolific child-bearing years. If you take the ratio of the average lifespan in the pre-diluvian age over the average lifespan today, and multiply it by the average birth rate today (2.43), you get a pre-flood average birth rate of 29 children and 420 grandchildren per family. Life was very different before the flood. It's hard to imagine what it would have been like to keep track of all of those grandchildren and their birthdays! Moreover, Adam would have still been alive when Noah was born, ten generations later, making for billions of relatives! But why does this primeval revelation focus in upon the line of Seth and ignore the rest of Adam's children? Over one thousand years of world history is summarized in this chapter in the form of a single genealogy. Consider that God's revelation is all that is necessary to equip His people (2 Tim. 3:16, 17), and He did not want to include unnecessary, irrelevant, or spurious information. Why then does this revelation boil 1500 years down to a list of names? Well, it is no ordinary list of names. This is the line of the children of God, beginning with Seth, continuing with Enoch, and ending with Noah. God keeps track of His own people. Others died out, and God killed most of them in the flood. In fact, of all the people born before the flood (assuming a birth rate of 29 children per father and mother), 99.94% of them would have died in the flood waters: a total of 33 billion people.

The major difference between the city of God and the city of man becomes obvious when you compare the lines of Cain and Seth. Cain was building cities, establishing power bases, and developing polygamy and power-oriented, family fiefdoms. Meanwhile, Seth was calling upon the name of Yahweh God, and his great, great grandson Enoch was walking with God in relationship. It was clear from the outset that the city of God was more about relationships than building power bases. Interestingly, both Enoch and Lamech were the seventh generation from Adam. At the same time that Lamech was usurping God's prerogatives in defiance of God, Enoch was enjoying a loving, submissive relationship with God.

This genealogy is important because it is the first record of the church, a group of people who, to this day, in the pattern of Seth, "call upon the name of the Lord" (Gen. 4:26; Rom. 10:13; 1 Cor. 1:2). Genealogies like this one are simply lists of the names of fathers who represent households that are considered part of the church of God. We find similar lists later, in the book of Numbers. In the book of Revelation, the Lamb maintains a Book of Life containing those who call upon the name of the Lord.

Noah's father, Lamech, was a man of faith—evidenced in the naming of his son, and in his prophetic declaration:

> *"This same shall comfort us concerning our work and toil of our hands, because of the ground which the Lord has cursed."*

The name "Noah" literally means "to give rest." In his prophetic statement, Lamech referred to the curse that Yahweh placed upon the ground. By faith, he believed that God would one day bring rest to the world through Noah's seed. The salvation that God brings to this world includes more than the human soul. Lamech called for God's mercy on His creation, "which groans and travails together until now" (Rom. 8:21). While much of the world had gone the way of Cain, Lamech still had hope in the promised seed that would crush the Serpent and break the curse God had placed upon the earth after the fall. Lamech's faith was well-founded. As it turned out, Noah was that seed, as the progenitor of the Lord Jesus Christ!

How does this passage teach us to walk with God in faith and obedience?

1. The two lines of Cain and Seth continue to this day. Some people highly prioritize the projects of the city of man, and others highly prioritize the projects of the city of God. Either we will put our relationship with God first, and place high priority on our family and church relationships, or we will put our pursuit of power and money and the construction of the city of man first. Life will feed us tests every day concerning our ultimate commitments. When we receive these tests, we will either structure our lives by God's priorities or by the priorities of sinful "mammon."

2. The Old Testament saints looked forward to God's future plans to save His people from the curse of the fall. Today, we are even more privileged in that we can look back and see clearly what God has done to redeem the world by His Son. They looked forward, but we look backwards. The

hopes of these old saints were fulfilled in Christ. Now, we should rejoice in the completed work of God's redemption in Christ. In a world of sin, misery, and death, Jesus came to give life and blessing. He destroys the power of sin over us, and restores all things in this life and in that which is to come.

Questions:

1. What are the themes of Chapters 1 through 5?

2. What does it mean for a son to be born "in the image of his father?"

3. How was Seth's Line different from Cain's Line?

4. Who were the pre-diluvian men that had some faith in God and in His salvation (according to this scriptural revelation)?

5. Who was the seventh descendant from Adam on Cain's side? What sort of man was he, and what kind of life did he live?

6. Who was the seventh descendant from Adam on Seth's side? What sort of man was he, and what kind of life did he live?

7. What does the name "Noah" mean? How did Lamech manifest faith when he named his son?

Family Discussion Questions:

1. What is the focus of our family? What priorities drive the decisions we make in our lives? Do we put our energies into building relationships and building the city of God, or into breaking relationships and building the city of man?

2. Does our family walk with God as Enoch did? What does walking with God look like? Do we call upon the name of the Lord, as Seth did? What does this mean?

CHAPTER 6

Flood Plans

And, behold, I, even I, do bring a Flood of waters upon the earth, to destroy all flesh, wherein is the breath of life, from under heaven; and every thing that is in the earth shall die. But with thee will I establish my covenant; and thou shalt come into the Ark, thou, and thy sons, and thy wife, and thy sons' wives with thee. Gen. 6:17–18

Events:

1. The sons of God intermarry with the daughters of men.
2. Much violence corrupts the earth.
3. God announces His plans to destroy the earth and to save Noah and his family by means of an ark.
4. Noah builds the ark over a period of 120 years.

What does this passage teach us?

Verses 1–5. This is a mysterious passage, but an important one, because it gives us the conditions of the earth before it was destroyed by the Flood. Interpretations vary widely concerning the marriage of the sons of God to the daughters of men. Some have taken up the far-fetched idea that the "sons of God" who married the daughters of men were angels, but this would not comport with Jesus' statement that angels do not marry nor are given in marriage (Matt. 22:30). Who, then, are these "sons of God?"

From the beginning, God claimed special ownership of the children of the righteous (Ezek. 16:20–21; 1 Cor. 7:14), blessing them with the promise that they would be mighty in the earth (Psalm 112:1–2). Thus, you can see that there is a special grace that attends the descendants of a man who fears God. Regrettably, the children of godly men do not always pursue the interests of the kingdom of God. When the children of godly men cross over to the side of the city of man by adopting its ideas and lifestyles, or by marrying its daughters, they take the remnants of God's blessing with them. This synthesis of the godly with the unbelieving is deadly, because the strength of that godly heritage is used for foul ends. When this happened before the flood, the world was cursed with the Nephalim, evil men with access to the power and character that could bring about much destruction on the earth. The Hebrew word "Nephalim" may be translated "giant" or "tyrant." Because these men were powerful, violent, and infamous, we must conclude that they were more than physical giants. They were men who were able to centralize power in order to tyrannize vast numbers of people. It is possible that they created a one-world government or established very large empires whereby thousands or millions were exterminated. We do know that God destroyed the world because of the sheer magnitude of violence in the earth, brought about by the Nephalim.

Recent world events are reminiscent of this early precedent. During the 20th century, modern governments murdered somewhere around 200 million of their own populations. Of the evil tyrants of the last century, Adolf Hitler stands out as one of the worst, and Frederich Neitzche, the son of a Lutheran pastor, was the philosopher who most influenced him. Josef Stalin was another tyrant of the 21st century. Despite his mother's intentions to raise him to the priesthood in the Orthodox Church, he became a strident atheist and turned into one of the most powerful mass-murderers since the pre-flood Nephalim. Hitler and Stalin represented the last remnants of a Christian Europe, and they demonstrated radical rebellion against the faith in preference for a godless, atheist state. In the antediluvian world, a similar synthesis occurred. As the children of God mixed with the children of the godless, wickedness proliferated. Not only were the thoughts in the hearts of men wicked continually, but they also expressed their sin in destructive ways. This bloodshed and violence before the flood could have easily eclipsed what we have seen in recent centuries.

In this passage, the Lord describes the condition of the world as corrupted, indicating that men had engaged in terribly destructive acts, no doubt including murder, abortion, euthanasia, homosexuality, and mass purges. Shortly after the Flood, Yahweh enacted capital punishment for murder.

Whenever a society allows the shedding of innocent blood without due punishment, it corrupts itself and it will not last long.

Verses 6–7. Here we read that Yahweh repented of having made man on the earth. Some interpret this to mean that God had not expected all of this disobedience, and that it took Him by surprise. Such explanations go beyond the words of the text. Throughout the corpus of Scripture, it is a well-established fact that God knows the future and He is sovereign over all things, including the free actions and evil actions of men (Gen. 50:20, Acts 2:23, Is. 46:11, Dan. 4:35). When studying a text such as this, it is important that we draw a distinction between the purposes of God and the emotions of God. These words "repent" and "grieve" describe a shift in emotional regard concerning the situation at hand. At the same time that God works His sovereign will through the evil events that happen (whether it be the crucifixion of His Son, or any other evil event), He may concurrently feel sadness or anger towards the perpetrators of the dastardly deed. To think of God as if He were an emotionless computer program that controls all things without feeling, is to misconstrue the nature of God. It is true that God purposed to make man and He purposed that man would corrupt himself over time. But He also purposed that He would at some point feel disgust towards the people He had created.

Verses 8–12. In the middle of all of this murder and mayhem, there was one man with whom God did not feel disgust. "Noah found grace in the eyes of the Lord." The text does not say that Noah merited God's favor, or that there was something in Noah that God found attractive. It is true that Noah was the recipient of a godly heritage, and that he had continued to walk with God in faith, as did his father Lamech and his great-grandfather Enoch. In 2 Peter 2:5 we discover that Noah was a preacher of righteousness. He was a man in relationship with God, and Yahweh is tender-hearted towards those who look to Him in fear (Ps. 103:11,17).

Verses 13–22. Yahweh God announced His plans to Noah that He would destroy the earth with a flood. But this was not the end of the story. God was not finished with man yet. His plan of redemption was still in the works. Over 1500 years earlier, He had promised Adam that the seed of the woman would crush the head of the evil serpent. God could not break

His covenants. Before bringing destruction upon the whole earth, Yahweh God confirmed that covenant in the line of Noah (v. 18), and promised to save the man and his family from destruction.

This continued the pattern of God working His grace through a man's family line. This godly line had been preserved through Seth, and now it was continuing into the line of Noah. Later it would branch off into the line of Shem, and then on into Abraham's line. God is gracious to work in our families from generation to generation. How would Noah have felt if he had been saved from this terrible Flood while his wife and children were destroyed? That would have been devastating for him. Because of the covenantal, organic unity that God institutes in a household by marriage, He could hardly avoid being gracious to a man without being gracious to his entire family at the same time. Therefore, the Lord included Noah's entire household in the promise of salvation.

At the end of the chapter, Yahweh provided specific instructions for the building of the Ark. It was a huge boat—450' long x 75' wide x 45' high. We also see God's care for the animal kingdom, in providing a vessel large enough to contain two of each kind of animal. Christian biologists suggest that there would have been no more than 35,000 individual vertebrate animals on the ark (mammals, birds, reptiles, and amphibians). There is no way of knowing how many "species" were capable of inter-breeding prior to the flood, so this is a high-end estimate. If all of these animals were the size of an average animal such as a sheep, they would have filled about 15% of the ark's capacity.

How does this passage teach us to walk with God in faith and obedience?

1. True religion is keeping ourselves unspotted from the world, according to James 1:27. In 2 Corinthians 6:17-19, God calls us to "come out from among them and be separate." This separation has defined true believers since Adam fell in the garden. Some of the sons of God who lived in the pre-Flood earth did not do this, and the results were disastrous. It is critical that our children do not marry unbelievers and that they keep themselves from the world's ungodly ideas and practices.

2. This passage teaches us that God is merciful to those who call upon Him. But it is also a warning to those who turn away from Him. If we refuse to call upon God as faithful members of Seth's line did in ancient times, we will one day be destroyed in hell, even as many were destroyed in the worldwide Flood some 4,500 years ago. If we trust in the Lord and walk with Him according to His Word, seeking His guidance in prayer, He will preserve us from the fires of hell as He preserved Noah and his family from the flood waters. We pray that our whole family will walk with God, and be saved in the Ark of God's Savior, the Lord Jesus Christ.

3. A civil magistrate must deal with the crime of murder, or God will intervene Himself with severe force. Human society simply cannot permit sinful violence and murder whether it comes by anarchy or tyranny. Yet this has become the legacy of the humanist nation-states of our day. Fully one third of the babies conceived in the United States are murdered before they are born. In other humanist nation-states, the percentage is much higher. Moreover, multiple bloody revolutions and socialist purges killed hundreds of millions in the last century. In the face of this mayhem, we must believe (as Noah did) that God simply will not stand by and allow this to continue indefinitely. He is patient. He may wait a few hundred years while the remnant builds a boat. Eventually, He will bring His judgment on individual nation-states that refuse to oppose the murder of innocents.

4. We can learn much from the last verse (v. 22). Upon receiving God's instructions, Noah embarked on a project that may have taken 120 years to accomplish. Without even the slightest prospect of a flood or even of rain, Noah continued to work on the Ark in careful obedience to God. This is the mark of a righteous man. May God help us to obey Him in everything` that He calls us to do!

Questions:

1. What are the themes of Chapters 1 through 6?
2. The sons of God married the daughters of men. What does that mean?
3. Describe the Nephalim.

4. What do we learn about God when we read that He grieved over His creation of man?

5. What did God plan to do in His covenant with man? Who is included in this covenant blessing? Who did God save from the flood waters?

Family Discussion Questions:

1. How much has our family mixed into the world's ideas and lifestyles? Are we committed as a family to make sure our children marry believers? What sorts of associations and life habits might result in children from Christian homes marrying unbelievers?

2. Do we believe that God will save our whole family like He saved Noah's family from the Flood? Does God love our family?

3. Are we willing to obey God even in areas that may seem strange or inconvenient? Would we build an Ark over a period of 120 years without the immediate prospect of rain?

CHAPTER 7

The Flood

And the Flood was forty days upon the earth; and the waters increased, and bare up the Ark, and it was lift up above the earth. Gen. 7:17

Events:

1. Yahweh gives Noah last-minute instructions seven days before the Flood begins.
2. Noah, his family, and all the animals enter the Ark.
3. The water that was stored in the firmament above the earth and under the ground fills the whole earth over a period of forty days.

What does this passage teach us?

Verses 1–4. Seven days before the Flood, God provided Noah with several last minute instructions. First, Noah was to load the ark with two of every unclean animal and seven of every clean animal. Evidently, there must have been some knowledge concerning the differences between clean and unclean animals well before Moses received the law on Sinai. Although the godly were still governed by the vegetarian diet law issued by God at Creation, this was soon to change (Gen. 9:3–4). Until the flood, God's people used the clean animals for sacrifice and presumably for clothing as well. So to guarantee a good supply of these animals for Noah and his descendants, God gave the order to take seven clean animals onto the Ark.

Verses 5–16. Acting in faith, Noah obeyed God's commands. They all entered the Ark, and Yahweh Himself sealed the door. This divine act must have been a great comfort to the family inside, taken as a tender symbol of the Lord's care for His people during the most horrible catastrophe in the history of the world.

Verses 17–24. Just as God had declared, this Flood was a worldwide catastrophe of epic proportions. The waters destroyed billions of men and animals. It was far more devastating than any other cataclysm recorded in the annals of world history. Other catastrophes took down empires such as Rome or Babylon, and city states like Sodom and Gomorrah. But there has never been and never will be another flood or other worldwide cataclysm of this magnitude until the end of the world.

Many professing Christians today reject the idea that the Flood covered the entire globe. But if this flood was limited to a single valley or plain as they would like to believe, then it is doubtful that it would have taken almost an entire year for the waters to abate. Assuming the biblical record is God's truth, why would God provide a 120-year warning and ordain such a radical and unwieldy method of saving the animal population? It would have been much easier for Him to have sent Noah to a land well beyond the immediate area of the flood. The plain reading of this chapter upholds a universal, global flood. It is impossible to read it in any other way.

> *"The waters covered the high hills under the whole heaven... All in whose nostrils was the breath of life, of all that was in the dry land, died. And every living substance was destroyed which was upon the face of the ground... All flesh on the dry land died. All men died and only Noah and his family remained alive."*

Is there any room for equivocation on the universality of the flood in these words? Verse 21 also specifies that all the birds died in the great catastrophe. You would think that some of the birds might have escaped a local flood, particularly since there are birds that can make it across the Atlantic Ocean in 24 hours of continuous flight!

There are also physical geological evidences everywhere around the globe that point to a major cataclysm in the past, a disaster that far exceeds the magnitude of the most severe earthquakes and volcanoes men have witnessed over the last several thousand years. We find billions of dead animals buried in rock layers all over the earth. By scientific observation, we know that fossils form only when there is rapid solidification of sedimentation, and this usually occurs during a catastrophic flood of some kind. If there were huge earthquakes and volcanoes erupting during the flooding, this would contribute to a rapid solidification process. This is precisely what is described in Genesis 7! Moreover, fossilized sea creatures are often found buried in rock layers at the top of the largest mountain ranges in the world. How did these creatures make it to the tops of these mountains? How were they so quickly captured in watery sedimentation and fossilized? It is hard to imagine that these little clams crawled up a mountain to die there in a flash flood of some sort. A worldwide cataclysmic flood is the most obvious explanation for this physical evidence.

Finally, the story of the Flood is imbedded in the history of every ancient culture in the world, including the Babylonian Gilgamesh epic tale (ca. 2000 BC). This story contains so many similarities to the Genesis account that most rational people would conclude that the two writings refer to the same event. According to the Gilgamesh story, the deluge was divinely planned, the impending catastrophe was divinely revealed to the hero of the deluge, the hero was divinely instructed to construct a huge boat, the hero and his family were delivered, birds were sent forth at intervals, the hero worshiped after his deliverance, and the specified duration of the flood also concurs with the biblical account. Do you recognize this story?

The earliest confirmed Chinese orthography dates back to 1200 BC, so it should be no surprise to see references to the worldwide flood in the characters of the Chinese language. The character for "ship" ("chuan") is made up of three sub-characters: the character for the number eight, the character for "people" or "mouth," and the character for "vessel." It comes as no surprise that the memory of the flood is everywhere, though most cultures would never have incorporated the story of Abraham and the children of Israel (or even Christ) into their oral traditions. If the entire world was destroyed by a flood and only eight people survived, it would have been impossible to forget such a remarkable event! Such an experience would have been indelibly recorded in the hearts and minds of Noah and his family for a thousand years or more. That is why this story is so deeply imbedded in the language and folklore of so many ancient cultures.

How does this passage teach us to walk with God in faith and obedience?

1. Whenever we find a fossil of a sea creature somewhere above sea level, we need to remember that God's judgment came to this earth almost 4500 years ago. The world around us rejects the metaphysical idea that God could bring His righteous judgment to our world at any time. That is what makes the worldwide Flood so offensive to the ungodly. They do not like to think that God has an ethical interest in their lives and that He might bring judgment upon them. But we look at a fossil and we fear the God who destroys a world because of the sin of man. The apostle Peter reminds us in 2 Peter 2:9 that God will most certainly punish the unjust at the end of the world, even as He brought a severe judgment upon the ancient world.

2. Let us also remember that God is always merciful, even in His judgment. Just as He prepared the Ark for Noah and his family, He has prepared an Ark for our family in Jesus Christ. Noah believed God, trusting in His plans for the Ark as a means of saving his family from the worldwide Flood. Then Noah obeyed God by building the Ark and taking his family into it. In similar fashion, we believe in God's provision of Jesus Christ as our Savior. People may have laughed at Noah as he entered the ark. They could not believe that God would ever judge the world. After all, it had not rained from the beginning of Creation, and they had never seen the judgment of God demonstrated in a mighty flood before. The world may laugh at us too, as we present Jesus as the only Savior for man. But one day, judgment will come. Once again, all those that believe the Word of God will be saved, and those who refuse to believe will be destroyed in eternal fire.

Questions:

1. What are the themes of Chapters 1 through 7?
2. How many of each clean and unclean animal came onto the Ark? Why did God require more clean animals than unclean animals on the Ark?
3. Who closed the door of the Ark?

4. How does this catastrophe compare with the destruction of Sodom and Gomorrah, or the destruction of Pharaoh's army in the Red Sea?

5. What are the indications from Scripture that this flood covered the whole world?

6. What evidence do we find in geology that might substantiate a worldwide flood?

7. What evidence do we find in various cultures and traditions that might substantiate this worldwide flood?

Family Discussion Questions:

1. How certain is God's presence and God's hand of judgment in your mind? When you pick up a fossil, do you tremble just a little to remember how God destroyed our earth in 4500 BC? Why do you think God's judgment might be something less than real in the minds of men? Why is the reality of God so faint and distant in the consciousness of so many people today?

2. Does our family relate to Noah as he built the Ark? Do we believe in the Ark of God's salvation? Are we in the Ark of God's salvation? How do we know that we are in that Ark?

CHAPTER 8

The Dove

And the dove came in to him in the evening; and, lo, in her mouth was an olive leaf plucked off: so Noah knew that the waters were abated from off the earth. Gen. 8:11

Events:

1. The Flood waters begin to abate.
2. Noah sends a raven and a dove from the Ark to determine whether there is dry land.
3. Noah, his family, and the animals leave the Ark on the mountains of Ararat.
4. Noah offers burnt offerings to Yahweh.

What does this passage teach us?

Verses 1–14. "God remembered Noah." Elsewhere in Scripture we read that God remembered Rachel in her barren condition. He also remembered His covenant with Abraham. What great comfort to know that God remembers His people at all times and in all circumstances. God's people may face severe trials that last a very long time, but we can be assured that God will never forget about us, His people. We are not left to the hands of senseless fate. We are a people in relationship with the true and living God, and He has promised that He will be with us "even unto the end" (Matt. 28:19, 20). Noah's family was the only family left in the world. There they were, floating in a solitary Ark on a watery planet, lost in an enormous universe. But the important thing was that God Himself loved these people, and He would continue to preserve them. God remembered Noah.

God marked the progression of the Flood according to Noah's birthday. This signified the cutting off of the old world and the beginning of the new world, with Noah as the only connection between the old and the new. What follows is the progression of events of the great Flood, taking up a sum total of about 14 months.

(Noah's 600th year) 2/17	:	*The rain fell and the Flood began.*
3/27	:	*The rain stopped and the Flood reached maximum level.*
7/17	:	*The Ark arrived in the Ararat mountain range.*
10/1	:	*The tops of the mountains were seen from the Ark.*
10/10	:	*Noah sent out the raven and dove.*
11/17	:	*Noah sent the dove out again, and it returned with an olive leaf.*
11/24	:	*Noah sent the dove out again. It did not return.*
(Noah's 601st year) 1/1	:	*The waters were dried from the earth.*
2/27	:	*Noah and his family exited the Ark.*

From the calendar of events provided in the text, it is clear that Noah and his family remained in the Ark for a little over a year. The picture of salvation is inescapable. During the worst catastrophe in the history of the world, God saved this family from the imminent destruction that swallowed up the rest of mankind. During those weeks and months in the Ark, Noah and his family trusted in God's promises. They had no other basis for hope, and no other guarantee of safety. They may have been tempted to lose hope in the future. Would plants ever grow again on the earth? Would the planet ever sustain life again? In those darkest moments, they had to trust in God.

Meanwhile, Yahweh did not leave them without some encouragement. On the 270th day, an olive leaf appeared, carried by the dove. It takes weeks, or even months, for a plant to germinate and grow, so when Noah saw the olive leaf, he must have concluded that the waters had abated at least long enough for plants to grow. But, by God's orders, Noah continued to keep the animals with him until there was sufficient food on the earth to sustain them once they left the Ark.

Verses 15–19. Finally, Yahweh gave Noah orders to leave the Ark. Once again, we witness the faith and the patient obedience of this man throughout the entire ordeal. For a full 220 days, the Ark had rested on the mountains of Ararat while the waters continued to abate. Surely the family must have wanted to leave the Ark during the long wait, but Noah patiently held off for God's orders.

Verses 20–22. Immediately upon leaving the Ark, Noah built an altar to Yahweh in order to worship according to the method prescribed in the Old Testament. Although we are not told how many "kinds" of clean animals were on the Ark, it must have been a fairly limited number. These were the last animals alive on the earth. Yet, Noah did not hesitate to take one of each of the clean animals and sacrifice them to the Lord. Godly families have always given their first fruits to God, and Noah is no exception to the rule, even after going through the worst catastrophe in history. Offering sacrifices of prayer and thanksgiving before a meal is basic to a godly family culture, and we see that Noah was showing his family that worship was a priority.

This is only the second reference to animal sacrifice in Scripture, following Abel's sacrifice in Genesis 4. These are early reminders in Scripture that sinful man cannot approach a righteous God except by sacrifice. As the smoke rose from the altar, the burning bodies of the animals produced a sweet odor for Yahweh, and He promised not to curse the earth again in this way.

God's promise to Noah was very important for the future of life on earth. If men were going to take dominion of the earth by building houses, developing technology, and establishing communities, then they would have to rely on this promise. Why would you want to build farms and businesses if the next worldwide flood could wipe you out within five years? Therefore, God assured Noah that this kind of cataclysm would not happen again until the end of the world.

God also promised to regulate the world by giving it seasons, natural cycles, and patterns. This promise provided the regularity in nature that was essential for scientific development in all kinds of technology. The scientific method itself assumes that everything operates according to regular patterns. For example, if scientists have determined that a scientific law is in place today, such as the Second Law of Thermodynamics, we can count on that law holding true tomorrow. We assume that the same cause-and-effect relationships that existed yesterday will continue today and tomorrow. We would never plant seeds unless we trusted in the regularity of nature. If certain seeds germinated in the soil and yielded fruit last year, similar seeds will germinate this year—given the same conditions.

David Hume was one of the most important philosophers of the modern world. His theory of knowledge rested on empiricism and scientific enquiry. By the end of his life, however, he gave way to skepticism, because he could not account for the principle of induction. He could find no basis for the assumption that nature operates according to a principle of regularity.

If I drop ten balls and they fall to the ground today, would they fall to the ground again if I drop them tomorrow? Of course, we believe they would. That is because we believe in the principle of regularity. But unbelieving scientists do not believe in a God who maintains the order of the universe. They have no reason to believe that tomorrow's scientific experiments will yield the same results that they did today. If all unbelieving scientists admitted this inconsistency in their system, they would have to resign from their commissions. They have no basis for assuming that nature operates according to regular patterns. However, we do have a basis for this regularity, and we find it in the promises of God.

How does this passage teach us to walk with God in faith and obedience?

1. Noah trusted in God, and his faith was marked by his obedience to every order that God gave him. How often do you say that you trust in God, but then refuse to do what He tells you to do? While God's orders to us may not be as specific as the orders He gave Noah, we still must look to His Word to direct our thoughts, motives, words, and actions every

single day. By His laws, He governs our interactions with others. He tells us how to think, how we are to do business, how we are to educate our children in God's Word, and how we are to govern in the civil magistrate. All of this is found in all 66 books of the Bible. Our children should be well acquainted with the books of Exodus, Deuteronomy, Proverbs, the Gospels, and the Epistles. Every moment of our day ought to be governed by the imperatives found throughout the Word of God. If we trust in God, we will trust His Word for guidance in our day-to-day activities. Let us obey God even as Noah obeyed Him.

2. God received Noah and promised a respite from judgment because of his animal sacrifice. No one can approach God without sacrifice; this is why we must approach God through the sacrifice of His only begotten Son. Let us give thanks to God that He removes all threats of condemnation on us, because of that once-for-all Sacrifice at the cross!

3. As Christians, we live our lives believing in the promises of God. We do not live in constant fear that a comet will destroy the earth this year or the next. Some may believe that the earth will slow its revolution and begin producing thirty-six-hour days, because they refuse to believe God's promises in Genesis 8:21, 22. If we believe in the truth of these promises and if we trust that God is in absolute control over this world, then we can count on the regularity of natural processes. Our job is to work hard and take dominion of this world. God has promised that we will be blessed as we apply ourselves to our work. That should be enough to keep us from a sense of futility. Of all men on earth, we have the strongest basis for science. Therefore we should produce the best scientific work of all, and do it with strong hope and faith in God.

Questions:

1. What are the themes of Chapters 1 through 8?

2. How long did Noah and his family remain in the Ark?

3. How many times did Noah send out the dove from the Ark?

4. What was the impetus that led Noah and his family to disembark?

5. Give several examples of sacrifices that we present to the Lord.

6. What were the two promises that God gave Noah at the end of the chapter?

Family Discussion Questions:

1. Drop a pen on the floor ten times. What did you observe? Do you believe that this pen will fall to the floor the eleventh time if you drop it again? How can you be sure that this will happen again?

2. How does our family handle trials? Do we patiently obey God through severe, lengthy trials as Noah did so many years ago?

CHAPTER 9

The Rainbow

And I will establish my covenant with you; neither shall all flesh be cut off any more by the waters of a Flood; neither shall there any more be a Flood to destroy the earth. Gen. 9:11

Events:

1. God makes a covenant promise to Noah.
2. Ham sins and Noah curses the line of Canaan.

What does this passage teach us?

Verses 1–4. God's relationship with man is ethical in nature, which means that He institutes His law and expects man's obedience. In accord with His original instructions to Adam and Eve, God also told Noah to "be fruitful and multiply." God loves replication, and He built this into His creation. That is why pine trees are designed to drop literally hundreds of pine cones on the ground—each of them filled with seeds. God wants His world filled with trees and people. This sets itself in sharp contrast with the modern humanists who work very hard to depopulate the earth. In their ill-fated attempts to "save the earth," these social-planners break God's laws and destroy His creation; they do this particularly by their enthusiastic advocacy of abortion and infanticide. When the birth control pill was first introduced in the early 1960s, social planners never thought twice about its abortifacient qualities. How many millions of babies lost their lives somewhere between the fallopian tubes and the uterus in the 1960s, 1970s, and 1980s?

Are we to believe that God's command to Noah has no bearing on the world today, because Margaret Sanger and other liberal humanists placed the future of the world in the hands of the social planners? These are the Nephilim of the the 19th and 20th centuries, and their negative influence on society is indisputable. In point of fact, the birth control pill has brought about the largest worldwide demographic shift since the worldwide flood! Over 80 nations around the world are experiencing birth implosions in the 21st century: a phenomenon which will certainly negatively impact the world economy in years to come. Crucial to a dominion agenda is this desire that families will bear many children who will populate and cultivate the earth. In general, Christians should be far more interested in bearing children and raising them for the kingdom of God than anybody else, because believers are the ones who truly desire to fulfill the will of God in their lives. They trust in God's provision, and they trust in His command—"Be fruitful and multiply!"

Yahweh also revealed several new laws by which man was to be governed. From the beginning, God maintained complete control over man's diet. Because He is God, He may modify what He expects of man according to His own pleasure, and we see this happening with the dietary laws provided in Scripture. In this particular passage, He allowed for the consumption of meat for the first time since creation. Later on, He forbade the consumption of unclean animals, but in the book of Acts, even this restriction was removed.

What about the present day? Does God restrict our eating in any way? Every family ought to conduct their own study of Scripture on this subject. For now, suffice it to say that God forbids the excessive consumption of alcohol (Eph. 5:18), and He continues to disallow the consumption of blood as first revealed in the Mosaic law (Lev. 3:17, 7:26, 17:12, 19:26; Deut. 12:16, 15:23), and affirmed again with the New Testament church in Acts 15:20 and 29. God has the right to tell us what to do. God tells us it would be a sin to drink the blood of an animal. God requires a certain respect for the life of man and animal, and these specific commands are meant to demonstrate that respect. It is interesting that pagan nations, in direct violation of this holy law of God, will often revert to the evil practice of drinking animal blood.

It also appears from this passage that man's relationship with the animal kingdom would be even more strained than it was prior to the Flood.

Verses 5–7. Up to this point in God's revelation to man, there has been no reference to civil government. That is what makes these verses important in the unveiling of God's plan for fallen man. The specific law provided here is the basic civil law concerning the crime of murder. While it is appropriate to kill animals for their meat, human life is to be considered precious. If man or beast sheds man's blood, the justice of God insists upon retribution, blood for blood. Human life is precious and must be protected by such a law, because man was made in the image of God. He will not tolerate the violation of His image. If an artist spent six years of his life working on a masterpiece, he would take great offense indeed, if some malicious vandal tore the masterpiece into a thousand pieces. Should it be any surprise to find God taking great offense at the heartless destruction of His creation, which He made in His own image?

Since God has ultimate authority and since He established the sphere of civil government (Rom. 13:4), then He is the only One that can dictate its purview. From what we can tell from biblical records prior to the flood, the violence and murder that was on the earth was frightening, arbitrary, and extensive. It led to the destruction of that world. So God in His mercy established civil government to maintain social order, especially in this area of violence and murder; and He does so by means of a law requiring capital punishment for the murderer. This single law constitutes the basic foundation of a biblical jurisprudence. If a government fails to administer this law, it undermines its own authority to act as a civil government. This is the most basic civil law for all civil governments on earth.

Verses 8–17. Yahweh God showed His love for Noah and his family by providing them with a covenant promise. Any time that God revealed a promise to men in biblical times, it was a demonstration of His sovereign grace and mercy. In this case, He even included the animals in the promise, a unique element to this particular covenant. His careful planning had preserved the animals in the Ark during the Flood, and given that man was assigned the task to rule over creation, it was appropriate that Noah took the responsibility of carrying out God's wishes in caring for the animals on the Ark. Now, with this covenant after the Flood, Yahweh promised Noah and the animals that He would never destroy the earth again by a Flood until the end of the world. This does not preclude occasional localized disasters in which some cities and countries are consumed by the judgment of God. When the tsunami wave destroyed northern Japan and unleashed a huge nuclear disaster on that country, it was the largest financial loss of any natural disaster since the worldwide flood. Even so, this disaster only affected a small percentage of the land mass on the globe. God promised that the entire earth would not be flooded again, until the end. As a sign that He would preserve the world from such a cataclysm in the future, God placed a rainbow in the sky for a sign and seal of His commitment.

Verses 18–29. This final chapter in the story of Noah is a sad one, a rude reminder that sin made a deep imprint upon the nature of man. First, Noah committed the sin of drunkenness by consuming an excessive amount of wine. This led to Ham shaming his father by looking on his father's nakedness. Although the text does not provide much detail regarding the sin of Ham, it is plain that his action was intentional, disgraceful, and dishonoring. Ham's sin was further exacerbated when he told his brothers about his father's shameful state. The Bible explicitly forbids the shameful uncovering of father or mother in Leviticus 18:7.

Children ought rather to honor their parents, as Shem and Japheth did when they covered their father's nakedness. While the Bible is not very specific on principles modesty in the home, it is important that families thoughtfully consider household rules for interpersonal decorum. Of course, we want to be careful not to separate the heart from the actions. It is not necessarily immoral for a son to see his father undressing or undressed. But hearts that are in the wrong place can shame their loved ones by paying undue notice, by inappropriate contact, or by mockery.

When Noah discovered Ham's dishonoring actions, he cursed Ham's son Canaan. Noah did not extend the curse to all of Ham's sons, as some commentators have suggested. But this curse was still binding upon the children of Canaan, and later this tribe would come to be known for its gross immorality in future generations. They apparently carried on the sinful patterns that were present in the life of Ham. Later, God would send the Israelites into that land to wipe out the descendants of Canaan.

How does this passage teach us to walk with God in faith and obedience?

1. God's covenants include both promises and ethical requirements for those with whom He makes the covenant. The old promises He made to Noah after the flood, and the promises he made to Moses (within the 5th commandment) still hold true today. We can count on God's promise signified by the rainbow, and we can know for certain that He will withhold His judgment until the end of the world. Moreover, the commands given to Noah are also applicable and relevant in our own day. When an animal kills a human being, the animal must be put to death. This law was confirmed again in Exodus 21:28, as part of God's moral and legal requirements for life on earth. This is why we are still bound to kill a dog if it fatally mauls a person.

2. Of all the civil laws given in the Bible and issued in the history of jurisprudence, the most basic and the most important is the law first revealed to Noah—capital punishment for murder. Any country that refuses to properly address the crime of murder is a nation that is destined for God's judgment. That is what makes the abortion problem in America such a major concern for Christians. From what we read in the Bible, there appears to be nothing more displeasing to God than the shedding of innocent blood, but regrettably, the shedding of innocent blood has become common in this country in just the last forty years. God takes these things seriously, even if human civil governments will not. If we learn anything about the nature of God and His demeanor towards nations in His holy revelation, then we should take bold action to oppose the shedding of innocent blood. Whenever we have an opportunity to cast a ballot for our leaders, we are duty bound to vote for leaders that will stand by this covenant and commit to putting murderers to death.

3. Modesty is essential in the home. Because clothing provides a covering for the shame of our nakedness, we should always wear clothes in the presence of our parents, our brothers and sisters, friends, and neighbors. When children are very young they do not understand these things, but it is important that every child learns the importance of modesty in their home during their early years. If you accidentally come upon somebody

who is not fully dressed, show them some respect by turning your eyes away from them. This consideration in clothing is an important difference between pagan societies and Christian societies.

4. The story of Ham's dishonoring behavior and Noah's curse comes across as a little odd in an age where the honor of parents is old-fashioned and awkward. But the fifth commandment is the basic cultural commandment. It is the "first commandment with promise." When children fail to honor their parents, things do not go well with them in the land. Societies and whole civilizations break down. At this seminal stage in the development of human civilization, Ham made a fatal mistake. He planted bad seed, and this did not bode well for his future and the future of his son Canaan. Yet in spite of Ham's dishonor to his father, Shem and Japheth honored their father by carefully covering his shame. Children ought to be careful not to share the sins and shame of their fathers and mothers with others. When you begin to speak of the sins of others in public, it is somewhat like opening up their underwear drawer. It would be better to close the drawer, and move on. This is becomes especially important when it regards the sins of your father and mother.

Questions:

1. What are the themes of Chapters 1 through 9?

2. Every person born on this earth has descended from Noah's three sons. What were the names of Noah's sons?

3. How did man's diet change after the Flood, at least for those who followed the commandments of Yahweh God?

4. What was/were the first civil law(s) that God gave to Noah after the Flood?

5. When you look at a rainbow, it should remind you of the covenant promise God made with Noah. What was that promise?

6. How did Ham's behavior differ from his brothers' in relation to their father?

Family Discussion Questions:

1. How can we be more careful to maintain the principle of modesty in our family? Are there situations where you might turn your head to avoid looking upon somebody's nakedness (e.g. motion pictures, billboards, etc.)?

2. Are we careful to speak honorably of our own fathers and grandfathers? How should we deal with the sins of our fathers?

CHAPTER 10

Noah's Line

Now these are the generations of the sons of Noah, Shem, Ham, and Japheth: and unto them were sons born after the Flood. Gen. 10:1

Events:

1. The sons and grandsons of Japheth are given.
2. The sons and grandsons of Ham are given.
3. The sons and grandsons of Shem are given.

What does this passage teach us?

This is the only recorded history of the early earth. There is no other book or document bearing the names of the fathers of all mankind after the Flood. Of course, other documents from these early days may have existed, but only the Bible has been carefully preserved for thousands of years without any appreciable corruption. This is a wonderful testimony to God's providential care of His revelation.

The Bible is careful to record genealogies from the Old Testament through the New Testament. Of course there must have been thousands of tribes and millions of people that lived in the ancient world who are not included in these lists. But there are some key names recorded in these ancient documents, because they are the special people with whom God chose to focus His attention and love. For some reason, God chose to work with certain fathers and their progeny in the line of Seth, Noah, and Shem. This chapter presents the line of Noah and his three sons. As time goes by, we find God narrowing in on the line of Shem (in exclusion of Japheth and Ham). Then He focuses on Abraham and Isaac (in exclusion of Ishmael), and then Jacob (in exclusion of Esau).

It wasn't long before the immediate descendants of Noah began building communities and cities throughout the Middle East. Sadly, many of them continued the legacy of Cain, and they were far more interested in building cities and empires than worshiping and serving the living God. It is amazing how quickly they forgot about the flood, the judgment of God, and the wonderful salvation He provided Noah and his family!

As the memory of God quickly faded from these tribes, these tribes did not fade from God's knowledge. He continued to record their names in His book. For the succeeding 2,500 years, God would work primarily through the line of the children of Shem (Abraham's children). It shows God's grace that He would include the descendants of Ham and Japheth in these lists. They are included because they are the sons of Noah, God's covenant man. But they are also the ancient fathers of the Europeans, the Africans, and the Asians, many of whom have learned about God's grand salvation plan through the Lord Jesus Christ.

Verses 1–5. The first section of the chapter presents the children of Japheth. Later biblical accounts and extra-biblical records indicate that these people eventually settled in the "lands of the north," which include Europe and parts of Asia.

Verses 6–20. These verses list the descendants of Ham, who mainly settled in Africa. Mizraim, as one of Ham's descendants, is an important character in history, as he became the namesake for the land of Egypt. To this day, the Hebrew or Semitic name for "Egypt" is "Mizraim." Whether this man or one of his children settled in the country we now call Egypt, we do not know. But it is clear that Egypt is among the first and oldest nations in the world. The family of Put settled in the modern nation state of Libya, while Cush and his clan settled in Ethiopia, south of Egypt.

Nimrod, the grandson of Ham, is one of the important fathers in the line of those who opposed God and His people. A father's faith is often revealed by the names he gives his children, and very often these names strongly influence the lives of his children. Our sons and daughters really do live up to their names! With that it mind, think of how Nimrod might have been affected by his name, which meant "We will rebel."

Prior to the Flood there were mighty men and tyrants who accumulated great power and brought about massive violence and destruction on the earth. In verses eight and nine, Moses described this man Nimrod using the very same word for "tyrant" as he used for the wicked "tyrants" or "Nephilim" who lived before the flood (Gen. 6:4). Here again, Nimrod would carry on the horrible tradition of the wicked men who built their kingdoms on centralized power and tyrannical violence before the Flood. While some translations describe Nimrod as "a mighty hunter before Yahweh," it would be better said that Nimrod was "mighty against, or in defiance of Yahweh."

Nimrod's big achievement was the creation of Babel. This was mankind's first major empire following the Flood, an attempt to construct a "one-world government" or "new world order." Ever since man had fallen in the garden, he had been working hard to create the kingdom of man, or what Augustine referred to as "the city of man." Throughout history, we see that the kingdom of God was growing at the same time that men were trying to build their kingdoms without God. This pattern has continued through Babylon, Egypt, Greece, Rome, the Holy Roman Empire, Spain, France, England, and lately, with the European Union and the New World Order.

It was Ham's son Canaan who received the curse from his grandfather Noah, and then settled in the land of Canaan, where his descendants made up the Jebusites, the Amorites, the Girgasites, and the Hivites. Because of their great wickedness, God later destroyed the people of Canaan by the hand of His people, Israel. It is interesting that the line of Ham quickly produced much more rebellion against God as these descendants emulated Ham's rebellious character. Inevitably, the dishonoring of fathers will lead to evil empires and wicked cultures.

Verses 21–32. The final verses in this chapter name the children of Shem, the line from which Abraham, David, and Jesus will come. Most of these tribes settled in the Middle East, including modern day Arabia, Iraq, Armenia, and Turkey.

How does this passage teach us to walk with God in faith and obedience?

1. Genealogies are important because family is important. Revolutionary cultures work hard to cut off the memory of previous generations, divorcing themselves from their fathers and their heritage. Sadly, this marks the time in which we find ourselves. To their shame, many who live in modern cities and empires today cannot name their own great grandfather or great grandmother. May God revive an interest in our heritage! Honoring our heritage is part and parcel of obeying the Fifth Commandment: "Honor your father and mother, that it may go well with you, and that you may live long upon the earth."

2. While men like Nimrod work hard to build a kingdom without reference to God, it is the duty of all Christian families to work to build the kingdom of God. It is possible to build a home and a family, or to work a job, without any interest whatsoever in the kingdom of God. However, what makes the difference between a Christian nation and a wicked empire is the God that we serve. To the extent that we will not worship God and apply His law to our social systems and ethics, we give up on building the kingdom of God in favor of another kingdom. Have we turned ourselves into a god, or do we worship, serve, and obey the God who made heaven and earth? When we set out to build a country (like America), are we building it for the kingdom of God or the kingdom of man? Our families should be "kingdom outposts for Jesus Christ."

Questions:

1. What are the themes of Chapters 1 through 10?
2. Where did the children of Japheth eventually settle?
3. What Hebrew or Semitic word is used for the nation state of Egypt?
4. Which grandson of Ham began to build the city of man in the land of Babylon?
5. From which son of Noah did Abraham and the Jews come?
6. Men have been building two different kingdoms since the time of the Flood. What are they?

Family Discussion Questions:

1. Can you name your great grandfathers and great grandmothers on your father's side? On your mother's side? Why is it important to honor your heritage?

2. What kingdom are we building? Is our family building the kingdom of God or the kingdom of man? How do we do this? What is the difference between the kingdom of God and the kingdom of man?

CHAPTER 11

Shem's Line

These are the generations of Shem: Shem was an hundred years old, and begat Arphaxad two years after the Flood. Gen. 11:10

Events:

1. God puts an end to the building of the tower of Babel.
2. The line of Shem is given.
3. The line of Terah is given.
4. Terah, Abram, and Lot move north out of Ur to a town called Haran.

What does this passage teach us?

Verses 1–4. During the first 2,000 years of world history, man in his fallen state built cities and established power centers, and then used that power to bring about great works of evil. When men wander from God, they seek to turn themselves into a god, and they do this by increasing the power of government and centralizing that power in one office, one city, or one major institution. This was the motivation behind the men who built the tower of Babel. It was simply a continuation of what Cain started and what the powerful tyrants consummated prior to the Flood. The text specifically indicates the motivation of those building the tower—*they wanted to make a name for themselves.* To this day, men still work hard to establish political and cultural systems whereby a few leaders and cultural icons make it to the top and become the "men of renown." Instead of allowing political power and cultural systems to decentralize into smaller villages and regions, these men press for the construction of large cities and centralized power bases. Naturally, it is under these circumstances that citizens are easily controlled, and they begin to seek security in these big governments instead of putting their trust in the living God.

We should also note that these people were disobeying God's command to "fill the earth." It was God's explicit intention that no part of the earth be a barren wasteland. But when men congregate in a few large cities as they did in Babel, they are ignoring this mandate and opening themselves up to the proliferation of wickedness, the anonymity of city life, and the tyranny of government.

Verses 5–9. Yahweh God understood the danger of people congregating in one centralized area. It was this very problem of the powerful Nephilim that brought about so much evil prior to the Flood. Now, man was moving in this direction once more. Concerned that this centralized power base would provide little or no restraint to those who were inclined to performing great, terrible acts of evil, God was pressed to action.

We witness a similar pattern in recent history in the western world. Wherever power bases form in large cities like San Francisco, Detroit, Portland, New Orleans, Chicago, Los Angeles, Denver, New York, Atlanta, Boston, and Washington D.C., the sins of abortion, thievery, and homosexuality predominate. Typically, voters from these cities also elect the most tyrannical leaders to rule over them. When power comes to rest on one man or one centralized government, that government is opened up to unspeakable, bloody purges. This is the legacy of the Roman Caesars, as well as the modern tyrannies established by men like Josef Stalin, Fidel Castro, Kim Il Jung, Pol Pot, and Mao Tse Tung.

God nipped the problem in the bud at Babel by removing one of the important cultural norms that unifies the people of a land—their language. Since they began to favor different languages, they could no longer relate to each other and this initiated the great dispersion—a migration into the far reaches of Europe, Africa, and Asia.

This also established the Babel principle. For the remainder of human history, men have continued to build their empires only to see them collapse. As the Christian philosopher-historian, Francis Schaeffer put it, "Men build their towers so high that they fall down." From Babel, Egypt, Assyria, and Rome in the ancient world, to Spain, France, and England in the modern era, the empires of men grow in force only to dissipate away. Immigrations, imperialist insurgencies, civil wars, internal corruption, cultural diversity, and natural disasters dismantle the towers that men build. Directly following Babel, civilization was reduced to small city states. The same thing happened after the fall of Rome, and it will happen again after the empires of the modern era fade away.

Verses 10–26. These verses give us more specific detail concerning the descendants of Shem, focusing on the line of Abram. This sets the stage for the remainder of the Old Testament, which concerns itself with the children of Abraham. Until the time of Christ, God's kingdom was confined to one family—the family of Abraham, Isaac, and Jacob.

In this early revelation concerning the history of the world, God saw fit to provide the precise number of years that elapsed between the Flood and Abraham's life. Most modern historians and scientists would disagree with this history of man on the earth. But should we trust their dating methods implicitly? Scientists have attempted carbon-14 dating on certain specimens and have found them to be 60,000 years old. But carbon-14 dating assumes certain starting conditions, and it assumes that the carbon 14 - carbon 12 ratio remains constant over the lifespan of the specimen. But this is impossible to establish beyond any doubt. Some scientists even doubt that the ratio is at equilibrium in the present atmosphere! In the final analysis, there is no empirical method by which scientists can verify God's truth. Those who believe in God must believe that He is both truthful and wise in His revelation (and capable of preserving that revelation). He speaks with far more authority and He is far more trustworthy than scientists who employ their historical guesswork and questionable dating methods. Based on these ancient biblical records, the Flood must have happened on or near to the year 2347 BC (or about 4,360 years ago).

Following the Flood, the lifespan of men declined rapidly. Noah lived 950 years, Shem 600 years, and eight generations later, Terah lived only 205 years. This is partly due to the removal of the firmament of the heavens during the Flood. It is thought that the firmament provided a barrier from the sun, without which the human body would deteriorate much more rapidly.

Verses 27–32. The rest of the chapter lays out the line of Terah. He was the father of three sons: Abram, Nahor, and Haran. Leaving Ur of the Chaldees, they moved north to a city called Haran, where Terah died. It is from this place that God called Abram into the land of Canaan.

How does this passage teach us to walk with God in faith and obedience?

1. The early founders of America understood the danger of power consolidated into one government. For example, George Washington warned that, "Government is like fire—a dangerous servant and a cruel master." These men maintained a biblical perspective concerning the nature of man. But that all changed over the 19th century. The American federal government has managed to consolidate almost 30% of the Gross National Income into federal expenditures, up from 2% to 3% during the first fifty years of the Republic. Most of the other modern nation states have also ignored the "Babel principle" that God put in place thousands of years ago. When a government consolidates power, it will always tend to employ that power towards evil and destructive ends. But there are limits to how great God will allow this power to grow. On many occasions throughout history, God has crushed empires and powerful governments for their prideful attempts to centralize power. You can be sure that He will do it again in the future. These proud, modern nation states that have centralized power since the 1850s, beyond anything the ancient world ever achieved, will come to an end as well. The Bible limits the power of the state to no more than 10% of the people's income (1 Samuel 8:15ff). Therefore, God-fearing men will always oppose the efforts of the humanists and the socialists to perpetually increase the power of the state.

2. The only thing that can safely unite the people of the world is the kingdom of Jesus Christ. This is the city of God. If the city of man tries to unite all of the people without Jesus, their efforts will only result in more death and destruction. True unity can never come about by powerful civil governments. Rather, the preaching of the Gospel around the world is the only way that brothers from Africa, Asia, and Europe may safely unite. It is only when we gather to worship the Prince of Peace that peace and love

will prevail upon earth. No other unity is possible without suffering the consequences of great evil and destruction. This is the lesson of Babel.

3. Let us not give way to a desire for power. In humble obedience, we ought to take only that power and authority which God has given us. Sometimes children will assume power that does not belong to them by taking command over their brothers and sisters without permission to do so. This is a usurpation of the authority of parents. Satan's first sin was grabbing for power, and mankind is still powerfully tempted to this sin. Let us humble ourselves before God and cease from seeking power that does not belong to us.

Questions:

1. What are the themes of Chapters 1 through 11?
2. Why did the people of Babel want to build a tower?
3. Why was God concerned about this?
4. Name several dictators who became quite powerful and murdered a great many people.
5. How did God stop the Babel tower project?
6. What is the only safe way to bring about world unity?
7. Who was the father of Abram, and where did he die?

Family Discussion Questions:

1. What are the ways in which we usurp authority that does not belong to us?
2. How can we oppose the centralization of power and the building of tyrannical governments? How might we be unwittingly contributing to the building of stronger power bases for evil men?

CHAPTER 12

Abram Called

So Abram departed, as the LORD had spoken unto him; and Lot went with him: and Abram was seventy and five years old when he departed out of Haran. Gen. 12:4

Events:

1. The Lord tells Abram to move out of Haran.
2. Abram is called to the land of Canaan with Lot and his family.
3. A famine in the land forces Abram to take refuge in the land of Egypt.
4. Abram misleads the Egyptians about his wife, and God judges the Egyptians.

What does this passage teach us?

Verses 1–3. In the previous chapter, we learned that Abram resided in the land of Haran, located about 350 miles northeast of Jerusalem. When we catch up with Abram in Genesis chapter 12, the old man is still childless at 75 years of age.

Nearly 425 years after the flood, God made contact with this man Abram. In similar form to His previous revelations to Adam and Noah, God again provided him with both instructions and promises or sanctions. "You do this, and I will do this," is the pattern of these covenants. So here He instructed Abram to move south to the land of Canaan, promising that He would turn his family into a great nation. He also promised a blessing to those who would bless Abram's family and a curse to those who would oppose him. It was a promise that Yahweh God would act upon right away through Abram's interaction with the Egyptians later in the chapter. He also promised to bless all the nations of the earth through Abram and his seed. Such promises are relevant and precious to those of us who benefit from these blessings, including those of us who are reading this right now! Indeed, we are the ones who have been blessed through this man Abram, and specifically through his Seed, the Lord Jesus Christ. Today, there are Japanese, Sudanese, Brazilians, Samoans, Chinese, Swedes, and saints all around the world who are clearly blessed because of Abram and his Seed.

But why should God choose this man Abram out of all the millions of other families on the earth? This question is answered in Deuteronomy 7:7–8 where the Lord explains that He chose Abram because... He chose to do so. He loved Israel, because He loved Israel. As it turns out, the Bible offers no other basis for God's call on Abram and the generational blessings that followed.

Verses 4–9. We discover right away that Abram was a man of faith because He obeyed God's command and made the move to Canaan. Then, he built an altar and called upon the name of Yahweh. This is exactly the same language used to describe Seth's faith in Genesis 5. When a man calls on God, it is an expression of his utter dependence upon God. As he calls on God, he must believe first that God exists, and that He will reward him with His salvation, and that He will answer these heart-felt prayers. In 1 Corinthians 1:2 and Romans 10:13, Paul describes God's people as those who "call upon the name of the Lord Jesus Christ." Throughout thousands and thousands of years of world history, in both Old and New Testaments, men and women of faith make up the same "exclusive" club of those who "call upon God." When Abram called upon Yahweh, he spoke to Him on familiar terms as a friend would call upon a friend. In the New Testament, we call upon Christ, the Son of God, as our Friend, our Deliverer, and our Refuge in the day of trouble. God is not a friend to everybody. It is only those who approach Him by faith and through sacrifice (as Abram does here), who can properly call Him "a true friend." Of course, our Sacrifice is found in His Son, the Lord Jesus Christ.

The Lord appeared to Abram a second time and promised the land of Canaan to his family. All of these promises are important to us as well. Before Jesus Christ came, there were very few people who had access to the revealed Word of God, or what we call "The Bible," outside of Canaan. But now, the kingdom of Jesus Christ extends well beyond the borders of

Canaan. His people and their influence have spread over every single land mass, and every single institution of man, everywhere around the world. Remember that Jesus is the Seed of Abram, and these promises are fulfilled in Him. Whereas the inheritance of the land was once a tiny sliver on the eastern shores of the Mediterranean Sea, now these promises extend to the entire world (Matt. 5:5; Eph. 6:2–3). According to Jesus, the meek shall inherit more than Canaan. "The meek shall inherit the earth!"

Through Jesus Christ, Abraham's family of faith now spreads over Canaan, Saudi Arabia, Japan, Australia, North America, Greenland, and Antarctica. Obviously, this kingdom is not realized instantly. It takes time for the mustard seed to turn into a tree that expands into every nook and cranny of this world's geographical and institutional territories. At the very least we can say that Abraham and his Seed have blessed millions and millions of people the world over, especially since AD33.

Verses 10–20. During a time of famine and drought in Canaan, Abram took his family down into Egypt for survival. Abram was sensitive to the potential dangers facing his family in Egypt, realizing that where there is no true faith in the living God, there will be a great deal of danger to godly families. This is as true in the big cities today as it was in the ancient Egyptian power center. Abram took several measures to protect his family from these potential dangers, and told the Egyptians that Sarai was his sister—which was partially true. She was his half-sister. But still, he failed to mention the fact that she was also his wife. The text does not further clarify his actions, nor does it provide any statement that would commend or condemn him in this. We must be very careful not to go beyond what the Bible gives us in this ethical scenario. God is the one who defines our ethics and He has the right to draw the lines where He sees fit. What we do know is that Scripture commends Sarai's humble submission to her husband in these untoward circumstances. According to the Apostle Peter, she obeyed her husband without fear in what we would refer to as "the gray area" in ethical decision making. In so doing, this faithful wife set an example for all godly wives (1 Pet. 3:6). In the end, God showed His preferential treatment for His man Abram while in Egypt, and protected his family. This certainly provides a beautiful picture of God's mercy on this man in very challenging circumstances, where his faith may not have been the strongest.

How does this passage teach us to walk with God in faith and obedience?

1. This passage is relevant to every person, Jew or Gentile, who reads the Bible in the 21st century. We are blessed in Abram, because we are part of Abram's family. Of course, many of us are not part of the blood line of Abram, but we are still adopted into the family of Abram. This is the point Paul makes to the Gentiles in Galatians 3:29—"And if ye be Christ's, then are ye Abraham's seed, and heirs according to the promise."

Those who belong to Christ are indeed Abram's children and partake in the promises given to Abram (including the promise of the land). Anyone who has faith in Jesus is a child of Abram and part of Abram's family (Gal. 3:7–9). If we share the faith of Abram, we will receive the promises, the inheritance, and the blessings of Abram. Indeed, we are all part of a great nation called "the kingdom of God." We build this kingdom according to the principles contained in the Word of God.

The kingdom of God was just a fledgling work during the time of Abram, especially in comparison with the great Empires of Egypt and Babylon, but God's kingdom has grown slowly but surely over the last two thousand years. Jesus has already inherited territory *through our family*, in that our home, our property, our businesses, and our ministries are all part of His inheritance. To the extent that we apply biblical principles to every area of our lives, (including our real estate and the businesses that God has given us), we have turned that part of the world into the kingdom of Jesus Christ.

2. We too must be a family of faith, which means that we should both obey God's Word and call upon Him in worship. That is why we participate in family worship, in prayer, and in worship with the saints on the Lord's Day. After 5,000 years, we are still following in the footsteps of Seth and Abram, who called upon the name of Yahweh.

3. Sarai provided a good example of a wife who obeyed her husband in faith, even under difficult and dangerous circumstances. Of course, there

are clear instances in which a wife should obey God rather than her husband, yet when it comes to the gray areas, she should submit to her husband and trust in God to protect her and her family.

Questions:

1. What are the themes of chapters 1 through 12?

2. Where did Abram move to, after living in the city of Haran?

3. How does God bless all the nations of the earth through Abram? Who are those that receive the promise and the blessings of Abram today?

4. God promised the land of Canaan to Abram and his children. How does this promise apply today? Do Abram's children still inherit the land?

5. Why did Abram have to go down to the land of Egypt?

6. What does Peter commend Sarai for in 1 Peter 3:6?

7. What did Abram tell the Egyptians while he and Sarai were in Egypt? What did God do for Abram in the land of Egypt?

Family Discussion Questions:

1. How has our family been blessed because of Abram and his Seed, the Lord Jesus Christ? How have we inherited the earth for Christ and His Kingdom? What resources are we using for the sake of Christ in our family?

2. How has God protected our family despite our weaknesses, lack of wisdom, and sin? Provide one or two examples of God's provision and protection.

CHAPTER 13

Lot Chooses

And Lot lifted up his eyes, and beheld all the plain of Jordan, that it was well watered everywhere, before the LORD destroyed Sodom and Gomorrah, even as the garden of the LORD, like the land of Egypt, as thou comest unto Zoar. Then Lot chose him all the plain of Jordan; and Lot journeyed east: and they separated themselves the one from the other. Gen. 13:10–11

Events:

1. Abram's family returns to Canaan from the land of Egypt.
2. The families of Abram and Lot are forced to separate, and Lot takes the land in the valley, which is populated by the cities of Sodom and Gomorrah.
3. God again promises to give Abram many children and grandchildren, as well as the land of Canaan.
4. Abram is called to the plains of Mamre and builds another altar there.

What does this passage teach us?

Verses 1–4. Abram returned to Canaan with substantial wealth. God had blessed his family greatly while they sojourned in the land of Egypt. For many folks, wealth provides a major distraction and deterrent from faithful service to God (1 Tim. 6:9, 17–18; Jam. 5:1–5). This was not the case for Abram. He was constant in his faith and continued to worship and serve Yahweh in the land of Canaan. After returning from Egypt, he worshiped at the same altar in Bethel that he built years earlier. From the Genesis record, we learn that this was a regular occurrence in Abram's life. In fact, no less than twelve times in the biblical record do we find Abram worshiping God and communicating to Him by way of sacrifice. In this way, Abram sets the example for every godly patriarch who has ever lived. God's men are characterized by one main thing: they worship Yahweh, the true and living God, with their families.

Verses 5–13. By this time, the families of Lot and Abram had gained considerable wealth, and this resulted in conflict between the two households over the grazing land. Again, Abram demonstrated his faith in God and his considerable generosity by giving Lot first dibs in the choice of land. Lot took the land that appeared most fertile down in the Jordan valley, which also happened to be in the vicinity of Sodom and Gomorrah. How often do people place economic well-being above the spiritual well-being of their families! When moving into an area to take advantage of a lucrative job offer, many Christians fail to consider whether the spiritual climate, the quality of churches, or the moral environment of the neighborhood will contribute positively to the health of their families. Then, after living in a spiritual wasteland for twenty years, these men watch their families deteriorate spiritually, while they prosper materially. This is the sad story of Lot and his family, and it has been repeated in the lives of millions of families to this day.

Verses 14–18. In these final verses, Yahweh reminded Abram of the initial covenant promise revealed before he moved his family to Canaan. Abram would be the father of a great number of children, greater than the number of dust particles on the earth. This extraordinary promise must have been quite a challenge of faith, especially for an old man who did not have a single child!

In a very real sense, Abram was alone on the earth. He lived far away from his extended family, and he had no church or fellow believers with whom to worship. Here was one solitary man on the earth walking in relationship with the living God, the Creator of heaven and earth. One day, Abram's family would cover the earth and inherit a land as far as eye can see—a land without boundaries in the earth. This great promise is finally realized in the present age, where millions, if not billions, of people have inherited Abram's faith and are counted as his seed.

How does this passage teach us to walk with God in faith and obedience?

1. Riches can be a major trap for those who are tempted to rely on their wealth rather than trusting in the living God. This is especially true of the average American today. Contemporary men and women see little need to bring God sacrifices of praise and tithes on the first day of the week, because they have little need for God. They have wealth far beyond what it takes to survive. If at any point we begin to put our material comfort and our wealth ahead of worshiping God, then we must repent of it.

2. This passage provides a basis for the institution of private property ownership. In general, families should not share property. God calls each man and his family to take dominion of some area of this earth, whether for the purpose of farming, commercial business or ministry. If God expects each of us to own our own land, buildings, and tools, then it stands to reason that stealing or the forced redistribution of that property is sinful.

3. Abram provided a great example of selflessness and generosity. Truly, "It is more blessed to give than to receive," and nobody ever achieved happiness by living a life of self-centered greed. How often do children and adults alike seek their own comfort first before seeing to the needs of others? Whenever dessert is served, it may be tempting to grab the first piece of cake or the biggest slice of pie. But don't give in to that temptation. Hold back, and see what God will do for you when you serve others first. Greed betrays selfishness in the heart, but it also demonstrates a lack of faith in God to provide what is best. Seek the good of others first, and trust that God will supply your needs. When greed dominates a family, the results are often tragic—as in the case of Lot, who would eventually lose everything in the destruction of Sodom.

4. It is not always easy to believe God's promises. Sometimes we look at the challenging circumstances that test us, and we cannot see how God will turn these things to our good as He promised in Romans 8:28. Again, Abram serves as an example for us, as he trusted God for decades. Let us

not give up on God. He will test our faith and our ability to wait on Him over the years. These are always faith-growing experiences. Although it may not appear that God will or can intervene, we must believe that God will be true to His Word, and He is powerful and wise enough to keep every one of His promises.

Questions:

1. What are the themes of Chapters 1 through 13?

2. How many times did Abram call on the name of Yahweh, as recorded in the book of Genesis?

3. How did Abram show himself to be generous with his nephew Lot?

4. What was the geographical location of the good land that Lot chose for himself? How did this choice work out for Lot later on?

5. What might have made it difficult for Abram to believe God when God told him he would have many children and grandchildren?

Family Discussion Questions:

1. Does our family prioritize the spiritual condition of our home over our economic condition (something that Lot failed to do)? What are the important things to consider before moving into a new area?

2. What are the sorts of things that are testing the faith of our family right now? What challenges to our faith have we encountered in past years?

3. When cake is served for dessert, do you ever reach for the biggest and best piece? If so, why is it so difficult to deny yourself and serve others first?

CHAPTER 14

Lot Captured

And when Abram heard that his brother was taken captive, he armed his trained servants, born in his own house, three hundred and eighteen, and pursued them unto Dan. Gen. 14:14

Events:

1. Four kings make war with the kings of Sodom and Gomorrah and the surrounding areas.
2. Lot and his family are captured.
3. Abram pursues and overcomes the enemy.
4. Melchizedek blesses Abram.

What does this passage teach us?

Verses 1–13. It wasn't long after Lot chose the best land for himself down in the Jordan valley that he found himself in serious trouble. Since the hearts of sinful men are so filled with pride and envy, they always seek to build their empires by war. This was the legacy of the first murderer, Cain. It is carried along in the sinful hearts of men, and the wayward generations of Shem, Ham, and Japheth after the flood. War between nations is inevitable as long as pride and hatred dominate in the hearts of men. Until children cease fighting over who gets the biggest piece of cake, and unless neighbors can work out their differences with humility and long-suffering, the wars of nations will never cease. As it turned out, the city states of Sodom and Gomorrah were also drawn into these wars. They lost a key battle, and the enemy dragged away Lot and his family.

Verses 14–17. This key passage provides the first example of a godly system of government and defense. It is of vital importance to any Christian who might want to address the area of civil government according to God's righteous principles. First of all, Abram covenanted (or confederated) with other leaders in the area. He wasn't controlled by the same imperialist zeal that later consumed men in America and that would fuel the colonialist mercantilism of Spain, France, England, and other European empires. Nor was he so hungry for power that he formed an unwarranted alliance with foreign dignitaries. This lure of foreign power is practically irresistible to sinful men, but Abram was not interested in centralizing power. No God-fearing Christian ever has been interested in this. Christians would rather covenant together by means of a contract or constitution, and carefully limit the bounds of that covenant by written stipulation. This was the original intent of the founders of our American federal republic, until the nation was radically transformed into a single centralized state in the late 19th century. Some of our early founding fathers, like Patrick Henry, argued that the United States Constitution should have begun with the phrase, "We the States," instead of, "We the People." Rather than drawing all of the people under one powerful government, Henry wanted to covenant the states together mainly to provide for a common defense from the powerful European empires. Covenantal thinking always marks the minds of men who think like Christians.

Secondly, Abram engaged in a legitimate defensive form of warfare. Several wicked nations had unlawfully pillaged the cities on the plains and had kidnapped Lot and his family in the process. Though there have been a few exceptions in Christian history, every justly-fought war has been a defensive war as Abraham's war was a defensive war.

If there is something to glean from this passage in respect to Abram's actions against these kings, it is a godly view of violence and war. Clearly, there is allowance for some level of self-defense and family-defense within a biblical system of ethics. When faced with offensive military action, good men will rise to defend family and homeland. Generally, it is the responsibility of the civil magistrate to protect us from invading kings and armies, but when there is no government to defend and protect, it is the responsibility of the head(s) of households to protect their families and relatives from those who would kill, plunder, and steal. The basis for the Second Amendment to the United States Constitution lies here. This passage also gives us biblical approval for keeping and using weapons, such as guns and swords. We also find this topic in the New Testament, when Jesus advised his disciples to have swords for defense (Lk. 22:36).

Verses 18–24. On Abram's victorious return from the battle, two men approached him—a man named Melchizedek, and the king of Sodom. Melchizedek was a mysterious character, though it is clear from this passage and others that he was a true priest of the true God. By His providential, all-wise purposes, the Lord worked in surprising ways with individuals such as Melchizedek and Ruth who came from other tribes besides the line of Abraham. The Lord used Melchizedek as a prefiguring of Jesus Christ. Like Christ, this man served as both a priest and a king in the city of Jerusalem. However, the Old Testament priests were drawn from the line of Levi, and Christ would not have been qualified to serve as a priest, since He was of the tribe of Judah. Yet, Psalm 110:4 and Hebrews 7:17 place Christ's priesthood in the legitimate order of Melchizedek. It is God's prerogative to establish two legitimate orders of priests. According to the book of Hebrews, Christ's supremacy in His person and position was established when the great grandfather of Levi, Abraham, submitted himself to Melchizedek by giving him a tithe of his goods.

Melchizedek also provided hospitality to the men returning from the battle. This is the first reference to hospitality or "love of strangers" in the Bible. We know from this and other Scriptures that hospitality is a way of life for true believers. Regrettably, this practice has been sadly neglected of late, in favor of an institutionalized, commercialized form of hospitality. People seldom open their homes to wayfaring strangers today. Some are even uncomfortable with opening their homes to their own relatives! But hospitality was common for thousands of years among godly families and even among pagans. Hospitality should especially mark the lifestyle of those who lead in New Testament churches (1 Tim. 3:7-8).

Melchizedek blessed Abram in a similar fashion as the Levitical priests blessed the people (Num. 6:23). If these priests are acting as intercessors between God and man, then we must believe that such blessings are effectual and important in the lives of the ones who they bless. The second individual that met Abram upon his return was the pagan king of Sodom, who was obviously advantaged by the recent military victory. Abram's rejection of the offer of material reward from this king is an interesting addition to the story. From Abram's testimony it is clear that his motivation was the glory of God. By lifting his hands to God, he testified that all blessings come from Yahweh in heaven. This marked Abram's perspective throughout his lifetime. In Egypt, he fully expected maximum resistance from Pharaoh, but God forced Pharaoh to bless Abram. Then, Abram offered the first choice of land to Lot, such that nobody could say that Abram had squeezed Lot out of the best land. Nor did Abram want anybody to think that a pagan king had made him rich. By faith, Abram would wait for God to write his paychecks and increase his goods.

How does this passage teach us to walk with God in faith and obedience?

1. "Every good gift comes from above." God gives us our paychecks. If some king or employer sees himself as the ultimate source of our blessings and happiness, we ought to outright reject that notion. Moreover, we should never look at our success as the product of our own hands. Just as Abram did in this passage, let us always give God the glory for any success, power, or riches that we achieve.

2. It is appropriate to raise our sons to defend their families as Abram did in Genesis 14. This is a responsibility God gives every man. Following Abram's lead, Nehemiah also instructed the men of Israel to fight for their wives, sons, and daughters (Neh. 4:14). Also, Psalm 82:3 encourages us to "defend the poor and fatherless: do justice to the afflicted and needy. Deliver the poor and needy: rid them out of the hand of the wicked." This is the duty of all faithful men.

3. Following our father Abram who paid tithes to this priest and king in Jerusalem, we bring our tithes and offerings to Jesus our Priest, after the order of Melchizedek. We accept His sacrifice and His blessing, and we submit ourselves to His kingly rule in all parts of our lives.

Questions:

1. What are the themes of Chapters 1 through 14?

2. What does this passage teach us concerning self defense or family defense? Would the Bible prioritize self-defense or defending the person or property of others?

3. From what city did this mysterious priest and king, Melchizedek, come?

4. Who is the priest that comes from the priestly order of Melchizedek?

5. Why did Abram refuse to take a reward from the King of Sodom?

Family Discussion Questions:

1. What sort of effort have we made, or should we make, to show hospitality to strangers?

2. How are we preparing our sons in our family and church to be faithful in their Nehemiah 4:14 duties?

CHAPTER 15

Covenant Confirmed

In the same day the LORD made a covenant with Abram, saying, Unto thy seed have I given this land, from the river of Egypt unto the great river, the river Euphrates: Gen. 15:18

Events:

1. Abram has a vision and asks God for confirmation of the covenant promises.

2. The covenant is confirmed by the sacrifice of animals.

3. The Lord prophesies the captivity of Israel and their eventual deliverance.

What does this passage teach us?

Verses 1–6. Genesis is a book of firsts, and that is what makes this book so fundamental in the progressive revelation of God to man. As this revelation unfolds, we learn something about God, something about man, and something about God's relationship to man. For the first time in this developing revelation, Abram learned that God was his Savior. Using words like "shield" and "exceeding great reward," Yahweh presented Himself to Abram as his Savior. In the Gospels, the angel announced the coming of a Savior as the One who would "save His people from their sins" (Matt. 1:21). Thus, we are called to trust Jesus, the Son of God, as our Savior, even as Abram was called to trust God as his Savior. There is really very little difference between the Old Testament and the New Testament, except that Abram did not know that this Savior's name would be Jesus, and that He would be born in a manger and die on a cross. But Abram did know the basic fact: God was his Savior.

Since the fall, man has not been able to deny that he has a problem and needs a Savior. But still he makes two mistakes. He defines the problem wrongly and seeks salvation in himself or in some false god, rather than in the only One who is capable to save.

This is the third time that God promised a seed that would produce a huge number of descendants for Abram. This formed another test of faith for Abram, who was still childless, even as an old man. Did Abram waver in faith here, when he pointed out to God that he was still childless? What about when he offered the "helpful" suggestion that perhaps one of his servants could have a child who would carry on the family name and inherit the promises? Even if Abram wavered for a moment, he still received God's correction when Yahweh rejected Abram's suggestion outright and demanded faith on Abram's part. So Abram believed God. There was no more argument, no more doubting, and no more equivocation. Abram believed God. Verse 6 is one of the most important verses in the Old Testament, quoted by the Apostle Paul in the book of Romans. "And he believed in the Lord; and He counted it to him for righteousness."

The way of salvation has not changed since the earliest days. In the New Testament, Paul tells us that we are saved by grace through faith (Eph. 2:1). Abram was also saved by grace through faith. So you see that salvation always belongs to men and women of faith. Although God's promises may have seemed far-fetched to some, Abram believed the words that God spoke to him. He believed in the promises of God. Because of his faith, he was counted a righteous man in the eyes of God. Therefore, you can see from the earliest times that no one is saved or counted among the righteous for performing "X" number of good works. We are considered righteous because we believe the promises of God and are willing to hang our lives on those promises.

Verses 7–11. Abram asked for a confirmation of these covenant promises and Yahweh provided that confirmation by means of a common form used for covenants and contracts in the Middle Eastern countries at that time. Today, men sign written contracts when they come to an agreement of some kind; in ancient times, men cut animals in half and the parties walked between the pieces and thereby confirmed the covenant (Jer. 34:18). In fact, the Hebrew word for covenant is rooted in the word "to cut." Thus, if you understand the nature of these contracts, you know that Abram was only asking God to sign the contract between them. Abram cut three animals in half (a cow, a goat, and a ram), and made a path between the pieces of the dead animals.

This is a mysterious text, introducing a number of interesting questions. Why did Abram drive the birds of prey away? Why was he so concerned that they not feast upon the dead meat? What is the light, and the smoking furnace that passes through the pieces? Comparing Scripture with Scripture, we find that birds of the air sometimes represent the Devil attempting to steal away the Word or the covenant from God's people. Smoke is a reference to God's judgment, and light is a reference to His truth and salvation. The smoke and light represent God Himself. You may remember that the presence of God in the wilderness was signified by a cloud by day, and fire or light by night (Exod.13:21–22).

Verses 12–21. Towards the end of the chapter, Abram received a prophetic vision from the Lord. This time, Yahweh provided him with future insight concerning the next 400 years. Although God had promised the land to Abram's descendants, this promise would not take place immediately. There was to be an interim period of 400 years in which the children of Abram would labor under the affliction of a foreign power. God would orchestrate the events of history to assure that Jacob (Abram's grandson), Joseph, and the rest of the family would make it to Egypt. For several hundred years, they would remain in the land of Egypt as slaves. All of this constituted God's glorious plan for Israel's redemption, the testing in the wilderness, and eventual taking of the Promised Land. Why the four hundred year delay? God had a plan for His people's redemption, and for the judgment on Egypt and Canaan. According to what we read here, the land still had to wait until the corruption of the Canaanites had reached some intolerable limit. Abram learned to wait with patience and faith for the fulfillment of God's promises. We must learn from this that the wait itself is a test of faith. As we trust God's promises, we must also believe that God's plans are never frustrated.

How does this passage teach us to walk with God in faith and obedience?

1. The Bible contains many promises issued by God concerning our salvation. In it, He describes Himself as a Savior, using hundreds of expressions, forms, stories, and examples. The pages of Scripture are filled with promises. Therefore, the questions that face us today are the same as those which faced old Abram: Are we willing to take God at His Word? Do we believe that God is good to fulfill His promises to us? Is He really our Shield and our Savior, as He was for this man Abram, the father of all believers?

2. The Bible tells us that the "meek shall inherit the earth." The fulfillment of God's promise comes in different ways at different times. Abram's faithful seed did inherit the land of Canaan, and his seed of believers now continues to inherit the entire earth, as was promised. We see that millions of believers follow in the footsteps of this father of faith, and when they do, they inherit larger portions of the globe and rule their families and their communities according to the principles contained in the Word of God. Yet we believe, with Abram, that there is a better country and a final consummation of this great promise, which will be ours at the end of time. "For he looked for a city which hath foundations, whose builder and maker is God… But now they desire a better country, that is, an heavenly: wherefore God is not ashamed to be called their God: for He hath prepared for them a city" (Heb. 11:10,16). God is true to His promises. He ratified the promise of the land and the promise of a great posterity of children for Abram. He signed the contract, and we will continue to witness the fulfillment of this promise. In the meantime, it is for us as Abram's children to simply believe the promises of God.

Questions:

1. What are the themes of Chapters 1 through 15?

2. Why was it so hard for Abram to believe God's promises?

3. Did Abram earn his way to God by good works? How was Abram accounted righteous before God?

4. How did God ratify the covenant?

5. The promise of the land was going to be delayed for 400 years. What did God prophesy would happen to Abram's family during those

400 years? Why did God put off the fulfillment of the promise for 400 years?

Family Discussion Questions:

1. What is our basic problem and who is our Savior?

2. Do you believe the promises of God? How do you know that you believe them? How do you know that these promises apply to you?

3. Have you ever had to wait for God to fulfill His promises? Did this serve as a test for your faith? Explain.

CHAPTER 16

Hagar's Son

And the angel of the LORD said unto her, Behold, thou art with child, and shalt bear a son, and shalt call his name Ishmael; because the LORD hath heard thy affliction. Gen. 16:11

Events:

1. Abram takes Hagar as a second wife.

2. Sarai becomes jealous of Hagar when she becomes pregnant.

3. Hagar escapes into the wilderness, where the angel of Yahweh meets her and sends her back to Abram's home.

4. Upon her return to Abram's home, she gives birth to Ishmael.

What does this passage teach us?

Verses 1–6. This is the first recorded instance of polygamy within a righteous line in the history of mankind. As is clear from Genesis 4, Cain's line introduced polygamy through Lamech, who made a great show of his rebellion to God. But now, Abram took this woman Hagar at the suggestion of his wife. To this day, there are still sects and cults that recommend polygamy as an acceptable or preferred lifestyle. Yet from the beginning God never intended three people to form the nucleus of a household. He created one woman for Adam, and the two became one. This was the ideal, established from the beginning. Otherwise, God would have created multiple wives for Adam in paradise.

Polygamy created a pronounced dysfunctionality in family life from the beginning. Although there are no clear, universal prohibitions on polygamy in the Old Testament, the general tenor of Scripture is biased against it. As you consider the stories of the Old Testament through sanctified eyes, you will find the fruits of polygamy as anything but peaceable and righteous

(Jam. 3:18). Right away, jealousy and contention erupted between Hagar and Sarai. Something similar is seen between Hannah and Peniniah, and between Rachel and Leah. Regrettably, the fruits of Abram's polygamy produced thousands of years of contention between the children of Israel and the children of Ishmael. Later, in New Testament revelation, Paul forbids polygamy in the eldership of the church of Christ.

Therefore, this "Plan B" was nothing less than a breach of faith on the part of Abram and Sarai. After ten years of waiting, Abram and Sarai failed to believe that God could actually produce a child in Sarai's aging womb. So they resorted to a half-baked "Plan B," which, as it turned out, was not God's plan for Abram's seed. If this was a breach of faith, then of course it was a sin, by the Apostle Paul's definition of sin in Romans 14:23. "Whatever is not of faith, is sin."

Verses 7–16. Unable to bear Sarai's jealous opposition, Hagar decided to run away from Abram's home. It is instructive that Yahweh was still tender and kind to Abram and his household in spite of their failures. Their faithlessness, jealousy, and contention notwithstanding, God was still good to this home that held to a modicum of faith. Although the Ishmaelites failed to take on the faith of their father Abram, God still visited this people with a temporal blessing of prosperity and power. The modern Arabs trace some of their lineage back to Ishmael. Nevertheless, there were negative consequences that played out towards Isaac's family as a result of Abram's disobedience. The angel prophesied that Ishmael would fight against his brother, and fight he did. To this day, some 3,600 years later, the wars in the Middle East rage on. The animosity between these brothers in the Middle East will only abate when the Gospel of the Lord Jesus Christ penetrates the hearts of both the descendants of Isaac and Ishmael.

How does this passage teach us to walk with God in faith and obedience?

1. Abram failed as the spiritual leader in his home. Of course, a man should listen to the wise counsel of his wife. But in the case at hand, the advice was faithless and Abram failed to discern it. Abram also failed to

take responsibility for Hagar and his child when Sarai drove them out of the home. Thankfully, God intervened. But this is an important lesson to all fathers and to all sons who will be fathers some day. If you will be a father, you will be the spiritual leader in your family, and God holds you responsible for the spiritual condition of your home. Abdicating your responsibility will only result in chaos, contention, and moral failure.

2. So very often when we are in a pinch, or when we are tempted or tried, we look for some way of escape that involves moral compromise. Instead of praying and seeking God's will through His Word and patiently waiting on Him, we want to take the shortest path out of the trial. So in our impatience and lack of faith, we choose our own way and sin against God. Abram's patience was tried for eleven years before he gave in to the ill-fated Plan B. Eventually, God did give him a son, but twenty-five years passed before that happened. Are we willing to go through 25 years of patient waiting through a trial without giving way to sin? God always tests the resilience and intensity of our faith by raising the heat in the furnace of the trial and leaving us there for longer periods of time.

Questions:

1. What are the themes of Chapters 1 through 16?
2. Why did Abram take a second wife?
3. Who was the first man to take two wives?
4. What happened when the Old Testament saints took more than one wife?
5. Can you think of several bad things that ensued as a result of Abram taking a second wife?

Family Discussion Questions:

1. Have we ever gone through a long trial that seemed like it would never end? How did we handle it?
2. How does a father exercise spiritual leadership in his home?

CHAPTER 17

Covenant Sign

And ye shall circumcise the flesh of your foreskin; and it shall be a token of the covenant betwixt Me and you. Gen. 17:11

Events:

1. Yahweh reminds Abram of His covenant with him.
2. Yahweh institutes a sign of the covenant.
3. Abraham circumcises all of the men and boys in his household.

What does this passage teach us?

Verse 1. This passage outlines the covenant which God made with Abram. As the chapter unfolds, you will discover that covenants provide a basis for a relationship. A husband and a wife are in relationship, but what would that relationship be without the marriage vows, the witnesses, and the covenant seals (in the signed covenant and the rings)? Both parties in the marriage enjoy a huge sense of comfort and security knowing that the relationship is bound in a covenant. God's covenant with His people is not much different from this. In this chapter we find that God's covenant stipulates the parties, promises, signs, and requirements. When a contract or an arrangement is sealed with blood, the serious nature of the covenant is confirmed and solidified. Such was the case with the covenant God made with Abram. He sealed it with the blood of beasts in Chapter 15, and here Abram sealed it with the circumcision of the foreskin of his own flesh.

The parties in this contractual arrangement are laid out in verses 1, 2, 4, 9, 10, 11, and 19. Party #1 in the covenant is God Himself. As He introduced Himself in the first verse as "El Shaddai," or "Almighty God," it is clear that Abraham was covenanting with the one and only, sovereign Lord of the

Universe. There is no other god that is supreme over Him. There can only be one God who is all powerful. Because His power is absolute, nobody can thwart His purposes. He most certainly would uphold His end of the contract. The second party in the covenant is mentioned multiple times throughout the passage—God made the covenant with Abram and his seed. It was not just Abram. God was in covenant with a people, not just a person. Thus, we begin to see how God relates to both individuals and to corporate bodies. In the New Testament, we find God relating to a visible church body. The Church of Thessalonica was "in God and in Christ" (2 Thess. 1:1). The candlesticks of Revelation 2 and 3 represented local, visible churches in Asia Minor. It was these churches that were in relationship with Christ Himself.

Verses 2–9. These verses enumerate the expectations placed on Abram in the covenant. He must walk before God's face with sincerity. The word sometimes translated "perfect" is better rendered as "sincerity." To walk before the face of God is to maintain a right relationship with God. It is to love Him and to desire His presence. In each of our relationships in life, we experience times of closeness and times of distance. We may even offend one another from time to time. But it is quite another thing to break a relationship and to cease all fellowship with one another. A relationship is broken when the parties separate and will have nothing more to do with one other. So, according to the stipulations of this covenant, Abram must continue to walk in relationship with God, with sincerity of heart. A similar idea is expressed in 1 John 3:6. "Whosoever abideth in Him sinneth not: whosoever sinneth hath not seen Him, neither known Him." Any whom God has saved will hate their sin. They cannot bear to live with it. When they do sin, they confess and repent of that sin because of their love for God. This is the walk of faith and love.

Yahweh also outlined His part in this covenant. Reiterating many of the blessings already laid out in previous encounters, He promised that Abram would be the father of many nations. Kings would issue from him. The promise of land was also included. But now the heart of the covenant is found in verse 7: "I will be a God to you, and to your seed after you." This same covenant promise is repeated many times throughout the Old Testament (Zech. 8:8; Hos. 2:23; Jer. 7:23, 30:20). It is also repeated for Gentile Christians in Romans 9:26 and 2 Corinthians 6:16. This is why many Gentile believers consider themselves included in this original covenant made with Abraham.

Do note that God made this covenant with both the father and the children. The same wording is used in the New Covenant promise in Acts 2:38, where the promise of the regenerating and sanctifying Spirit of God was given to the fathers gathered to hear Peter's sermon. Peter told these men that the promise was to them and to their children. This is standard operating procedure for the covenants God makes with men. Therefore, can we say that the promise is extended to both the men listening to Peter's sermon and to their children? For 1600 years, the descendants of Abraham believed that the promise extended to both them and to their children. Was Peter going to disenfranchise them of this idea in his first sermon after Christ's ascension? Of course, he made no such clarification. That is why many families to this day believe that their children may be included in these covenant promises. They are just as much a part of the visible people of God on earth as Abraham's children were in the Old Testament.

Verses 10–14. Following the introduction of the parties and the terms of the covenant comes the outward sign of the covenant. A sign is an outward indication of an inward spiritual reality. In other instances, God has provided outward visible symbols of spiritual realities, such as the rainbow after the Flood and the blood of the Passover lamb placed over the doorways of Israelite homes during the Exodus.

The outward sign of this covenant is circumcision. Since the flesh to be removed in the circumcision is only found on men and boys, women were exempted from this circumcision throughout the history of the Old Testament. Why should God limit the circumcision rite to the males in the household? The same question may be asked of the Deuteronomy 16:16 mandate requiring only the "males" to appear before God three times each year for the feasts. Furthermore, it was the "males" commissioned by the Apostle Paul to pray "everywhere," in households or in churches, with the "lifting up of holy hands" (1 Tim. 2:8). Since every man is the head of his home, as Christ is head of the church (Eph. 5:25), and every boy is a head-in-training, the mark of the covenant was deemed unnecessary for the women.

It is clear that God is very serious about this sign of the covenant, as those children not circumcised would be "cut off from the people" with whom God was establishing a relationship. The visible body of the Old Testament church was made up of those who were circumcised into it.

In order to be a member of the church in the New Testament, one must be baptized. Circumcision is no longer necessary. Both circumcision and baptism are signs of the removal of the "filthy flesh." They are both pictures of cleansing and regeneration. Yet, there are several important differences between baptism and circumcision. While both of them signify the regeneration of the heart, circumcision is a painful and somewhat arduous experience, involving a bloody excision. Baptism is a simple bath, or cleansing, using water. Also, as already mentioned, women and girls were not circumcised. However, the first references to women baptisms are found in Acts 8:12 and Acts 16:14.

Verses 15–27. A man's name will define him, especially if God gives him the name. And that is what happened with Abram when God changed his name to Abraham, which means "the father of nations." Appropriately, He also changed Sarai's name to Sarah, or "princess." Still, Abraham was somewhat weak in faith concerning the promise of a posterity. He still suggested Ishmael as a suitable "son of the covenant" who might walk before Yahweh in covenant faithfulness. But God again rejected the son of the bondwoman in the covenant blessings, though He still promised him temporal blessings. From this we learn that even those who are circumcised into the covenant people of God may eventually find themselves excluded from the covenant.

Finally, God declared in no uncertain terms that Sarah would have a son. The name Yahweh assigned for this covenant lad was "Isaac," an ironic twist on the word "laughter." The laughter of incredulity would transfer to a laughter of joy and celebration upon the birth of this little boy. To this day we all have reason to laugh with joy upon hearing of the birth of Isaac, for our Savior came from the line of this man. The chapter ends with a testimony to Abraham's faithful obedience as he circumcised his entire household, both sons and servants.

How does this passage teach us to walk with God in faith and obedience?

1. The Bible presents our relationship with God in terms of both covenant bodies and individuals. Thus, anybody who was circumcised in the Old Testament or baptized in the New Testament has been initiated into the visible church of God. This body of the church is actually in relationship with God, but this does not mean that everybody participating in the visible church is really circumcised of heart, regenerated, and guaranteed to be saved in the end. Although God expects heart regeneration of all those who have received the "sign of the covenant" in Deuteronomy 10:16, heart regeneration is not always the case. You may be a member of a church that is in relationship with God, but your own heart has yet to be regenerated and you have yet to establish a personal relationship with the Lord. Hence, it is not enough that our children be baptized and be members of a church. They must believe in the Lord Jesus Christ and walk with Him in relationship all the days of their lives.

But why does God bother instituting a covenant using these outward signs if everybody making up the visible church may not be truly saved in the end? We must conclude that God chooses His own means of relating to His people and bringing them to salvation. It is for the same reason that God instructs us to read and preach His Word. Not everyone who hears the Bible preached gets saved, but that should not deter us from preaching the Word! Certainly, if we did not preach the Bible, few would be saved. Not everyone who comes into the visible people or church of God by circumcision or baptism are saved in the end.

2. Keep in mind the heart of the covenant—God will be our God, and we will be His people. The New Testament speaks of us belonging to the family of God (1 Tim. 3:15). Indeed, God counts us as belonging to His "group," His family, when we are in the covenant. We can call Him "our Father" because we are in His family.

Questions:

1. What are the themes of Chapters 1 through 17?

2. Who are the two parties in this covenant deal that God makes?

3. What does God require of Abram in this covenant?

4. What does God offer to Abram in the covenant?

5. What does the name "Abraham" mean?

6. What are the similarities between circumcision and baptism? What are the differences?

7. For those who want to be part of the visible church today, must they be circumcised? What sign does God require for those who join the church in the New Testament?

Family Discussion Questions:

1. Are we in covenant with God? How do we know that we are in covenant with God? Why are the outwards signs of the covenant important to God, and to us?

2. What is the state of our relationship with God right now? Are we walking in close relationship with Him, or has the relationship become more distant?

CHAPTER 18

Sarah Laughs

Therefore Sarah laughed within herself, saying, "After I am waxed old shall I have pleasure, my lord being old also?" And the LORD said unto Abraham, "Wherefore did Sarah laugh, saying, Shall I of a surety bear a child, which am old? Is any thing too hard for the LORD? At the time appointed I will return unto thee, according to the time of life, and Sarah shall have a son." Gen. 18:12–14

Events:

1. Three men visit Abraham on the plain of Mamre.
2. Yahweh again promises that Sarah will have a son.
3. The three men leave for Sodom.
4. Abraham negotiates with Yahweh to save Sodom from judgment.

What does this passage teach us?

Verses 1–8. At the outset of this chapter, Abraham receives an important visit from three strangers. Most likely they were angels appearing in the likeness of human flesh (Heb. 13:2). It is also possible that one of the three men was a physical representation of the second person of the Trinity, the Lord Jesus Christ. Occasionally throughout the interchange between Abraham and his visitors, the Scriptures refer to the speaker as Yahweh Himself. Evidently the three strangers came down to earth for two reasons. They came as harbingers of mercy… and judgment.

But first, the life of the believer is beautifully exemplified in Abraham's treatment of the strangers in this passage. According to Hebrews 13:2, true believers will always be marked by a commitment to hospitality. In fact, the word used for "hospitality" in the Hebrews passage is phileoxenia, literally translated as "love of strangers." Despite the fact that most wayfaring strangers today usually end up in hotels and restaurants where they pay for their "hospitality," Christian society is to be patterned after the lifestyle of Abraham. When Christian brothers and sisters are traveling through our area and need a little food and shelter, it should be our honor and pleasure to provide them with whatever they need, without any expectation of remuneration (1 Pet. 4:9; Rom. 12:13). Abraham's initiative to show hospitality is evident by his quick response to the needs of these men. Instantly, he hurried into the tent to alert his wife, and then he ran to the herd to find a suitable calf for the meal.

Verses 9–15. While the three strangers consumed the meal, Yahweh promised Abraham for the fifth time that he would have a son in his old age. His aging wife would bear the child. Do you see how the repetition of these promises could help to buttress a wavering faith? We have already seen how Abraham's faith was not always as strong as it could be, and Sarah gave way to doubt when she laughed at the announcement of her pregnancy. But God is gracious to us. Each time we hear God's promises through the faithful preaching of the Word of God, we are challenged to believe these promises and our faith grows.

Yahweh was still patient with Abraham and Sarah. He corrected their doubts by posing a pointed question, "Is there anything too hard for Yahweh?" Much hinges on such a question, does it not? If we truly believe that Yahweh created heaven and earth, and sovereignly disposes of nations, and carefully ordains the growth pattern of each of the 40,000 hairs on our heads, then why should we question His ability to bring forth a child from a ninety-year-old woman? Faith demands an answer to this question: "Is anything too hard for the Lord?" Before we face any of our enemies, before we pray any prayer, before we bring any need before God and cry out for His salvation, it is good for us to answer this simple question: "Is anything too hard for the Lord?"

Despite Sarah's unbelief, God was still faithful to His promises and followed through by providing the promised child. Sarah is later commended in Scripture for her faith and obedience. What tremendous hope this inspires in us who live by faith, but are also occasionally overcome by bouts of faithlessness!

Verses 16–21. This passage provides some interesting insights into the nature of our God. He conversed with Abraham as a friend, as a man talks with his neighbor on the front patio. He also consulted with Himself on whether He should include Abraham in His plans to destroy Sodom. Though we treat these as anthropomorphic descriptions, it is still clear that God has a Personality and an Imminence that His Transcendence does not obliterate. He is above and over all, but He still interacts with His friends whom He created!

Yet, why did God find it necessary to visit Sodom? Didn't He already know the moral condition of the city? While God is certainly omniscient, knowing everything in heaven and in earth, it does appear that there are varying levels of intimacy within this knowledge. From elsewhere in Scripture, we learn that God knows the way of the righteous (Ps. 1:5). But the way of the proud He knows "afar off" (Ps. 138:6). Therefore, when Yahweh set His face towards Sodom to "see whether they have done according to the cry of it," He put His face, as it were, a little closer to the manure pile and took a sniff. Such intimate knowledge concerning the sin of Sodom brought swift and terrible judgment on that city and the surrounding land. As we consider the deep truths of God's omniscience and omnipresence, we must be careful not to forget the connection that God has with His creatures. We must not think of Him as if He is a computer RAM assimilating data, for He personally and emotionally relates to every aspect of His creation.

Verses 18 and 19 give us further insight into God's perceptions of Abraham. He chose to include Abraham in His plans to destroy Sodom and Gomorrah for several reasons. Since He had already entered into a covenant with this man, and the land concerned was included as one of the stipulations of the covenant, Abraham would have had a vested interest in this matter. Also, God gives vision to men of vision. Abraham is an example of a true visionary father in the kingdom of God. In Abraham we find the great prototype, the archetypal father working to establish a generational vision for the kingdom. In the heart of Abraham, there was such a commitment to God, such an overwhelming zeal for the kingdom, that he would see to it that his children would walk in God's ways. He was a man with the faith and vision to see the expansion of the kingdom through his children and grandchildren. To this man, God revealed His plans for Sodom and Gomorrah.

God's plans should always serve as a warning to God's people, and a comfort. God will clear the land of a wicked people, in order that the righteous may inherit the earth. Do not entertain the idea that the wickedness of great cities and empires of the modern world will continue indefinitely. Within 40-50 years, perhaps 100 years, it will be over for them. This is what happens to the legacy of disobedience and rebellion.

Verses 22–33. Upon hearing of Yahweh's plans to destroy Sodom, Abraham tried to intervene in an attempt to save the city. Previously, Abraham had fought for the defense of the city of Sodom against the seven nations that were unlawfully pillaging the cities on the plain. Also, his relationship with Lot gave him some concern for the future of this city. Further insight into the character of Abraham's relationship with God is found in this passage, as he proceeded to negotiate with God over the fate of Sodom. The relationship of God's sovereignty to man's desires and actions appears to come under conflict here. Do our petitions change God's mind or in any way impact the outcome of a certain event? From Scripture we learn of both the absolute sovereignty of God and the effectual nature of fervent prayer to bring about a certain outcome (Jam. 5:16). Here Abraham prays fervently with Yahweh God over the future of these cities. His boldness in these negotiations with the Almighty is astonishing to us! But even more surprising, is God's response to his appeals. In the end, the Lord settled with Abraham that he would save the city if there were only ten righteous men living in Sodom. At a time when the cities of Canaan did not exceed much over 20,000 in population, the ratio of the God-fearing righteous to the wicked would still have been less than 1 percent. What tremendous insight into the patience and mercy of God we have here! What a great influence is borne by a few righteous men within a community! Could it be that God would preserve our cities if there were but a few thousand righteous people dwelling in them? Evidently, by this time, there was only one righteous man left in these cities. In the following chapter, God would destroy Sodom and Gomorrah.

How does this passage teach us to walk with God in faith and obedience?

1. Abraham is a great example of a father of faith who has a wholehearted commitment to God and His standard of righteousness. Let us emulate this man of faith. Even when God's kingdom was nothing but a single family, a tiny, fledgling camp on the plains of Mamre west of the Jordan River, Abraham could still make out what God would do in the following generations! He believed that God would pull it off and turn his family into a huge nation. Armed with this kind of a vision, Abraham couldn't help but communicate that to his family through his teaching and example.

2. Nothing is too hard for the Lord, though it may be hard for us to believe that God is able to fulfill every one of His promises. Think of some of the tough trials you are going through right now. Do you believe that the Lord will work these out for your good? If so, then you will not be worried about the future and you will rejoice in what God is going to do.

3. Many of the modern nation states have destroyed the family and entertained the sin of sodomy, like the first Sodom of long ago. For the first time since the Roman days, the sin of homosexuality has come into vogue in the social systems of Europe and America. It is even touted in public schools and in the legislatures as a moral good. Now, Christians are increasingly persecuted for taking a stand against this sin in a public forum. All of this brings up the question, "Will the Lord destroy this country also?"

4. If this chapter provides any insight into the workings of God in heaven, then there must still be hope for any city that claims a few righteous families. If there are enough people who refuse to support the sin of Sodom or the murder of the innocents, God may still save this nation. Occasionally, a righteous candidate will run for political office against two or three other candidates who support the sins of the day (such as sodomy and abortion). It is not unusual for this righteous candidate to lose an election with a paltry 4% to 5% of the vote. However, consider that in no place does God's Word bind us to support the "winning candidate!" What we do find is a requirement to choose able men who fear God and hate covetousness to represent us in government (Exod. 18:21). If He

will preserve this nation, God will find a small remnant here who will take a courageous stand for righteousness against all odds. Sadly, there are precious few righteous candidates who are willing to take that stand, and it is our task to find them. Our family must be careful to always vote for righteous candidates, and always stand for righteousness whenever we get the opportunity.

Questions:

1. What are the themes of Chapters 1 through 18?
2. Who were the three visitors that came to see Abraham?
3. How did Abraham show hospitality to his visitors?
4. What did Sarah do when she heard that she would have a son?
5. How many righteous people would have had to live in Sodom for the Lord to withhold judgment from that wicked town?

Family Discussion Questions:

1. When people we have never seen before come to church, are we quick to open up our homes to take care of them? How might we improve our hospitality and "love the strangers" in our midst?
2. Will our children carry on our legacy of faith? Will our children keep the way of the Lord and stand up for righteousness? To what extent does this depend on the fathers who lead their children in obedience to the Lord?
3. Should we vote for leaders who encourage sins like abortion and homosexuality? What if there is no possibility of a righteous candidate winning the election?

CHAPTER 19

Sodom Destroyed

And the men said unto Lot, "Hast thou here any besides? Son in law, and thy sons, and thy daughters, and whatsoever thou hast in the city, bring them out of this place: for we will destroy this place, because the cry of them is waxen great before the face of the LORD; and the LORD hath sent us to destroy it." Gen. 19:12–13

Events:

1. Two of the visiting angels proceed to the city of Sodom.
2. During the angels' stay with Lot, the men of Sodom attempt to break into Lot's house to kidnap the visitors.
3. The messengers from God strike the men of Sodom with blindness.
4. In the morning, the angels take Lot, his wife, and his two daughters out of Sodom, and God destroys the cities.
5. Lot's wife looks back and is turned into a pillar of salt.
6. Lot settles outside the city of Zoar, and his two daughters have sons by him.

What does this passage teach us?

Verses 1–11. Of the three visitors that enjoyed Abraham's hospitality in the previous chapter, only two proceeded to Sodom. They are referred to as angels, or more accurately, "messengers" or "ambassadors," in this chapter.

There is a question in the minds of some today as to the nature of the sin of Sodom, but this is easily addressed by a quick read of Leviticus 20:13-23. According to verse 23, the sins of these Canaanite nations that were especially bothersome to Yahweh God are listed in the previous portion of the chapter. One of those sins was the sin of homosexuality. Verse 13 clearly condemns the sin of homosexuality, and the nature of that sin is simply and plainly defined for us. There can be no debate on this. When a man lies with a man in the way that a man lies with a woman, he has committed an abominable act. In fact, the sin is so heinous in God's eyes that He requires civil magistrates to enact the death penalty on both parties who commit the act.

Homosexuality had virtually disappeared from the western world when Christianity gained influence in the latter part of the 4th century. For the crime of a "man coupling like a woman," the punishment was death under the Theodosian code. For over one thousand years, this sin was hardly an issue in the western world. By the 1790s, liberals like Jeremy Bentham lamented that homosexual behavior in Protestant countries like Scotland and the Netherlands appeared only once every hundred years or so. Sadly, the situation is far worse today. Almost every western nation in Europe and North America has turned into Sodom. There are literally thousands of cities like Sodom in the developed world today! This corruption and moral decay is thorough-going, and sins like homosexuality are extremely commonplace and socially acceptable.

The behavior of the homosexuals in this chapter is not unlike what we find in major cities today. To further compound the evil of their condition, homosexuals and heterosexual fornicators tend to prefer anonymous relationships. They abandon all notion of the biblical family with its long-term, nurturing relationships, and give way to the kind of animalistic relationships one would find among dogs or cows. This foul, bestial passion was apparently working powerfully in these Sodomites. As the biblical record has it, these men were anxious to "know" the new visitors in town. A similar scenario played out in Gibeah with the wicked Benjamites in Judges 19. What is described in this chapter is the lowest form of social and moral degradation. It is sickeningly familiar in the present social situation.

There is some question as to why God destroyed the city of Sodom. Some have attributed it to the inhospitable treatment the angels received when they visited Lot's home. But, other biblical references clearly attribute this judgment to their sins of pride, fullness of bread, self-centeredness, and abominable sexual sin (ref. Ezek. 16:49–50 and Jude 7). It is almost impossible to miss the correlation between fullness of bread (lack of gratitude to God) and moral corruption. The wealthiest cities and states almost always debase themselves with the worst possible abominations and entertainments. When men speak of the big cities as interesting and fun, where there is "lots to do," they are usually using code words for the bar scene, where anonymous, illicit relationships are cultivated and God's laws are violated.

Verses 12–22. The Creator of heaven and earth proceeded to destroy Sodom and Gomorrah for their gross violation of His holy law. For the love that God had for His man Abraham, though, he mercifully delivered Lot out of the destruction. The behavior of Lot throughout the story provides an interesting representation of what the Bible calls a "righteous man." He was weak. He seemed unable to convince his own family of his faith and commitment to Yahweh. He dragged his feet when leaving this wicked city. When the men of Sodom threatened his visitors, Lot offered to toss his own daughters out to the raging mob. Yet God was merciful to this man with all his weaknesses and sins. What an encouragement to know the mercy of God towards those of us with whom He has made a covenant, in spite of our own failings!

Verses 23–29. Lot did not cooperate very well with his rescuers throughout this entire ordeal. Having grown accustomed to city life, he resisted the idea of moving to the mountains. Although the angels had warned his family not to look back upon the condemned cities, Lot's wife could not resist the temptation. She remains an example for all generations of that person whose heart is inclined towards the world. She found something in the world of more value than her own soul. She demonstrated a lack of commitment to God. Her ultimate love was for the cheap offerings of this world, and she could not leave it all to follow Jesus. Even with all of the foul, wicked behavior manifest in the inhabitants of the cities, and the real and present judgment of God on them, she still loved the cities more than she loved God.

Verses 30–38. Another shameful episode caps the story of Lot's life. Ever since Adam fell into sin, men and women seek out every possible way to oppose God's order in the area of marriage and intimacy. First, there was polygamy, then homosexuality, and now the sin of incest. God forbids a man from marrying his own daughter and holds men and women to proper boundaries of intimacy in familial relationships. At the very beginning,

God told Adam that a man should leave his father and mother and cleave to his wife. This first injunction disallowed a man from marrying his mother, or a daughter from marrying her father. Sadly, Lot's two daughters failed to obey God's law in this matter, and both bore sons by their father. These two sons became the fathers of the Moabites and the Ammonites, both enemies of God's people throughout the Old Testament. But the story did not end here. Despite the shameful, sinful works of men, God showed His mercy in amazing ways. Over 800 years later, a Moabitess woman sought the God of Israel. This humble, godly woman married Boaz of the tribe of Judah. As the story played out, Ruth became the great-grandmother of David, in the line of our Saviour, Jesus Christ. Here once again, God turned men's disobedience to His own ends, and accomplished great things despite their sin and failings.

How does this passage teach us to walk with God in faith and obedience?

1. There are two kingdoms that continue to coexist in time and space—the kingdom of Christ and the kingdom of Satan (who is the god of this world). We must be careful here, for there are actually two different uses of the word "world" in Scripture. On the one hand, there is the world God created—the world of dirt, people, beagles, civil governments, and families. God loves this world (John 3:16). Yet God calls us to hate the other world of lust and pride (1 John 2:15,16). It is best to define this world as everything that is opposed to Christ in thought, word, and deed. Satan is the prince of the world that is dominated by lust and pride. As Christians, we live in the world made up of dirt and people, governments and culture. Because so much of this world is contaminated by lust and pride, we must be careful that this world does not dominate our lives. Instead, we should consider all that is lustful and prideful as our mortal enemy. Therefore, it would be a tragedy if our children would become unequally yoked with those who thrive on lust and pride. This would be akin to marrying the enemy! If you remember, this is what happened to Lot's daughters, who had husbands who were men of Sodom.

Let us learn a lesson from Lot's family, and commit today to avoid all synthesis with the world. Certainly, Christian children should marry committed Christians who are not held captive by the world of lust and pride. May we seek out those who truly love Christ and who seek His kingdom first! Since the latter part of the 19th century, hundreds of millions of young people have turned away from their Christian families and left the Christian church. It is almost the exception to see any children from Christian homes saved "from this present evil world." Slowly but surely, these young people come to love that world with all of its sin and rebellion. They are drawn to the symbols, the lifestyles, the attitudes, the music, the sinful behavior, and the belief system of the world. As with Lot's wife, they gaze longingly after all that is in rebellion to God. Even though it may be under the fiery judgment of God, brimstone flying from the heavens, they still want to run back to it! This passage is a warning to us all. Remember Lot's wife.

2. Above all, this passage requires from us more fear of God. In the western world, if we were to point to Sodom as an example of God's righteous judgment upon a city like San Francisco (where homosexual behavior proliferates), we would be severely mocked or even imprisoned. These people cannot believe that God would ever destroy a nation! Whatever gods they serve have nothing to do with this God of the Old and New Testaments. They may claim a Christian religious background, but they have long apostatized, and their picture of "God" or "Jesus Christ" is only a construction of their own imaginations. They recoil in horror from these biblical stories only because they do not fear God. Be very sure that their refusal to reverence and fear the true and living God (who is a consuming fire) will not exempt them from His wrathful judgment! If we were the last people on earth to believe these stories, we would do well to cultivate a healthy reverence for God. He has brought His judgment to many cities, nations, and empires over the last 3500 years since Sodom was destroyed. The nature of God and the standards of His righteousness have not changed. In fact, He is even more insistent now than in times past, that all men everywhere come to repentance (Acts 17:30). He could very well bring judgment on this nation by disease or weapons of mass destruction. May we faithfully preach righteousness with every opportunity we get, and repent of our own rebellion against the Lord. If there had been only ten righteous people in Sodom, God would not have destroyed it. Perhaps, we

shall be a few of the names on the list of those who love and serve the true God in our city.

Questions:

1. What are the themes of Chapters 1 through 19?
2. Why was Lot considered a righteous man?
3. What were the sins of the city of Sodom?
4. In what ways do men pervert marriage and sin against God?
5. Why was Lot's wife turned into a pillar of salt?
6. What were the names of Lot's two sons birthed by his daughters?
7. What famous woman in the Bible came from the Moabites?

Family Discussion Questions:

1. How much love do we have for the world? Are we more drawn to the worldly thinking and life that rejects God, or to the worship of God and the life of Christ?
2. How has God been merciful to our family despite our own half-hearted obedience to Him?

CHAPTER 20

Abraham's Sister

And Abraham journeyed from thence toward the south country,
and dwelt between Kadesh and Shur, and sojourned in Gerar. And
Abraham said of Sarah his wife, "She is my sister:" and Abimelech king
of Gerar sent, and took Sarah. Gen. 20:1–2

Events:

1. Abraham misleads King Abimelech, who then takes Sarah into his household.
2. God chastises King Abimelech.
3. King Abimelech releases Sarah and blesses Abraham with goods.

What does this passage teach us?

Verses 1–2. Here is yet another instance of Yahweh's fierce affinity for Abraham. He carefully protected the man and his family as they traveled into unfriendly territory. Again, Abraham worked his way into an awkward situation when he told the people in the land of Gerar that Sarah was his sister. You may remember that this was a half-truth, for she was his half-sister—and his wife. In those days, a king's political power was determined by the wives he married (which was also the case with the kings of the 15th and 16th centuries). King Abimelech took swift advantage of the situation, seeing that Abraham and his group might become a political threat to his little kingdom. He removed Sarah from Abraham's household in preparation for betrothal.

Verses 3–8. In the unfolding history of family life in Genesis, a number of sins emerge, including polygamy, homosexuality, and incest. Yet another form of marital sin is mentioned in this section of Scripture, as God warned King Abimelech about taking another man's wife. "You are a dead man!"

Yahweh God told Abimelech. The severity of the warning is in concert with later revelation, where God mandated the death penalty for anyone who dared to take his neighbor's wife (Lev. 20:10).

In response to God's remonstrance, this king vehemently insisted that he was acting out of pure motivations, and that he was misled by Abraham's reference to Sarah being his sister. In God's merciful and sovereign providence, He prevented Abimelech from following through on this potentially adulterous relationship. Where such misunderstandings might lead a man astray, it is clear that God in His sovereignty is well able to turn the situation around. The biblical view of a sovereign God is a far cry from the impersonal and amoral Greek fates that led Oedipus to murder his father and marry his own mother without even knowing it.

Whether it was news about Sodom and Gomorrah's recent demise or some other reason, it is clear that there was some true fear of God in this man Abimelech (reference also verse 11). Evidently, the news of Abraham's God had preceded him, enough to concern Abimelech that God might "slay" his nation also.

So Yahweh God demanded the return of Sarah to her lawful husband. Although it appears to us that Abraham miscalculated Abimelech and handled the situation poorly, you wouldn't get this out of the chapter. God makes no apologies for Abraham's behavior. There is only support and blessing for God's man. In the end, He leaves the fate of Abimelech and his kingdom in Abraham's hands. What tremendous loyalty and blessing God provides for the man with whom He makes covenant!

Verses 9–18. The king confronted Abraham with this misunderstanding and offense. Abraham then provided his "side of the story," but he did not confess any particular sin in the matter. Nevertheless, it seems that this interchange was sufficient to clear the air between the two men. Once again, God blessed Abraham materially through the whole ordeal. Since God put Abraham in the "driver's seat" concerning Abimelech's situation, it wasn't until Abraham prayed for Abimelech that God restored fertility to his people. Already, we are seeing the temporal fulfillment of the first promise given to Abraham in Genesis 12:3, "I will bless them that bless you, and I will curse them that curse you."

How does this passage teach us to walk with God in faith and obedience?

1. God always protects His own. His control of our circumstances and His care of us is absolute. If we are in covenant relationship with the living God, there is no end to where He will go to protect and defend us. Nothing will happen to His people without His permission.

2. Here, also, we find the mercy of God for His people even when they make unwise choices that put their families at risk. His mercy does not excuse a lack of wisdom on our part, but until we cross the river, we will always face our own finiteness, deficiencies, and sins; and it is only the grace of God that will sustain us along the way.

3. Sarah was commended by the New Testament Apostle for her obedience (1 Pet. 3:6). This is the only clear reference to Sarah's obedience. Therefore, we take this as a good example for married women in our churches today. Abraham's little charade seems to have been a harebrained scheme that could hardly have been necessary, let alone morally appropriate. His actions exposed his family to unwarranted risks. Yet Sarah cooperated with her husband through it all, and God blessed Abraham and Sarah at the end of it. God isn't telling a wife to submit to her husband out of some kind of blind trust in her husband's impeccable wisdom. No, rather she should submit to her husband out of blind trust in God, the source of all wisdom and blessings (who is pleased with a wife who submits to her husband).

4. Almost every developed nation around the world today is birth-imploding. While we may attribute the human cause of it to abortifacient birth control pills and other devices, God is still sovereign over the use of these scientific contrivances. The fact is that GOD is closing the wombs of billions of women all over the world, as He did with the little city-state in this story. May God have mercy on His own covenant people in the present crisis!

Questions:

1. What are the themes of Chapters 1 through 20?

2. Why did the kings of old think it was important to multiply wives for themselves?

3. How did Abimelech find out that Sarah was Abraham's wife?

4. What is the sin mentioned in this particular passage, that warrants death?

5. How do we know that Abimelech feared God?

6. How does Yahweh bless Abraham in this passage despite Abraham's failings?

Family Discussion Questions:

1. Have we ever found ourselves in difficult and dangerous circumstances such as what Abraham faced here? Did we trust in God, or did we rely on our own devices under these conditions? What would we have done in Abraham's situation?

2. How can a wife submit to her husband even when it seems like her husband is making some unwise choices? Is there any point at which she should not obey her husband?

CHAPTER 21

Isaac Is Born

And the LORD visited Sarah as He had said, and the LORD did unto Sarah as He had spoken. For Sarah conceived, and bare Abraham a son in his old age, at the set time of which God had spoken to him. Gen. 21:1–2

Events:

1. Sarah gives birth to Isaac.
2. Abraham sends Hagar and Ishmael away.
3. Abraham makes a covenant with Abimelech.

What does this passage teach us?

Verses 1–6. Abraham and Sarah had waited on God's promise for a full twenty-five years. Each day had served as yet another challenge to their faith. Each year that went by was one more year past the child-bearing age for them. Every year that God's promise was not fulfilled only demanded increased measures of faith to believe. But God did come through on His promise. After a 9,000+ day wait, and in spite of Sarah's faithless laughing and Abraham's attempt to circumvent God's will by producing a child through Hagar, Yahweh God fulfilled His promise and Sarah had a baby.

They named the child Isaac as God had instructed them. The name means "laughter." To fully appreciate the divine irony here, imagine naming your child "Laughing." Isaac was a constant reminder to his parents of God's goodness, their own lack of faith, and God's faithfulness to His promise.

This is the first instance of humor in the Bible, and it comes as a surprise to us that God Himself participates. People often laugh when something unusual and unexpected happens, such as when the punch line of a joke takes them by surprise. In the case of the birth of Isaac, the word "laughter" bears multiple meanings. Sarah's incredulous laughter turned into a laughter of joy and surprise when something very unusual and unexpected happened. A ninety-year-old woman gave birth to a baby! God told a joke when He named the child Isaac after Sarah's doubting laugh. No doubt, Sarah laughed some more on the birth of the child, and this time it was a different kind of laughter. Finally, she "got the joke," and she believed. This is the first clear instance of humor in the Bible, and it provides us a basis for appropriate humor and laughter in the home.

Verses 7–21. Sadly, family relationships are always undermined by sinful attitudes, words, and actions—and Abraham's family was no different. On the day that Abraham celebrated Isaac's weaning, sibling rivalry took the upper hand.

This portion of Scripture introduces a second form of humor known as "attack" humor. Paul refers to Ishmael's words as a "persecuting" scorn (Gal. 4:29). Good and godly humor will attack that which is evil and endear that which is good, but Ishmael used attack humor inappropriately to mock his brother Isaac. Instantly, Sarah realized that there would be competition for the inheritance. So she recommended removing the older son from the home. This put Abraham in a difficult spot. While he felt the responsibility for providing for the woman and child so as not to oppress the widow and orphan (his own son), he still needed to establish order in his home. But then, sinful actions always create complicated and impossible situations for families. In this case Yahweh graciously stepped in and agreed to care for Hagar and Ishmael Himself.

God's care for Ishmael must have been tied to the boy's relationship with Abraham, who was in covenant relationship with God. According to God's clear direction and intention, Ishmael would not take part in the covenant or share in its eternal blessings. Nevertheless, God still provided for Ishmael and blessed him with strength and vitality, which served to establish his family as an important nation in the earth. Any time that God provides blessings for unbelievers, it is because of His mercy. We call this "common grace." God is still more interested in blessing the godly, but He will bless the ungodly when they live in proximity with the godly (1 Cor. 7:14). We do know that God would not have destroyed Sodom and Gomorrah if there had been ten righteous people living there.

Verses 22–34. The Bible presents the "wandering," rootless life as an undesirable condition (Prov. 27:8; Num. 14:33; Acts 11:19; Deut. 28:64–65; etc.). Throughout the Old Testament, the people of God are instructed to be kind to the "strangers in the land." Jesus describes the stranger as similarly disadvantaged as those who are hungry, thirsty, sick, or imprisoned (Matt. 25:44). To properly understand the life of Abraham, therefore, we must first realize that the nomadic life is ultimately undesirable and an accursed state. Unfortunately, this transient lifestyle is very similar to the kind of life that many Americans lead today.

But God was gracious to Abraham and provided him some stability in his later years. "Settling down" has much to do with obtaining the rights to the land where you live and being without fear of government confiscation, war, or bank foreclosure. So by contract with this king Abimelech, Abraham obtained the right to occupy the land, dig his own wells, and "work his own ranch." This section of Scripture also establishes for us the importance of private property and boundary markers, as well as the value of covenants and contracts. It would be impossible to settle the land and personally enjoy the fruits of it without those things. Abraham also planted trees in Beersheba, another indication that he was going to be there for a long time.

In these final verses of the chapter, Abraham provided a good example for maintaining good neighborly relations. His desire was for peace, as this is the primary objective for any who will be part of the kingdom of God (Rom. 12:18, 14:17). God has called us to peace. As the father of all those who would make up this kingdom in years following, Abraham made peace with His neighbors. The ungodly will usually respond to conflict with angry words, bitter sentiments, and violent confrontation. But not so with this godly patriarch! First, he met face to face with the opposing party, then he provided a peace offering or a gift for his adversary, and finally established a clear and honest agreement with the man. Their future relationship would be governed by this standard of honorable conduct.

How does this passage teach us to walk with God in faith and obedience?

1. Humor is a wonderful thing, but let us be careful how we use it within our families. Far too often, families resort to the use of "attack" humor, sarcasm, and mockery in the home, and that is how family relationships are ruined over time. There is a place for satire and sarcasm when attacking the ideas of the world. But we are should never use this form of humor to tear down our brothers and sisters.

2. Ishmael was kicked out of the family for his rebellion against the covenant. In this case, he persecuted the son of the covenant, and was thereby demonstrating his rebellion against the covenant. This is a warning to all children born into a Christian home. There are some children that reach fifteen or sixteen years of age and scorn God's covenant child, the Lord Jesus Christ. Such rebellion is terribly offensive in God's eyes, as is plainly stated in Hebrews 10:29. Comparing New Testament rebellion to the Old Testament examples, the text concludes: "Of how much sorer punishment, suppose ye, shall he be thought worthy, who hath trodden underfoot the Son of God, and hath counted the blood of the covenant, wherewith he was sanctified, an unholy thing, and hath done despite unto the Spirit of grace?"

For this reason, it is important that even minor indications of rebellion in our children be carefully corrected. Otherwise, parents will see their children turning into what the book of Proverbs calls "a scorner."

3. This is a sad story. But it testifies to the fact that there are often deep and abiding consequences for sinful behavior. The whole problem began with Abraham taking a second wife. Then his son rebelled, and he had to expel him from the home. However, in the midst of the trial God was still merciful and He made a great nation out of Ishmael. There is both comfort and warning here for us. Let us be careful not to fall into gross sin, or we will suffer painful consequences. Also, we should be especially careful to play by God's rules in marriage. According to God's ordination, a man gets just one wife (until death separates them), and he must remain faithful and true to her.

Questions:

1. What are the themes of Chapters 1 through 21?
2. What did Abraham do to his son on the eighth day?
3. Why did Abraham expel Ishmael from his household?
4. How did God show mercy on Ishmael even though he was a rebellious son?
5. How did Abraham get his neighbors to respect his right to a piece of land?
6. What did Abraham do that indicated he was settling down around Beersheba?

Family Discussion Questions:

1. Do we employ a healthy use of humor in our home? How often do we resort to cutting sarcasm or attack humor?
2. How has God blessed us with stability and roots where we live? How transient are our lives? Do we move from place to place, or are we settling down in one particular area?
3. How is our relationship with our neighbors? What might we learn from Abraham about godly conflict resolution?

CHAPTER 22

Isaac Sacrificed

And it came to pass after these things, that God did tempt Abraham, and said unto him, "Abraham:" and he said, "Behold, here I am." And He said, "Take now thy son, thine only son Isaac, whom thou lovest, and get thee into the land of Moriah; and offer him there for a burnt offering upon one of the mountains which I will tell thee of."
Gen. 22:1–2

Events:

1. God challenges Abraham to sacrifice his son on Mount Moriah.
2. Abraham obeys, but God provides the sacrifice.
3. God blesses Abraham even more.

What does this passage teach us?

Verses 1–14. Beyond any other Old Testament Saint, Abraham patterned the walk of faith in this extended account of his life from the book of Genesis. Hardly any other person is dealt with so comprehensively in the Scriptures. Throughout Abraham's life, God subjected him to multiple tests, each of which was calculated to strengthen his faith in the promises of God. But here in this chapter we find the ultimate challenge in the trial of his faith. After the long and laborious wait for the birth of his son, his only son, now God asked Abraham to give the son back to Him by sacrifice.

Normatively, human sacrifice is contrary to the revealed law of God for men. Yet God retains the authority to determine right and wrong, and demand obedience of men. If God is the source of law, then of course we may not question the propriety of His commands. Therefore, Abraham quickly made preparations to kill his son and burn him on an altar on Mount Moriah as God instructed him. Clearly, these motions towards killing his own son in no way diminished Abraham's love for the little lad. According to the book of Hebrews, he moved ahead in faith, trusting that God could raise Isaac from the dead (Heb. 11:19).

Each action that Abraham took in order to prepare the sacrifice was an act of faith. The preparatory work involved collecting and assembling wood, fire, and stones for the altar. In those days, men had to carry their fire with them by means of a candle or torch.

Initially, Abraham thought that he would have to offer his son as a burnt sacrifice. However, it should also be noted that the word for "burnt offering" is *olah* in the Hebrew and does not always denote a sacrifice burned by fire. In its more fundamental sense, the word indicates something that is given entirely up to God. Effectively, this is what happened here. Abraham held nothing back from his God. He spent the entire day preparing the sacrifice. He bound the boy to the altar, and even lifted the knife to plunge it into the body of his beloved son. It was just at this point that God intervened and provided an animal for the sacrifice.

The story of Abraham and Isaac prefigures another sacrifice of another son: God's offering up of His own Son on the Cross. This time it was an efficacious sacrifice made for the sins of the world. Compared to the story of Abraham and Isaac, there was no less love for the Son on the part of the Father, and no less submission on the part of the Son to the will of His Father. With Isaac, we see a son willingly submitting himself to the will of his father as he was bound to the altar to face the ultimate test of faith. Nevertheless, we witness a far more wonderful incarnation of submission and love in Jesus Christ, who sacrificed Himself to save us from our sins.

Important and memorable events always warrant a name-sake for the place where they take place. Abraham commemorated the place by calling it Jehovah-jireh, which translates, "Yahweh provides." This is a highly significant reference to God's provision of the animal for the sacrifice, as well as a prophetic allusion to the sacrifice God would provide in His Son, the Christ. Men of faith in the Old Testament really believed that God would provide the efficacious sacrifice that would satisfy divine justice and reconcile God's people to Himself.

Verses 15–24. The story of Abraham's life contains these constant reminders of God's promises. How many times does God reiterate His promises to Abraham? This repetition is hard to miss in God's revelation to His man of faith. If Abraham's life is the prototypical life of faith, then our lives will be made up of two things—the constant reiteration of God's promises and an ever-increasing faith in God on our part. Our faith must be based upon the promises of God, that these promises are for us, and that He has what it takes to deliver on them. As in the case of Abraham, God keeps these promises before us, lest we forget and become disheartened on the way to heaven.

God promised, and it was up to Abraham to believe and obey the God of the promises. When Abraham obeyed, God promised to multiply even more blessings to him and his posterity. What part does faith and obedience play in our covenant relationship with God? Does God desire our faith, obedience, or both? Herein lies a controversial and important question! The Bible outright rejects a system of merit. God delights in the obedience of His children and loves to give them good gifts as a loving father gives gifts to his children. Even a human father will provide an inheritance to his children, who love and respect him, and we are careful not to think of this as a quid-pro-quo system of "merit." If we were to revert to a merit system within the life of the family, motivations would become self-oriented, and relationships would no longer be based upon love and service. If Mother cooks a meal for the family, should she charge each person $6.00 per meal? If one of the children cleans a bathroom, should he send an invoice to Father for $25.00? There would be a huge number of invoices flying around the home, if family life was reduced to a quid-pro-quo enterprise system. This is not the way households run, and this is not the way God runs His household for those He adopts into His family.

While it may appear that God "bases" his blessing upon Abraham's offering up of "his son, his only son," we reject the notion that Abraham earned God's favor in a merit-based judicial or economic sense.

God introduces yet another covenant promise, stating that Abraham's seed will rule over his enemies (verse 17). This also is finally fulfilled in the Lord Jesus Christ. As the Seed of David and the King of Israel, Jesus Christ ascended into heaven to rule on the right hand of the Father, until all of

His enemies were brought under His footstool (Acts 2:34–35). Those who were once enemies of Christ in places like China, New Guinea, South America, Africa, and Greenland now serve the King of kings and Lord of lords. This is the fulfillment of the promise, in the Seed of one solitary man who pitched his tent in the land of Canaan 3,400 years ago.

How does this passage teach us to walk with God in faith and obedience?

1. God demands our absolute allegiance. It may not be every day that He asks a man to give up his most precious possession, as He did when He asked Abraham to give up his only son on Mount Moriah, Nevertheless, at some point in our lives, God will challenge us to choose between something that is precious to us and our commitment to Him. Unless we are willing to leave everything for Christ, we cannot be His disciple.

2. For us, "Yahweh-yireh" means that God has provided our sacrifice on the mountain of Calvary. What a tremendous sense of relief and gratitude Abraham must have felt the moment he discovered that he did not have to plunge the knife into the heart of his only son! Let us not forget that it was Yahweh God Himself who stepped in and provided the sacrifice for Abraham. At the moment that we learn of God's provision of a Sacrifice for us in the form of His Son, might we also experience a similar sense of relief?

3. There are deeper contemplations for us, as we tread upon this holy ground of sin atonement. The world is horribly offended to learn of this Father who sacrificed His own Son on an altar. How could a father love his son and still lift a knife with the intent to kill him? The story of Abraham and Isaac combines the love of a father and son with an all-consuming submission to God. What bothers the ungodly who read this story is the whole idea of blood atonement. They hate the idea that their sin might require any form of atonement. Equally irritating to them is Abraham's willing submission to God's demands (up to and including his yielding up his son to God). These things are profoundly offensive to natural man whose heart is set in absolute rebellion against God.

But the deeper message pounded home to our hearts is the message of God's sacrificial love for undeserving sinners like us. There is no question that God the Father loved God the Son with an everlasting love. He loved His son far more that Abraham loved Isaac. So, for Him to sacrifice His only Son, there must have been some higher purpose for such a monumental action. He gave His Son because He loved the world (John. 3:16), but more fundamentally He did it for the praise of the glory of His grace in Christ Jesus (Eph. 1:6). What wondrous contemplations are found here at the Cross of Jesus Christ! What desperate measures our God employs to rescue sinners from the dark abyss of sin and eternal misery! What severe justice; what severe love! What incomprehensible purposes are found here!

Questions:

1. What are the themes of Chapters 1 through 22?
2. What was God's big faith challenge to Abraham in this chapter?
3. How do we know that Abraham was entirely willing to sacrifice his son on the altar?
4. What does the term Jehovah-jireh or Yahweh-yireh mean?
5. How is Abraham's Seed ruling over His enemies today?

Family Discussion Questions:

1. What earthly relationships or belongings do you consider most precious? Would you be willing to give them up for your love for God?
2. When we give presents to our children, are we paying off our children for being good? Would we be just as likely to give many gifts to children who were constantly disobedient, disrespectful, and hateful towards us? How do a father's gifts relate to a child's relationship with the father?

CHAPTER 23

Sarah Is Buried

And after this, Abraham buried Sarah his wife in the cave of the field of Machpelah before Mamre: the same is Hebron in the land of Canaan. Gen. 23:19

Events:

1. Sarah dies at 127 years of age.
2. Abraham buys the cave of Machpelah from the children of Heth.
3. Abraham buries Sarah in the cave.

What does this passage teach us?

Verses 1–2. This is the first text in Scripture that speaks of the pain and sadness of death. Following the fall in the garden, man's life on earth filled up with trials, danger, and tragedy. But there was no more painful consequence of sin than the curse of death. With the death of his life-partner, Abraham once again felt the emptiness and loneliness of a cursed earth. The sharp reality of death, broken relationships, and separation awakened deep sadness in him. Abraham wept over his loss for a time, but not as a man without hope. For the man of faith, earthly losses are only temporal because he hangs his hopes on eternal gains. It is only men without faith who grieve without reprieve. An endless grieving is a true manifestation of a fundamental lack of faith in the heart. Unbelievers cannot believe in the resurrection power of God, nor can they hope in eternity. Of all men, they are most miserable!

Verses 3–18. Abraham the wanderer bought a field from one of the children of Heth. It was a significant purchase for several reasons. In a world that was effectively owned and operated by tribes of men who were in complete rebellion to God, here was one man of faith who finally took ownership of one small piece of land. Also, the land of Canaan had already been promised to Abraham and his descendants. So the purchase of the cave of Machpelah was a small advance on the promise of the land. By faith, Abraham was sinking his roots in the land, still confident that God would one day provide his descendants with the rest of the land of Canaan.

Against the modern statist ideals that undermine property ownership by way of property taxation and eminent domain, the Bible affirms property ownership on the part of individual families. In the biblical record found here, property is defined by a purchase and a public record of that purchase (vs. 16). Abraham was no socialist. He was careful to provide a payment for the land so as to ensure that nobody else could "share" the land with him. When men take ownership of property, it should be understood that the property remains in the family unless it is sold or transferred by contract. There ought to be no expectation that the property is to be shared with others.

Verses 19–20. Abraham buried Sarah in a cave for which he spent a good deal of money. This established a pattern for burial that was followed by God-fearing people for about 4000 years. It is only among pagan tribes and nations where the practice of cremation and the burning of the body is more normative. After the fall of Rome, cremation virtually disappeared for almost 1,500 years in the Christian West. But with the return of pagan humanism and a breakdown of the Christian faith in the hearts of billions of Christians in the western world, this practice returned with a vengeance. It was only in the 1870s that the first U.S. crematory was constructed in Lancaster, Pennsylvania. By the 21st century, there were over 2,000 crematoriums in America. As might be expected, the states with the lowest percentage of Christians (Hawaii and Nevada), claim the highest cremation rates. The treatment of the body upon death is highly symbolic. For example, burial assumes imminent bodily resurrection. Cremation, though, is strongly suggestive of a lack of belief in the resurrection. It is more representational of annihilationalism, the pagan belief that the body and the soul are annihilated upon death (never to exist again).

A careful study of Scripture will find a good deal of information on the treatment of the body after death. That which is created in the image of God is not to be tampered with and mutilated at the whims of man

(Lev. 19:28; Deut. 14:1). God even condemns the Moabites for their ill-treatment of the body of the king of Edom in Amos 6:10. It is not for us to destroy the body. Under certain extraordinary circumstances God occasionally requires the burning of the body, but it is typically done for the "cleansing" of the land where gross sin was committed (Josh. 7:25; Lev. 20:14; Lev. 21:9; Gen. 38:24; 2 Kg. 23:20; Is. 30:33). As New Testament Christians following the pattern of 2000 years of Christ's church, we lay the body in the grave because we believe that the body will one day rise again from the dead. As we lay our brothers and sisters in the ground, we consider their bodies to be only sleeping. One does not burn a body of one who is sleeping! (Matt. 9:24; John 11:11; 1 Cor. 15:6, 18,20; 1 Thess. 4:13–15). It is only those who have no certain hope in the resurrection from the dead, that will think of burning bodies.

How does this passage teach us to walk with God in faith and obedience?

1. From this text we learn to respect the property that belongs to our neighbor. The modern Marxist notion that all property is held in common is unbiblical at its core. Although large portions of our country are now owned by the federal and state governments and it has become much more common for local and state governments to seize private property, God's Word upholds a strong respect for private property ownership. Therefore, we ought to be careful not to trespass on the property of others without their permission, and we should work hard to re-establish the right to property ownership in our country.

2. Abraham's insistence on paying the full value for his property is a lesson in personal integrity. On the one hand, he wanted exclusive use of the land, but on the other hand, he did not wish to defraud his neighbor of the value of his property. While it may be tempting to cheat our neighbor out of fair market value in our negotiations for their possessions, there are boundaries over which Christians must not pass. Granted, there may be a wide range of value depending on a hundred factors. But common sense should dictate that a car with a "Blue Book" value of $5000 should not sell for $500. Adjusting for private party sales, local demand, and other factors

might reduce the price of the car to $3000, but there should be a point at which an honest man will not want to defraud his neighbor.

3. We also learn from this text that God created both the body and the soul of man in His own image. That is why it is important that we respect the bodies of our loved ones, whether they be dead or alive. That is also why we do not desecrate graveyards or use human skulls as kick balls in sporting activities. Christians do not want to engage in wanton destruction of the bodies of their loved ones. When our people die in the hope of resurrection, it is appropriate to give them a burial fitting to that belief. The burial is like planting a seed with the expectation of new life in the morning (1 Cor. 15:42).

Questions:

1. What are the themes of Chapters 1 through 23?

2. How old was Sarah when she died?

3. Why did Abraham insist on paying for the field?

4. How do we respect the private property of others?

5. How did Abraham show respect for Sarah's body?

6. Why do Christians typically bury the bodies of their loved ones?

Family Discussion Questions:

1. How will we treat the bodies of our own close relatives upon their deaths? What are some good ways in which we might show respect for the bodies of ourselves and others, who are made in the image of God?

2. Are we careful to pay the true value for a product or service? Or would we be likely to defraud a poor widow at a garage sale?

CHAPTER 24

Isaac's Wife

And Isaac brought her into his mother Sarah's tent, and took Rebekah, and she became his wife; and he loved her: and Isaac was comforted after his mother's death. Gen. 24:67

Events:

1. Abraham sends his servant to the city of Nahor to find a wife for Isaac.

2. The servant asks the Lord for guidance at the well outside of the city.

3. God answers the prayer instantly when Rebekah volunteers to water his camels.

4. Rebekah agrees to return to Canaan with the servant and she becomes Isaac's wife.

What does this passage teach us?

Verses 1–9. As the story of the kingdom of God unfolds in the life of a family, the marriage of the son of the covenant forms a pivotal part of the account. It is a story that is relevant to every covenant family in our day. Far too many families have ruined their godly heritage by marrying unbelievers. In fact, this is what marked the sad demise of human civilization prior to the worldwide flood. When the sons of God intermarried with the daughters of men, they produced the wicked Nephilim. But for Isaac, the precious son of the covenant, Abraham did not want to make this fatal mistake.

Since the wicked Canaanites had already been singled out for God's judgment, Abraham was determined that his son would not marry a woman from one of those tribes. His absolute allegiance to that commitment is clear from the text. He had his servant swear by Yahweh in heaven that he would never allow Isaac to marry one of these women. So to obtain a wife for his son, Abraham resorted to the only place on earth where he knew there was still some respect for the God of the covenant. It was the land of his forefathers, roughly 300 miles north, in the cities of Haran and Nahor. So Abraham tasked his most trusted servant to find a wife for his son there.

The modern mind has a hard time comprehending the nature of these arrangements. It seems that, at forty years of age, Isaac would have been old enough to make his own decisions. In this account, however, he was the more passive participant in the process. How suitable is parental involvement in these matters? This hinges on the wisdom of the father, the love of a father for his son (or daughter), and the honor of a son (or daughter) for his (or her) father. Parental involvement in courtship and betrothal without robust and healthy parent-child relationships is usually counterproductive. The weakness of many marriages may be traced directly to the lack of honor in the hearts of sons and daughters for their parents. When a man leaves mother and father to cleave to his wife in marriage, it is especially important that he honor his parents in the process if the fifth commandment means anything at all. Once parents are no longer honored by their children, every other element of culture, economics, and family life comes unravelled. This is what we have seen in the 20th and 21st centuries.

Abraham also did not want his son leaving Canaan. This is because he was still holding on to the land promise for him and his posterity. If Isaac were to seek a wife for himself beyond the borders of Canaan, then he might settle there, especially if his wife was unwilling to leave the land of her people. You can see how Abraham was careful at every point to walk in the will of God, and each detail of this venture was considered to that end.

Verses 10–32. The aged servant then embarked on the most important journey of his life. It was an errand of monumental importance. As he stood at the well outside of the village of Nahor, the faithful man did what every man of God would do on such a critical mission. He prayed, and it was a remarkable prayer of faith. We may wonder, however, if his prayer for a sign crossed over the line into presumption. Jesus drew the line for the Devil when He rejected the temptation to take a flying leap off the pinnacle of the temple. Since there is nothing in the text that condemns the servant for his prayer, it is obvious that we should not condemn him. We see that he did lay out highly precise conditions by which he might ascertain the will of God in the matter. But there was also nothing in the prayer that would even approach the Devil's flagrant attempts to subject the Son of God to his whims (meanwhile advocating a violation of the Sixth Commandment—suicide). There is a thin line between presumption and faith in our walk with God. What matters is the heart of the one who prays. Is he subjected to the will of God or is he attempting to subject the sovereign God to his own will? Obviously, this man did not travel for twenty-one days to seek out his own agenda. It is clear that this man had already subjected himself to the will of his master, who himself was unquestionably submitted to the will of God in the matter of the marriage of his son. This was no impudent, presumptuous prayer. It was the petition of a humble servant who wished to be guided by the wisdom of God in this high-stakes game of selecting a wife for the son of the covenant.

The test the man chose to use on the prospective bride for his master is instructive to any young man seeking a wife. He carefully formulated a test that would identify the fine character traits of kindness, hospitality, and industriousness—all important features of a good wife, as also illustrated in Proverbs 31. Drawing sufficient water to satisfy a caravan of ten camels would have taken considerable time and energy, as this caravan would have consumed at least 300 gallons of water! Any woman who would gladly extend hospitality to an old man and his whole caravan is a woman whose price is far above rubies. Her hands extend to the needy, and she will not eat the bread of idleness (Prov. 31:20, 27).

This was a wonderful answer to prayer. Immediately after praying for a woman that would water his entire caravan, God brought a woman who volunteered to do exactly this! Rebekah's hospitality extended still further, as she invited the man to stay with her family. At this point in the proceedings, the servant was so overwhelmed with the goodness and power of God that he bowed his head to the ground and worshiped.

Verses 33–67. Rebekah's brother Laban came to meet the servant at the well. Right away he gave credence to the God of Abraham, employing His covenant name, Yahweh. Evidently there was a measure of belief in the true God still extant in the family of Bethuel (son of Nahor, Abraham's brother—Rebekah was Isaac's cousin's daughter).

Upon arriving at Laban's home, the servant wasted no time in laying out the purpose for his journey. He spoke of his trip from Canaan, his prayer to God, and the answer to his prayer. Instantly, Bethuel and Laban saw God's hand and direction in the matter. "The thing is of the Lord," they said. We may wonder ourselves if answers to prayers like these provide providential direction and give wisdom in our decision-making. We must understand that the first and primary means by which decisions are made is God's prior revelation in His Word. Abraham had already narrowed God's will for Isaac's spouse down to his extended family, based on God's prophetic Word concerning the Canaanites.

To refuse to frame their lives by the revelation of God's Word is the first mistake that many make when they set out to know God's will. In making life's decisions, we want to take the "wisest" and "best" approach to walking in God's ways and pleasing Him. But this does not happen without a heart that loves His Word, and a mind and will that are applied diligently to doing His revealed will. If God provides a special providence or an answer to prayer that points us to the way of wisdom, we ought to be grateful for this mercy. When Rebekah's father and brother approved of the marriage, the servant again fell prostrate to the ground and worshiped Yahweh God. What a remarkable example of faith and gratefulness to God! It is as if the man forgot everything else around him, overwhelmed by a sense of God's presence and goodness.

Thus far in the story, Rebekah had not yet been consulted. This seems foreign to an individualistic culture where each person makes his or her own choices in life. According to the biblical pattern, however, fathers, mothers, and brothers have a great deal to say about prospective marriages. It is only foreign to us because, for the last century or so, we have watched this individualistic, socialized culture dismantle the family unit. However, the basic integrity of the family, honor for parents, and love and concern for siblings were still in place in Rebekah's community.

Nevertheless, this was not a strictly pre-arranged marriage. In verse 58, Rebekah forthrightly agreed to the arrangement, and later Isaac himself received her as his wife and embraced her with true love and affection.

How does this passage teach us to walk with God in faith and obedience?

1. This chapter commends faith-filled prayers. It is probably accurate to say that most of us do not pray with enough faith. According to Christ, a mustard seed of faith will move mountains! (Mark 11:20-24) Of course, a prayer of faith should begin by ascertaining the will of God about moving the mountain concerned. If moving this mountain is what is needed for God's kingdom, and you ascertain that it needs to be moved, then pray that God will move that mountain! Be confident that you are in the will of God, and faith will be added to your prayer. But it all begins with having the wisdom to ascertain what God's desires are, as communicated through His Word and Spirit. As mentioned earlier, there is a thin line between presumption and faith in what we pray for. May God help us to identify it, and pray with robust faith according to the will of God.

In order to pray with faith for specific requests while being assured that we are in the will of God, we must rely on the Spirit of God, who "makes intercession for us with groanings which cannot be uttered" (Rom. 8:26, 27). The Spirit must direct our prayers because it is the Spirit that confirms in us the will of God through the testimony of His Word. If we are confident that we are in His will, then we will pray with more faith for more things in accordance with His will. May God strengthen our prayer life, embolden our faith, and show Himself to us in many answered prayers!

2. Our worship should be as spontaneous and as seamlessly integrated into life as it was for Abraham's servant in this passage. Twice, he interrupted the conversation by bowing his head to the ground and falling prostrate before God in thanksgiving and praise. (The Hebrew word for worship is "Shachah," which is literally translated "prostrate.") When God answers a prayer, never fail to thank Him for it. If the situation calls for it, fall on your face and worship the King.

3. There are few more important decisions for a man or a woman than the choice of a prospective mate. Such decisions cannot be made without faith in God, utmost submission to the will of God, and sincere prayer to God for wisdom. Should Christian fathers, mothers, and young people treat these matters lightly, their families will pay a price for it. May God increase

love for children in the hearts of parents, and honor for parents in the hearts of children! When fathers do not lead in faith and family members do not love each other enough, successive generations suffer from weak marriages, and the kingdom of God languishes!

Questions:

1. What are the themes of Chapters 1 through 24?
2. Where did Abraham send his servant to find a wife for Isaac?
3. How did Abraham's servant pray for the Lord to lead him to the right woman?
4. What good character traits did Rebekah exhibit in this chapter?
5. What biblical principles can we find in this chapter that relate to finding spouses?

Family Discussion Questions:

1. What are the sorts of spouses we seek for our children? How much involvement will we expect from dad, mom, brothers, and sisters in forthcoming courtships and marriages in our family?
2. In what situations might it be appropriate for us to fall on our faces and worship God? Have you ever fallen on your face in a public place and worshiped God?

CHAPTER 25

Abraham's Line

And these are the days of the years of Abraham's life which he lived, an hundred threescore and fifteen years. Then Abraham gave up the ghost, and died in a good old age, an old man, and full of years; and was gathered to his people. And his sons Isaac and Ishmael buried him in the cave of Machpelah, in the field of Ephron the son of Zohar the Hittite, which is before Mamre; Gen. 25:7–9

Events:

1. Abraham takes Keturah as a wife and has six more sons.
2. Abraham dies and is buried.
3. Ishmael is blessed with twelve sons.
4. Isaac and Rebekah are blessed with two sons, Jacob and Esau.
5. Esau sells his birthright for a bowl of red lentil stew.

What does this passage teach us?

Verses 1–6. Life was not over for Abraham following the death of his first wife, Sarah. He continued to live life to its fullest by marrying another woman and populating the earth with six more sons. Although Yahweh God had clearly established the covenant with Isaac alone (Gen. 17:21), Abraham was still being true to the basic dominion covenant God made with Adam and Noah. Both then and now, God intended for men to populate the earth, work the soil, and harness animals and minerals for the benefit of mankind. Though it is a sad reality in a fallen world, some children who are born into Christian homes do not remain in the covenant. Although we hope this to be the irregular case, it was not so for the sons of Samuel, David, and Solomon. But even when a disobedient, apostate son turns out to be a sorrow to his father and mother, this does not mark the end of all hope and purpose for the family. At the very least, godly parents are still fulfilling the dominion mandate when they raise children. They are still endeavoring to live life in obedience to God's will. Moreover, we also find that the covenant promises revisit a man's posterity in generations to come. It was out of the ungodly behavior of Lot's daughters and the unbelieving Moabites that Ruth came, and blessed God's people through furthering the line of David and the Lord Jesus Christ, Himself.

It is important to note that Abraham refused to provide any significant part of the inheritance to anyone but Isaac, the son of the covenant. When the interests of the kingdom of God are of primary importance in the eyes of the man of faith, he will want to put his resources on God's project.

Verses 7–10. Abraham died at 175 years of age, and his sons buried him in the cave that he had purchased from the sons of Heth. From these early records of divine revelation, those who read with eyes of faith will identify several clues pertaining to the afterlife. Very early in the history of the world, Genesis records Enoch's ascension to be with God. The man did not die. This was a strong sign to generations of faith afterwards that there was something other than death awaiting the righteous. As we read that Abraham was "gathered to his people," we cannot help but to think that this was a veiled, but hopeful allusion to a reunion of the living somewhere beyond death! We are those who believe in the resurrection ourselves, so we ought to use such references to death. While life on earth may involve separation from our roots—as is the case with the wandering vagabond and stranger—believers can rest assured that one day they will arrive at their final home for eternal fellowship with loved ones, never to part again.

As we approach the New Testament, we begin to find more explicit references to the resurrection of the body, centered on the bodily resurrection of our Lord. With the Old Testament writings, however, we find only veiled references to heaven and resurrection—but even these veiled references would have inspired hope in the hearts of believers. Sadly, the skeptical sect of the Sadducees in the time of Christ did not pick up on these references. They would not believe in the final resurrection. For all true believers throughout all time, the belief in the resurrection is one of the most basic truths of all.

Verses 11–18. The book of Genesis is organized mainly around family lines, beginning with Adam, Seth, and Noah, and ending with Abraham, Isaac, and Jacob. Chapter 25 then summarizes the line of Abraham, beginning with his oldest son, Ishmael. Some parts of God's covenant promises for Abraham materialized right away. True to God's promise, Abraham became the father of several nations immediately. Ishmael quickly rose to power and influence by way of his twelve sons, who themselves became powerful princes over cities. By God's providence, Isaac had to wait a generation for his twelve sons! Sometimes God's kingdom works slowly and somewhat surreptitiously. Nevertheless, the Edomites had no part in the covenant and so the kingdom they established was merely an earthly kingdom. Today the Edomites are gone. Their kingdom did not last. But the Kingdom of Christ, David, Moses, and Jacob continues to prosper, even to this day.

Verses 19–26. It should be pointed out that God's Word is most concerned with the people of the covenant. Until the Gospel reached Asia Minor, Greece, and Rome, very little was said about the great empires of men. A few paragraphs were afforded to cover Babel, Egypt, and Greece. The book of Daniel had a tiny bit to say about Greece and Rome. Although Ishmael produced a great nation, only a sum total of eight verses addressed his kingdoms. God is more interested in His own covenant people. The last half of the book of Genesis will provide minute detail concerning the descendants of Isaac and his covenant son, Jacob.

As is characteristic in the development of God's people, Isaac and Rebekah faced their own difficulties. They suffered through twenty painful years of barrenness before they added one more grain of sand to the posterity that was supposed to be more numerous than the sand on the seashore. Comparing the fertility and accomplishments of Ishmael with that of Isaac, it may seem at first that God was blessing the unfaithful more than the faithful. But He always has good reasons for what He does with His own. The meek do inherit the earth... eventually. But they have to be meek first. God carefully humbles His people in order that He might exalt them. This is how He works in history. Just so they will rely upon Him, God trains His people to patiently endure much difficulty along the way, as they grow His kingdom through the generations. Without question, He is testing their faith.

Under these trying circumstances, Isaac did not repeat the same mistake Abraham made, when his father took a second wife. Instead, he interceded to God for his wife. The Lord answered his prayer and Rebekah conceived twins. Still alive, Abraham would have been 160 years old when his grandsons were born. What a tremendous confirmation for Abraham and Isaac's faith!

Then we read that the two babies wrestled in Rebekah's womb through the pregnancy. Helpfully, the Lord God explained this ferocious prenatal competition to her. By His providence, He planned that these two children would form two nations. They would represent two sides of the great cosmic war that existed since the Garden. For hundreds of years, the Edomites would set themselves against the descendants of Jacob. To this day, the wars in the Middle East may still represent some of this dissension. Towards the end of God's revelation to Rebekah, we find an encouraging promise that remains a comfort to the sons and daughters of the covenant forever: "The older son will serve the younger." This was the preferred modus operandi by which the kingdom of God would play itself out in the succeeding millennia. Again and again throughout history, God would exalt the disadvantaged and humble the proud. The younger brother in the parable of the Prodigal Son got the fatted calf and received great mercy and acceptance from his father. This principle always renders hope to the downtrodden, the humble, and the needy, while at the same time checking the pride of the privileged and presumptuous.

So the younger emerged from the womb gripping the heel of his elder brother and he was named Jacob, or "heel holder." Throughout his life, Jacob demonstrated a strong competitive spirit, and an overweening inclination towards usurping the position of the elder.

Verses 27–34. As with all siblings, there were marked differences between Esau and Jacob—Esau was full of vigor and a hunter in the field while Jacob preferred to stay in the tent. For better or worse, Isaac and Rebekah played favorites with their sons. Certainly, Rebekah had good reason to choose Jacob as the favorite, having received God's revelation concerning the matter. The basis for Isaac's favoritism was less rooted in divine revelation than in his stomach. According to verse 28, Isaac was especially fond of the venison that Esau brought home from the hunt. As parents, our primary interest in our children should be their spiritual well-being, not the immediate gratification we receive from externalism and superficiality.

A man's values and priorities are eventually clarified at certain crossroads in his life. This is what happened to Esau the day he sold his birthright. On that fateful day, he clarified his own priorities in life by choosing a meal over his birthright in the inheritance. The importance of this event in Esau's life can hardly be overstated. In fact, the name used for his generational line is "Edomite," and refers to the "red stew" he ate that day in exchange for his birthright. Evidently Esau had little interest in the long-term promise of the land (which was still 400 years to follow). Nor was he all that interested in being part of the covenant line. His carnal, temporal commitments were manifest in his all-controlling desire to have something he could touch and taste and enjoy in the present.

How does this passage teach us to walk with God in faith and obedience?

1. Any one of us may die today. As Christians we must hang all of our hopes on a final resurrection. We must believe that we will be present on that day with Christ and all true believers, friends, and family members. For this reason, we do not have to be afraid of death.

2. Where are you in relation to the covenant and the kingdom of God? Are you an Esau or a Jacob? Do you look forward to the blessings of heaven or do you seek all your blessings in the present? Jesus told his disciples to lay up for themselves treasures in heaven. Sometimes you may have to deny yourself and suffer for Christ in this world. You will not find this so burdensome if you have faith that God has a great inheritance waiting for you in heaven. Without a solid faith placed in the promises of God, you will throw away that inheritance in exchange for a little pleasure here and now.

Questions:

1. What are the themes of Chapters 1 through 25?
2. What problem did both Rebekah and Sarah share?
3. What was the sin Abraham had committed that Isaac did not commit? How was Isaac to be commended in this chapter? How did he demonstrate weakness?
4. What do the names "Jacob" and "Esau" mean?
5. What did Esau do that demonstrated his lack of interest in being an heir to the covenant?
6. How did Esau come to be called Edom?

Family Discussion Questions:

1. What are the problems that may develop when parents play favorites with their children? When is it appropriate to commend a child for something? Is there any sin in preferring one child in the inheritance over another child?
2. Does it appear that Christians have the upper hand in our country at this time, or does it appear that the wicked are prospering? Is God humbling His people? Can we expect that God will bring the proud down as well?

CHAPTER 26

Isaac Blessed

And the LORD appeared unto him the same night, and said, I am the God of Abraham thy father: fear not, for I am with thee, and will bless thee, and multiply thy seed for My servant Abraham's sake. Gen. 26:24

Events:

1. God reiterates his covenant promise to Isaac.

2. Isaac seeks to protect his wife in Gerar.

3. Isaac avoids conflicts with the herdsmen of Gerar.

4. Isaac and Abimelech make an agreement to live together in peace.

What does this passage teach us?

Verses 1–5. In this chapter, we find that God's blessing for Abraham was reaching into the generations and touching the lives of Isaac and his family. But it wasn't all a bed of roses for Isaac. Like all the rest of God's people who walk this earth, Isaac faced difficulties throughout his lifetime. It started with a famine in the land that forced him to move south into the land of the Philistines. When families must move from place to place because of persecution, famine, or unemployment, they cannot very well establish roots or settle the land. They take on more of the role of a vagabond or a gypsy, who never have the opportunity to improve on their property and develop their communities. We continue to witness this transience in the life of Isaac, which might have eroded any notion of his long term inheritance in the land of Canaan. But God stepped in and reminded Isaac of his inheritance. It would have been tempting for Isaac to have taken his family to Egypt, for it was a large, prosperous empire. Warning him not to take his family into Egypt, Yahweh God reiterated the promises He made to his father, Abraham. God had bigger plans for Isaac and his heirs.

Verse five contains an important characterization of the life of Abraham. While we would not go so far as to claim sinless perfection for him, it is plain that he embraced a life of faithfulness to God. To keep the commandments of God is to keep the faith or guard the post. Abraham was like a careful sentry, looking out for the commandments and statutes which Yahweh had revealed to him. In other words, Abraham was a faithful son. He loved God as his father and God loved him as a son; and a father loves to reward an obedient son who is faithful to him. God blessed Abraham and Isaac, because Abraham kept God's commandments by faith. For the same reason that a good father will gladly turn over an inheritance to a faithful son, God provides an inheritance for His son. The fundamental basis for Abraham's reward was found in their relationship, not in that Abraham kept so many commandments and only broke a few along the way. At the end of the day, every good and perfect gift (including the gift of faith), comes from the Father of lights (Jam. 1:17). Likewise, there was nothing in Abraham's faith and obedience that would have merited his salvation or the blessings conferred upon him.

Verses 6–11. During his stay in the land of Gerar, Isaac repeated Abraham's actions. Isaac referred to his wife as his sister in order to protect his own life. In the case of Abraham, the reference to Sarah as his sister was, at the very least, a half-truth. For Isaac it was a clear falsehood, since Rebekah was his cousin. According to the cultural mores of the day, brothers were expected to take responsibility for their sisters in regard to their betrothals. Therefore, we must not think that Isaac failed to provide protection for Rebekah. Here again, the plan backfired when Abimelech saw Isaac interacting with Rebekah in an intimate way, as a husband would with a wife. You would think that Isaac would have learned from the failures of his father in this area. But God was patient as he worked with this family (of whom He had just said were faithful to His commandments)! For the third time, God circumvented the harebrained plans of His men and provided protection for the family. While the heathen king proceeded to chew Isaac out for his duplicity, the Lord God blessed Isaac an hundredfold in subsequent days. Isaac was in a covenant relationship with the sovereign God of heaven and earth.

Verses 12–24. When the Philistines saw Isaac's great wealth, they envied him because of it. There is no more destructive evil than the sin of envy. For, while the coveter wants to possess that which belongs to others, blind envy hates the prosperity of others and wants to destroy it! So the Philistines didn't even bother stealing Abraham's wells. These envious men ruined the wells previously dug by Abraham for his family. What a tremendous waste of productive work that could have yielded good profit for crops and herds. To make matters even worse, they provoked range war against the herdsmen of Isaac. War is just another unproductive and destructive use of resources, but that is what sinful heathen tribes spent most of their time on. Whether it be the megalomaniac nationalists or internationalists or pagan tribes like the Native Americans or South Sea Islanders, men are particularly drawn to fighting other men.

However, Isaac was a true son of God, the prototypical peacemaker in His kingdom (Matt. 5:9). There may not be many like Isaac on the earth, but where there are true Christians, there will be true efforts towards making peace. Isaac wisely refused to waste his resources on fighting a range war when he could simply dig another well in another location. Holding firmly to God's injunction, "Vengeance is Mine, I will repay," saith the Lord, this righteous man saw no need to require retribution for every act of evil done to him. He knew that his reward would neither come from the Philistines nor wells of water. His reward would come from the Father of lights. Surely enough, God continued to bless Isaac despite all the inconveniences caused by the Philistines. Being a part of God's family and a member of the covenant had its benefits. Along with His blessings, God also provided the comforting promise contained in verse 24, "Fear not, for I am with you." This promise is repeated many times throughout Scripture, and those who embraced it with iron faith became mighty men of God, both in ancient and recent times. Taking dominion of this world is not easy, and whether one is taking the promised land or taking the entire world for Jesus Christ, that promise resounds again and again throughout Scripture: "Behold I am with you, even until the end of the world!" (Deut. 31:6–8; Matt. 28:20)

Verses 25–33. In the end, Abimelech agreed to make a treaty with Isaac. First, Isaac pointed out the animosity that had developed between the two groups. Abimelech categorically denied this, acting as if his people had been faultless in all the strife. However, they were able to make an agreement similar to the one Abraham made at least eighty years prior. In commemoration of this new agreement, Isaac dug another well and called it Beersheba, which meant "well of the vow."

Verses 34–35. The last few verses of the chapter mention the rebellion of Isaac's oldest son, Esau. The state of this young man's heart was not good, as demonstrated in his selection of a wife. Not only did he practice polygamy (something his father did not do), but he also married Canaanite women. These were a people that God had condemned in the covenant promises. This rebellion saddened both of his parents.

How does this passage teach us to walk with God in faith and obedience?

1. Envy is a destructive sin. We should root out the sprouts of envy as soon as it shows up in our lives. We also ought to be careful not to encourage envy in others, by comparing ourselves with others or bragging about our accomplishments.

2. The story of Isaac is the story of respect for fathers. You may have noticed that in verse 18, Isaac kept the same names for the wells that his father had given to them. Indeed, this faithful son patterned his life after his father in many ways. He was careful to get along with his neighbors. He made covenants with them, and worked hard to avoid conflict with them. He even named a new well using the same name his father had used for another location ("Beersheba").

3. Some young people from Christian homes demonstrate the rebellion of Esau. They do not treasure their Christian heritage and they do not love the God of their parents. Often they find unbelieving spouses to marry, as Esau did. Watch out for the seeds of rebellion. It begins with a carelessness towards the things of the Lord—for example, preferring to eat red stew rather than to sit and listen to God's Word. It begins with dishonoring thoughts about fathers and mothers. It begins with a love for the world that displaces a love for Christ and His Word. If you see the seeds of rebellion

in your life, you must repent of them right away. Ask God's forgiveness and seek Him with all your heart today.

4. God is with us. If we really believed this, we would not be afraid of people or of dangerous circumstances. God has given us a commission to take His kingdom throughout the world. We should engage in this mission with vigor and faith, realizing that the God who created the universe is at our side. He has promised that He will never leave us or forsake us.

Questions:

1. What are the themes of Chapters 1 through 26?

2. When Isaac introduced his wife to Abimelech, how did he mirror what his father Abraham had done?

3. What did Isaac do to the Philistines when they began to fight over his wells?

4. What does "Beersheba" mean?

5. In this chapter, what promise has been a strong comfort to Christians who are alone in a dangerous world?

6. How did Esau manifest his rebellion to God and to his parents?

Family Discussion Questions:

1. What kind of legacy are you gaining right now from your father and mother? Will you honor your parents and carry on their godly habits and customs?

2. How can you detect envy creeping up in your own heart? How might you be encouraging envy in others?

3. What confidence do we have that Christ is with us, as we seek His kingdom?

CHAPTER 27

Jacob Blessed

And when Esau heard the words of his father, he cried with a great and exceeding bitter cry, and said unto his father, "Bless me, even me also, O my father." And he said, "Thy brother came with subtlety, and hath taken away thy blessing." Gen. 27:34–35

Events:

1. Rebekah aids her son Jacob in his duplicitous acquisition of the blessing.
2. Esau plots to kill his brother.
3. Rebekah sends Jacob back to Haran to her brother Laban's house.

What does this passage teach us?

Verses 1–4. This chapter describes a wholesale moral failure on the part of Isaac's family. Despite the sad failure of these men of the covenant, God's purposes are never frustrated. He gets what He wants one way or another!

God's revelation ought to trump human traditions, but there is no indication that Isaac considered God's Word to Rebekah in his plans for his sons' inheritance. Before the birth of the twins, God had told Rebekah that the elder would serve the younger. Initially, it seems that Isaac's priorities were set more towards lesser things than the kingdom of God. For a bowl of porridge, Esau forfeited his birthright. For a portion of venison, Isaac sought to pass the blessing to the one who shirked the covenant.

All of this chapter rests upon the assumption that the blessing of a father has some influence upon the future state of a son. Rightly so, both Esau and Jacob were strongly desirous of their father's blessing. All children ought to value a father's blessing. But it is still God who remains the One from whom all blessings flow. A father may pronounce a blessing that does not materialize, for the same reason that farmers plant seeds that do not germinate. Yet these blessings still mean something. When a father pronounces a thoughtful blessing upon his children, he plants seeds that may very well germinate. But God is still sovereign over the increase. This fact may have been missed by some of the players in this story. From the outset, it is clear that God fully intended Jacob to receive both the birthright and the blessing. Scripture tells us this. Clearly, God loved Jacob and He hated Esau (Rom. 9:13; Mal. 1:2).

Verses 5–40. Among the many problems in the life of this family were Isaac's failure at spiritual leadership, and a lack of unity between him and his wife. Apparently, Rebekah did not feel that her husband would receive her thoughts in the matter of the blessing. So she instigated a plan to deceive her husband so as to transfer the blessing to Jacob. Meanwhile, Jacob lived up to his name as "the supplanter" in this charade. He lied when his father asked him point blank, "Who are you?" God's Word puts the highest value upon truth and condemns all liars to the lake of fire, so it is important to understand something about what the Bible says about lies. There are various forms of what we call "lies" found in Scripture and human experience. These are summarized below:

1. Playful lies are told by actors in the theater, where everyone understands it is only an act.

2. Obliging lies are told to protect someone else (as Rahab did for the spies at Jericho).

3. Destructive lies are told when bearing false witness to harm our neighbor.

4. Wartime lies are deceptive actions taken to fool an enemy in a battle, as when the armies of Israel feigned a rout before the armies of Ai.

5. Revelatory lies are told to shock a sinner into realizing his ignorance and sin. For example, in Luke 24 Jesus allowed two men to believe that He was an ordinary man until the time was right to reveal Himself. Joseph did something similar with his brothers in Egypt; and in 2 Samuel 12, Nathan recounted a story to David to bring him to repentance.

There is wide disagreement among Christian thinkers and writers concerning these things. What constitutes a bona-fide falsehood and a moral sin? Some consider only destructive lies to be sinful. Others point to obliging lies and wartime lies as sinful behavior. Suffice it to say that God is the One who defines what is true and what is righteous—not us. If the Bible tells us that a certain lie is a sin, then that settles it. If the Bible condemns Nathan for misleading David, then we must conclude that his words were sinful and wrong. If we can find in the Bible some indication that what Rebekah did was a sin, then we must agree that it was sin. In the case of this particular story, it is not immediately clear whether Jacob told a destructive lie or an obliging lie. On the one hand, this lie could have been destructive to the future of Esau, yet it might have been obliging to Isaac who was (at least in the view of his wife, Rebekah) about to make a mistake in placing the blessing on Esau. However, Isaac accused Jacob of fraudulently usurping the blessing in verse 35. This is an indication within the text that Jacob was guilty of the sin of lying.

Despite Esau's protests to the contrary, Isaac refused to remove the blessing from his son Jacob. Does this suggest a change of heart on the part of Isaac in relation to Jacob's blessing? At this point Isaac must have been willing to submit to the will of God in the matter. What we do know is that God would never have allowed a blessing on Esau. That was not in accord with His eternal plan with regard to Esau and Jacob—a plan that He revealed at the birth of the twins.

Verses 41–46. Sadly, the true heart of Esau was revealed in his anger. When Rebekah heard of Esau's intent to murder his brother, she insisted that Jacob return to Haran and stay with her brother, Laban. In some respects, she was more committed to the covenant than her husband was. She was willing to do whatever was necessary to preserve the son of the covenant. We know Abraham could not think of his son marrying a daughter of the Canaanites, and Rebekah shared this commitment. According to verse 46, this was the most important concern of her life. She said her life would be a total waste if her second son married a Canaanite.

How does this passage teach us to walk with God in faith and obedience?

1. Although we would not say Rebekah behaved perfectly in this story, she did maintain something of a righteous commitment to the covenant. She may have chosen the wrong approach in pursuing this righteous commitment and securing the blessing for the son of the covenant, but at this stage, she exhibited a deeper commitment to the covenant than her husband did. Therefore, it would have been prudent for her husband to have listened to his wife. David listened to Abigail's warning when he was about to shed blood without due cause, and he received her respectful correction. In accordance with Paul's admonition, a wife should maintain a meek and tranquil spirit, and submit to her husband in the Lord. But this certainly doesn't preclude her bringing an important matter to her husband's attention, especially if it pertains to an element of God's Word. Nobody is closer to a man than his wife. Nobody loves a man more and nobody is as committed to a man's success as his wife. Of course, a wife should speak her wise counsel freely in her husband's presence, and he should be more than willing to receive it!

2. It is also appropriate that fathers speak a blessing on their children. Both fathers and pastors have been given some authority to pronounce a blessing. Even as the fervent prayers of a righteous man effect much within the sovereign rule of God, we can trust that our spoken blessings may produce similar effects.

3. Our first commitment is always to the interests of the kingdom of God. Our love for Christ and His kingdom should trump our love for our children and especially our love for good venison. Therefore, it is not for us to reward rebellion. If a child rebels against the covenant, the father should consider this when he plans out his blessing and inheritance.

Questions:

1. What are the themes of Chapters 1 through 27?

2. How did Isaac disobey God in his plan to bless Esau?

3. How did Rebekah and Jacob lie to Isaac?

4. What sort of lie did Jacob tell in this story? Was this lie a sin?

5. Why didn't Isaac cancel out the blessing he gave to Jacob?

6. What were the two reasons Rebekah gave for sending Jacob to Haran?

Family Discussion Questions:

1. Do we have a problem with lying in our family? Give several examples of sinful lies that may have been told in our family. Why do people engage in sinful lying?

2. What is the proper heart attitude a wife should have when she is about to provide an important piece of wisdom for her husband? What is the proper heart attitude her husband should have?

3. What sort of blessing might we provide for our children? Consider what would make an appropriate occasion for such blessings, and what blessing might be appropriate for each child.

CHAPTER 28

Jacob's Ladder

And he dreamed, and behold a ladder set up on the earth, and the top of it reached to heaven: and behold the angels of God ascending and descending on it. And, behold, the LORD stood above it, and said, "I am the LORD God of Abraham thy father, and the God of Isaac: the land whereon thou liest, to thee will I give it, and to thy seed."
Gen. 28:12–13

Events:

1. Isaac blesses Jacob a second time.

2. Esau takes another wife (from the daughters of Ishmael).

3. Jacob travels to Haran and on the way he has a dream in which God blesses him.

4. Jacob makes a vow to the Lord.

What does this passage teach us?

Verses 1–9. This chapter presents a different Isaac altogether. It is as if he awakened from a stupor with a great deal more enthusiasm for God's covenantal purposes. He was now fully on board, and ready to embrace his wife's better judgement and God's plan for his family. Now affirming the covenant promises God gave to his father, Abraham, he fully accepted and approved Jacob as God's appointed heir to the covenant. Hebrews 11:20 plainly testifies to this—"By faith Isaac blessed Jacob and Esau concerning things to come." Although the demonstration of that faith may have been imperfect in the beginning, Isaac's willingness to fully accept God's will was evident in the end. Faithless men might have steadfastly opposed God's will in stubborn pride, but this was not the case with Isaac. His humility and repentance were manifest.

Esau, however, did not take this view of the covenant. On the surface, it might appear as if his desire for the blessing signaled a return to covenantal faithfulness and a relationship with the God of his fathers. In truth, this was far from the case. Further on in God's Word, we find the Book of Hebrews comparing him to fornicators and profane persons. "Looking diligently lest any man fail of the grace of God; lest any root of bitterness springing up trouble you, and thereby many be defiled; lest there be any fornicator, or profane person, as Esau, who for one morsel of meat sold his birthright. For ye know how that afterward, when he would have inherited the blessing, he was rejected: for he found no place of repentance, though he sought it carefully with tears" (Heb. 2:15-17).

Esau's repentance was not genuine. In most Western countries today, including the United States, apostasy from the covenant is practically the norm among Christian families. Children quickly lose interest in the church and don't prioritize the kingdom of God. Following suit with the first apostate, Esau, they synthesize with the world by taking on its ideas and by marrying unbelievers who have no interest in raising mighty warriors for the kingdom of Christ. When it comes down to making the choice, they prefer a bowl of porridge over God's eternal blessings and precious promises.

Esau did take a third wife from a descendant of Abraham, but this comes across as a half-hearted attempt to regain his father's blessing. Besides perpetuating the problem of polygamy, he married into Ishmael's line that had already demonstrated similar separation from the covenant. Esau must have been incapable of discerning the priorities of the covenant.

Verses 10–15. As Jacob left his home for Haran, it is important for us to recall that this man was the root from which all Israel would come. He was the source of the church of God on earth. Alone and exiled from home, he represented the seed of God's people. In a world populated with millions of people, this solitary figure was the one man on earth with whom Yahweh God chose to perpetuate a covenant relationship. Jacob sleeping alone under the stars on a rock in a strange country is a picture of a vulnerable church protected by the hand of a sovereign God.

It is at this dramatic stage in the development of the church that God revealed Himself to Jacob in a marvelous way. Jacob dreamt of angels ascending and descending to the earth on a ladder, a representation of God's careful provision for His people. As we see throughout Scripture, angels serve as ministering spirits attending to the needs of the people of God. The ladder merely represented a connection between God and His people, transcending the distance put there by the sin of man. Today, we recognize that great mediation to be the Son of God Himself, the person of the Lord Jesus Christ.

The Creator of heaven and earth revealed His great promises directly to this lone man, lying in the dark wilderness somewhere on the east side of the Mediterranean Sea. It was a repetition of the Abrahamic promise already reiterated a number of times to both Abraham and Isaac. But there was something added here, which became a central element of the covenant promises given through Moses and our Lord Jesus Christ (Deut. 31:6–8; Matt. 28:19–20; Heb. 13:5). "Behold, I am with you, and I will keep you in all places whither you go." This was closely related to the early form of the Abrahamic promise, "I will be your God, and you will be My people." This promise to Jacob added the comfort of knowing that God would be in covenant with him wherever he went. This world is a dangerous place, and believers are almost always severely outnumbered. They rob the strong man's house when they preach the Gospel of Christ and extend the borders of His kingdom. Though the man of God be alone, outnumbered, or overwhelmed by the foe, he can count on one thing— God is with him. And that is enough! On the cusp of taking the promised land, Joshua received this same promise, as did the apostles of Christ as they prepared to take the entire globe for their Lord. When embarking on a project of eternal value and cosmic proportions, it is essential that we know and believe that our Savior is always with us.

Verses 16–22. When Jacob woke up, he was simultaneously overwhelmed with great joy and great fear. A genuine relationship with Almighty God must truly involve a complex web of emotions—fear, love, peace, and joy. Certainly, any who have caught a vision of Almighty God, Creator of heaven and earth, who connects with man by way of a heavenly ladder, or more strikingly, by the visitation and sacrifice of His only begotten Son, would respond in both holy awe and humble joy. Such a person would be afraid to take God's name in vain or to disobey His righteous orders.

It isn't every day that a man has such a close and meaningful encounter with the Lord of the heavens. It is appropriate to identify such times and places with a memorial. This is not for the purpose of turning the memorial into an idol, but it is so that God's people might remember the interest that He has taken in them and the special connection He made with them. Jacob memorialized the place with a stone and called it "Bethel," meaning "House of God."

Finally, Jacob made a vow in this place, hinging his faith on God's provision for him. If God could bring him back to the land of his fathers, then he would, in faith, accept God as his own. He further committed to giving one tenth of his income to the Lord in what is known as "the tithe." Jacob was equipped to live the Christian life of faith and obedience.

How does this passage teach us to walk with God in faith and obedience?

1. Let us not follow the path of Esau, who did not walk in thorough-going repentance. When a man repents only in order to receive an earthly blessing, he is failing to meet the real problem head-on. He betrays his basic heart commitments. There is no sin in delighting in earthly blessings, but when we are willing to trade heavenly blessings for earthly (if presented the opportunity), it is plain that our hearts do not yearn after God. In such a case, we do not believe God's promises, and we cannot believe that God has greater blessings awaiting us at the consummation of His heavenly kingdom. May God help us to seek a heavenly country, while we traverse this earthly pilgrimage.

2. God is with us. What an encouragement this is to those who are traveling difficult roads, fighting dangerous wars, and striving to acquire new territories for the kingdom of Christ. Those who are unfamiliar with the Christian life will find no comfort in these words. But for those of us in the heat of the battle, these words constitute a lifeline in our darkest hours. We must be strong and of good courage if we are to make any progress in this war. But even more importantly, we must never forget Jesus' promise, "I am with you, even until the end of the age."

Questions:

1. What are the themes of Chapters 1 through 28?

2. How did Isaac's second blessing for Jacob differ from the first?

3. How did Esau's repentance come across as insincere?

4. Where else does God's promise, "I will be with you," appear in the Bible?

5. What does the word "Bethel" mean?

6. How much did Jacob commit to give to the Lord as a tithe?

Family Discussion Questions:

1. What is thorough-going repentance? What does it look like? What would it have looked like in Esau?

2. How has God blessed our family? How have we realized that blessing? How might we memorialize these things?

3. We have received the same covenant promises that Jacob received, but ours come through Christ. What is our response to these promises? Will we commit to loving the Lord, worshiping only Him, and tithing ten percent of our increase? How much do we give the Lord in our tithe?

CHAPTER 29

Jacob Tricked

And Jacob served seven years for Rachel; and they seemed unto him but a few days, for the love he had to her. Gen. 29:20

Events:

1. Jacob reaches Haran and helps Rachel water her father's sheep at the public well.

2. Jacob works seven years for Rachel.

3. Laban gives him Leah instead of Rachel and requires him to work seven more years for Rachel.

4. Leah gives birth to four sons.

What does this passage teach us?

Verses 1–12. Always true to His promises, the Lord God saw to it that Jacob arrived safely in Haran. It was the town of his uncle's residence; Laban was Rebekah's brother.

The Fourth Commandment presumes that sons and daughters are about the business of their father's economies, since it requires the father to give his sons and daughters a one-day-in-seven rest from work. Although these family economies are very much missing in many homes today, this sort of life is basic to God's law-order. Rachel was feeding her father's sheep. This is what families did for 5800 years until the Industrial Revolution. Thanks to the absence of fathers from the home, the child labor laws, and compulsory school attendance, the family economy virtually disappeared over roughly 180 years. The disappearance of the family economy adds incentive to not have children, especially when people find out that it will cost $221,000 to raise a child[1].

---

1. Belkin, Lisa, *"$221,000 to Raise a Child?"* (New York Times Online: Aug 5, 2009) <http://parenting.blogs.
nytimes.com/2009/08/05/221000-to-raise-a-child/> accessed on Sept. 25, 2012

Historically, children were never considered a drain on the family economy, because they contributed to the family economy! For thousands of years, children worked with their parents, providing sustenance for the family and the advancement of its wealth. Later, we will find that Jacob's sons took care of his flocks. In the book of Acts we meet Aquila and Priscilla who worked together as tent makers (Acts 18:3). From the immediate passage, it is clear that Laban was wealthy enough to hire servants, but even this did not exempt his daughters from the work of the family economy.

Years earlier, Abraham's servant had come upon Rachel's aunt, Rebekah, drawing water at the well of Nahor, and she had become a fitting bride for Isaac. Such situations are unmistakably, providentially orchestrated by God. Certainly, Jacob must have recalled the story of his own mother's betrothal to his father, initiated by a prayer of faith and God's sovereign hand in the events there at the well. We have to conclude that it was God who now was guiding Jacob into similar circumstances, by His providential direction over all things. The same God who brought Rebekah to the well fifty years earlier had now arranged a meeting between Jacob and his future wife in the same context.

Jacob's behavior on meeting these strangers and distant family members was marked with kindly regard and tender brotherly love. He referred to the men near the well as "brothers," and proceeded to water their flocks. If you are accustomed to the more stilted, cold reunions that seem to characterize modern relationships between relatives, Jacob's tears and kisses might appear a little "over the top." It is especially strange in light of the fact that Jacob had never seen these people prior to this meeting.

Verses 13–29. Immediately, Jacob placed himself in the context of his uncle's household economy. From the outset, Laban offered him some reward for his labor and Jacob stated his interest in marrying Rachel.

In a day when the state did not provide welfare for single mothers, and family relationships bore great relevance in human society, every marriage involved important economic considerations. For example, what would happen to the daughter if her husband failed to provide for her or abandoned her? This was where the dowry came into play. It was an insurance of sorts, in case the husband defaulted on the covenant marriage arrangement. Because Jacob entered Haran with nothing but the clothes on his back, there was no way he could provide the bride price. Thus, Laban's request was not unreasonable. "He who finds a wife finds a good thing" and "her price is far above rubies" (Prov. 18:22, 31:10). Given that Jacob was seeking a very good wife, seven years of labor was clearly not out of the question for him. Truly, it is remarkable to see this man's patience, diligence, and self-control over the seven years he waited for Rachel.

Regrettably, Uncle Laban turned out to be unreasonable when the seven years were up. This scoundrel failed to live up to his original agreement and he swapped Leah for Rachel on the wedding day. Apparently, the brides in that day were covered with full-face veils during the wedding proceedings. Although Laban had an explanation for the switch, he was still guilty of violating the clear verbal contract that he had made with Jacob at the beginning of the seven years. After one week, Laban turned Rachel's hand over to Jacob, requiring him to work another seven years for her.

This story speaks to the old adage, "What's good for the goose is good for the gander." Clearly, Jacob had not been hesitant to dabble in a little deception, himself, to obtain the birthright and blessing. Now, as God's providence would have it, Jacob received a little taste of his own medicine.

Verses 30–35. Troubles began right away in Jacob's polygamous marriages to the two women. In the unfolding of God's revelation to man, we find that polygamy fails to meet the intent of God's creation mandate for families. There are Old Testament laws that regulate polygamy, and there is little explicit condemnation of it. Nevertheless, the Creation mandate laid out the standard of one man and one woman in the Garden. God did not create multiple wives for Adam and it would have been a sin for Adam to have taken one of his own daughters for a wife. Also, Jesus affirmed the Creation mandate of two becoming one (Mark 10:8), and Paul disallowed any polygamous man from the office of elder in the church (1 Tim. 3:2).

The troubles we encounter in Jacob's family include favoritism, pride, bitterness, and envy. In sympathy for Leah's lot, God compensated by opening her womb and closing Rachel's. Evidently, God is vitally interested in the care that a man shows to his wife. He pitied poor Leah who was despised by her husband. Clearly He interfered in Jacob's relationships (vs. 37). While it was contrary to God's design for Jacob to engage in polygamous relationships in the first place, Jacob made the condition even worse by treating Leah poorly. God could not tolerate this.

This story makes little sense to the present self-oriented, existentialist world of birth implosions. Over 80 nations around the world are birth-imploding presently, because men and women do not want children. They have come to consider children a curse. From the beginning, God hard-wired a desire for children into the hearts of women. Leah and Rachel desired children, because they knew that children would bring fulfillment to their lives. But large institutional forces have successfully destroyed natural affections in the hearts of millions of women. These forces include universities, media, seminaries and churches, government funding, and technology in the form of the birth control pill. That little pill with its abortifacient qualities has produced the largest demographic shift since the worldwide flood! When the natural affection of women for their children has become as suppressed as this, you know entire civilizations are in the process of extinction. When professing believers hold the same self-centered, materialistic values as unbelievers, the church as well as society is in a state of regression.

Leah named her four sons Reuben (which means "See, a Son"), Simeon (which means "To Hear"), Levi (which means "To Join"), and Judah (which means "To Praise"). God saw her affliction, God heard her cry, God joined her husband to her, and she praised God for the sons He gave her. Such names bear prophetic meaning, and from this we know that Leah was a woman of faith.

How does this passage teach us to walk with God in faith and obedience?

1. Jacob was inconsistent in expressing his love for his family. How well do we express love in our families? In a world that has systematically destroyed natural affection, we have a long way to go to express faithful love. Divorce is more egregious than polygamy in God's ethical framework (Mal. 2:16), but it is a constant reality in most churches today. Let us learn to treat each of our family members with affectionate love. Let us value the children that God gives to us, and treat them with tender affection. Children should also be affectionate with each other. When we are affectionate to others, we

are telling them that we appreciate them, we enjoy being with them, and we want to encourage them.

2. It is not unreasonable for a father to request a dowry from his future son-in-law, especially if the father cares about his daughter's future. Young men should think about preparing a dowry well before they marry. The dowry used to be an insurance policy for the woman, in case the young man defaulted on his responsibilities in the marriage. Certainly, no father who loves his daughter would want his daughter to marry a loser! At the very least, the young man should prove that he is able to provide for his own, lest he be considered worse than an infidel (1 Tim. 5:8). That is why we are raising our sons to be responsible men and diligent workers. One of the best things that ten-year-old boys can do to prepare for adulthood and marriage is to learn to work hard.

3. Troubles multiply when people refuse to do things God's way. Laban had two daughters, and Isaac and Rebekah had two sons. If the players in this story had been more concerned about God's will in their lives, things would have been different. Esau, for example, could have married one of Laban's daughters, and Jacob could have married the other. Instead, both families were consumed with rebellion, polygamy, contention, deceit, and synthesis with the Canaanite culture. Sin always has consequences, and we see unsavory consequences resulting from Jacob's polygamy.

4. A household in the Bible is an economic unit. That means the household functions together in the ways it gains wealth. Although it may be difficult to incorporate into the modern world, there are creative ways in which families can learn to function together as a team. We may not have sheep to raise, but we have dinners to cook, home businesses to run, and cars to repair. As our children grow older, they should become more helpful in supporting their household economy.

5. We must learn to keep our promises. Laban was dishonest when he offered Jacob a deal and then broke it. This was a clear violation of the Eighth Commandment and the Ninth Commandment. When we make promises, we must be prepared to keep them.

Questions:

1. What are the themes of Chapters 1 through 29?
2. What did Jacob do at the well to show his affection for his extended family?
3. What was the dowry that Jacob promised to give Laban for Rachel?
4. How did Laban deal fraudulently with Jacob on his wedding day?
5. What sins were prevalent in Jacob's family? What sort of troubles happened in Jacob's family when he married multiple wives?
6. How does the Word of God speak of polygamy? How does the Word speak of divorce?

Family Discussion Questions:

1. How can we create a better family economy in our household?
2. How well does our family keep our promises?
3. What reasonable expectations might we require of young men who are interested in courting our daughters?

CHAPTER 30

Laban Tricked

For it was little which thou hadst before I came, and it is now increased unto a multitude; and the LORD hath blessed thee since my coming: and now when shall I provide for mine own house also? Gen. 30:30

Events:

1. Bilhah gives birth to two sons for Jacob.
2. Zilpah gives birth to two sons for Jacob.
3. Leah gives birth to two more sons for Jacob.
4. Rachel gives birth to Joseph.
5. Jacob finds a way to obtain Laban's sheep, goats, and cattle.

What does this passage teach us?

Verses 1–25. Despite the polygamy and dissension in Jacob's household, God blessed the man by giving him eleven sons in six years! These were prolific years for Jacob indeed! Both Rachel and Leah pressed Jacob towards more polygamy, offering their maidservants to him as additional wives. Competing interests and competing moral values present themselves in this chapter. Apparently, the two sisters were unaware of the humiliation and dishonor to which they were subjecting themselves through this polygamy. When a man marries multiple women, he must divide his time, attention, and love amongst his wives. But these women were less concerned about their husband's time and affection than they were about getting the best of each other. This is the corrosive sin of envy.

At the same time that they rejected God's intentions concerning marriage, the sisters also ignored His sovereign control over the womb. They came to rely entirely on their own ability to manipulate causes in order to bring about the blessing of children. Granted, there are things that we can do to enhance the possibility of pregnancy. But men and women will often forget about trusting in God as they enthusiastically pursue pseudo-scientific methods to get what they want. The women in this story were desperate to get their hands on mandrakes, a walnut-sized fruit thought to improve fertility. Here, Moses under the inspiration of the Spirit, attests that the opening of Rachel's womb had far more to do with the hand of God than it did with the mandrakes. Rachel eventually attributed the blessing to God's hand.

Verses 26–43. Meanwhile, Jacob was busy working to produce blessing for himself out in the field with Laban's flocks and herds. While his wives were seeking to enhance their fertility by polygamy and mandrakes, Jacob was working to advance the family's wealth by another pseudo-scientific means. He peeled the branches of poplar and hazel trees and placed them in the water where the herds drank. As the theory went, if the sheep looked upon the stripes prior to conceiving their young, this would permanently affect the genetic code such that the lambs would come out striped.

Verse 30 elucidates the basic problem with Jacob's family at this time. Jacob told Laban, "Yahweh has blessed you since my coming; and now when shall I provide for mine own house also?" This is the same issue that Abraham struggled with when he took matters into his own hands and conceived a child with Hagar. Upon multiple occasions, Abraham and Isaac tried to deceive the pagan kings using their own ill-conceived means. Also, Rebekah arranged an extravagant deception in order to secure the blessing for Jacob. When push comes to shove, this family has a hard time trusting that the sovereign power of God would work things out for them. On the one hand, Jacob here acknowledged God's sovereign provision for Laban's family by way of his own hard work. But then he turned his eyes away from God's sovereign hand when it came to his own family, focusing instead upon his own responsibility to provide. Could not the same God who blessed Laban because of Jacob's presence with him also bless Jacob with equal or better provision? It was at this point that Jacob's faith in God wavered.

The truly astonishing element of this story is found in God's gracious condescension towards this unworthy clan. Although we know that striped sticks do not produce striped lambs and mandrakes likely do little to improve the fertility of a woman, God patiently "played along" with the silly antics of His people in this story. He provided them with children and striped lambs. He worked through Jacob's deceptive intent to effect what Jacob fully intended to bring about—the disenfranchisement of Laban. Indeed, God's judgments are unsearchable and His ways past finding out! In mercy, He did not give them their just desserts. At the same time, there would be consequences for polygamy and enviousness in the household in the lives of Jacob's sons.

How does this passage teach us to walk with God in faith and obedience?

This passage wisely instructs us concerning a godly view of science. Men are using science when they use previous experiences to assign cause and effect relationships to the world around them. But science should never be used to break God's laws. Neither should we wholly rely upon science to accomplish the things we want to accomplish. Because of the explosion of scientific technology and the consequent affluence that has followed, most western nations have abandoned any and all trust in the providential sovereignty of God. They now rely entirely on science for their medical cures, economic success, and psychological treatments. They look to their striped sticks and mandrakes for blessing. Often, they break God's law in the process by experimenting on human stem cells, aborting their children in the womb, debauching their currencies in their economic systems, and refusing to worship the living God. Fundamentally, they refuse to look to God "from Whom all blessings flow." It's highly debatable whether mandrakes and striped sticks will bring us the blessings of children or economic wealth. Even if there was a distant relationship or a partial cause and effect relationship, let us never forget that the outworking is always in the hand of God. Ultimately, our health and wealth come from God. Let us trust in the Lord and pray to Him for His blessing. This will always be far more effective than science and technology.

Questions:

1. What are the themes of Chapters 1 through 30?

2. What were the mandrakes supposed to do for Leah and Rachel?

3. What were the striped sticks supposed to do for the sheep?

4. Who is the source of blessing for Laban and Jacob, according to Jacob's testimony in verse 30?

5. What are the names of the eleven sons who were born to Jacob in six years?

6. According to the passage, what happened to Rachel that enabled her to have a son?

Family Discussion Questions:

1. In what ways might our trust in science and modern medicine displace our trust in God? Do we seek prayer from the elders of the church before going to see the doctors who play in science and pseudo-science? (Reference James 5:14)

2. Does the sin of envy and hateful jealousy ever infect the siblings in our family? Can you think of any examples of this? What are the destructive effects of these sins?

CHAPTER 31

Jacob Flees

And Jacob stole away unawares to Laban the Syrian, in that he told him not that he fled. Gen. 31:20

Events:

1. Yahweh God tells Jacob to return to Canaan.
2. Jacob leaves Haran with his family without telling Laban.
3. Laban pursues and overtakes him seven days later.
4. God warns Laban in a dream not to harm Jacob.
5. After making a covenant between the families, the two parties part ways.

What does this passage teach us?

Verses 1–16. After 21 years of disingenuous dealings and deception between Laban and Jacob, the relationship had almost completely disintegrated. But through it all, Yahweh was true to His promise. He did not forsake Jacob, the man He had called at Bethel. Despite Jacob's imperfections, God was still directing his life. In a dream, He told the man to leave Haran and return to the land of Canaan.

Laban exhibited a great deal of self-centeredness in his business dealings with Jacob. What a sad commentary on this man's lack of love for his own flesh and blood! One would think that he would have been happy to pass his assets on to his daughters and to the son of the covenant. But the man was controlled by his flesh. In spite of Laban's double-dealing and short-changing, God circumvented his foul purposes and blessed His man Jacob anyway.

The sojourn in Haran seems to have been a growing experience for Jacob. In verse nine, he finally acknowledged God's sovereign control over every aspect of his work and compensation (v. 9). At first, he might have relied a little too much on the peeled-stick-in-the-drinking-water technique to yield him striped herds, but now he was convinced of God's presence and blessing. In a dream, Yahweh confirmed that He was looking out for Jacob's interests. Surely, it was this revelation that solidified the man's confidence in God's sovereign provision. Can you see the great blessing that comes from being in covenant relationship with the God of heaven? He really does look out for the interests of His own.

Jacob is also to be commended for his diligent labor and productivity. While it is true that Laban did benefit from this massive agricultural enterprise, Laban was also blessed by Jacob's prodigious work. Comparing the character of these two men, we have to conclude that Laban was far more dishonorable and self-centered. He broke contracts, refused his own daughters any inheritance, cheated his son-in-law on his wages multiple times, and even dealt underhandedly in the marriage of his daughters. The word "scoundrel" comes to mind.

Verses 17–21. Is it any surprise that Rachel would also join the deception game that both her husband and father were playing? Before leaving Haran, Rachel snatched her father's Teraphim (or idols). Most likely, these golden idols represented a sizable portion of the family's wealth. Verses 14 and 15 indicate that Rachel was motivated by financial gain. She was especially distressed that her father would not provide her with any inheritance. This was one miserable family indeed! This is what happens when people live for themselves. Relationships suffer when sin, selfishness, and dishonesty dominate in the home. Regrettably, this selfishness is the story of the average family in our world as well. It is only by the grace of God and the indwelling of the Spirit of God that we are able to transcend the selfishness, covetousness, envy, and treachery that ruin so many family relationships.

Verses 22–42. Laban pursued Jacob for one full week. Imagine the kind of irritation, animosity, and vengeful thoughts that must have simmered in this man's heart as he bore down upon Jacob and the family. At this juncture there was real potential for violence. Thankfully, God intervened in the situation. By direct revelation in a dream, he warned Laban not to speak good or evil of His man Jacob. In other words, Laban was not to make any judgment concerning Jacob. Effectively, what God told him was, "Let it go. Just drop the issue and walk away."

Laban is a complex character in the biblical record. Clearly, it was the fear of the living God that restrained him from taking action against Jacob. He agreed to take a vow in the name of the God of Abraham. Yet at the same time, he was steeped in idolatry, contract-breaking, and materialism. How much different is this man from ourselves?

Back at Bethel, God had promised that He would not allow anyone to harm Jacob. All the way to this point, God held true to His promise. Laban did complain about the teraphim, and proceeded to search the tents for the idols, to no avail. In a sad addendum to the story, Jacob unknowingly cursed his favorite wife. He may not have expected Rachel to have stolen the idols from her father, but when Jacob placed a curse on the person that lifted the teraphim, God took his words at face value. It wasn't long after this that Rachel died, which very well could have been a consequence of her theft and her husband's curse. Let this be a lesson for all of us! Even if men do not take their words seriously, God is listening and He will hold us to the words we speak.

Verses 43–55. Finally, Jacob and Laban came to an agreement. They marked the place and promised never to pass over that boundary marker to harm each other. Jacob promised never to marry another woman or to hurt Laban's daughters. Together they sealed the covenant with a meal. This covenant supper is a common element in godly covenant-making in both the Old and New Testaments.

How does this passage teach us to walk with God in faith and obedience?

1. God writes our paychecks. A Christian does his work faithfully, but attributes every blessing to the Father of lights from whom all blessings flow. In this fallen world of deception and treachery, every single person will encounter some form of cheating or mistreatment at the hands of others. It is inevitable. But God is still in the heavens. As long as we are

His and He is ours we can be sure that He will take care of us under the most unjust and treacherous circumstances. It is God who controls all things. But it is for us to walk in relationship with Him and obey His commandments.

2. Jacob believed the promises conveyed to him in his dreams, and he knew that God would be with him. It is important for us to believe in the promises of God recorded in Scripture, that God is with us, that He will look after our better interests. If we are walking in relationship with Christ, the Son of God, then we know that He will be with us, even unto the end of the age (Matt 28:20).

3. Stealing is always wrong (Exod. 20:16). When Rachel stole the teraphim from her father, she broke the eighth commandment. Of course she was disappointed that her father did not give her an inheritance. But this did not allow her any good reason to steal the teraphim. Over the twenty-plus years of labor with Laban, Jacob learned by hook and crook to trust in God as the great Provider. Rachel should have witnessed this great truth. When our children are still very young they must learn not to take other people's things without permission.

4. Selfishness and greed erode family relationships. Let us always be on our guard against these terrible sins! If there are disagreements involving an inheritance or a will, let us always put relationships ahead of money. Why should we destroy family relationships over a few thousand dollars, or even a few million dollars? Is it really worth it?

5. When there are disagreements between in-laws, it may be a good idea to make agreements by way of written contracts. While Laban and Jacob marked the covenant with a monument, we mark our covenants by putting them in writing. God has called us to live in peace, even with unsaved relatives.

6. In the ancient world, men certified their covenants with a meal or even a glass of wine. By sharing food together, we certify our covenants. We engage in fellowship or "communion." This is why the church is warned not to "eat" with the unrepentant excommunicated church member (1 Cor. 5:9-11). Our covenant relationship with Jesus Christ is also sealed with a meal, whenever we share wine and bread in the communion service.

7. This passage gives us some ideas on how to make good decisions in our lives. Before he made the decision to leave Haran, Jacob looked at the situation through the eyes of Laban and his sons. He asked counsel of his wives and he received revelation from God Himself. First and foremost, we should be open to the revealed will of God found in the Scriptures. Yet this alone is not enough. There are always those who read God's Word and lack the wisdom to rightly understand it and apply it to life. Therefore, good decision making also requires sound wisdom that comes from prayer, from godly counsel, and from experience. Moreover, the Spirit-led, Spirit-filled man makes the wisest decisions when his decisions are saturated in love, joy, peace, longsuffering, gentleness, goodness, and faith (all fruits of the Spirit). God speaks to us both through His Word and by His Spirit.

Questions:

1. What are the themes of Chapters 1 through 31?

2. How did Jacob come to the decision to move back to Canaan?

3. According to Jacob's own testimony, how did he obtain his wealth?

4. Why did Rachel steal her father's teraphim?

5. In what way were Laban, Jacob, and Rachel "cut out of the same cloth?"

6. Why did Laban refrain from hurting Jacob and his family? Was Laban a God-fearing man? Why or why not?

Family Discussion Questions:

1. What is the state of our relationships in our family? Is there materialism, envy, and deceit amongst us that could create rifts in our extended family in years to come?

2. Have you ever been the target of "dirty dealings," and have you seen God look after your better interests? Give examples.

CHAPTER 32

Jacob Wrestles

And Jacob was left alone; and there wrestled a man with him until the breaking of the day. Gen. 32:24

Events:

1. Jacob meets a host of angels as he continues his journey back to Canaan.
2. Jacob makes preparations to meet his brother Esau.
3. Jacob wrestles with the Lord, seeking to obtain a blessing.

What does this passage teach us?

Verses 1–3. The prospects facing Jacob and his family at this stage were not pleasant. Having survived a potentially lethal confrontation with Laban, the party now was heading for an even more unpleasant engagement—a face-to-face meeting with Esau. Life is made up of an assortment of unpleasantries. We should fully expect to encounter difficulties, conflicts, and even catastrophic loss on this journey through life. It is better to settle this in our minds right now, than to be surprised by hardship when it comes. Certainly, Job knew what he was talking about when he said that "man is born to trouble as the sparks fly upward" (Job 5:7).

Such was the case for Jacob as he prepared to meet Esau. Twenty years earlier, when he left his family in the land of Canaan, his twin brother was in a vengeful rage. As Jacob now stood at the edge of these dark waters, contemplating the challenge of wading into the trial, surely he must have felt deep consternation.

But remember that God had promised that He would be with Jacob wherever he went. As Jacob prepared to walk through this difficult trial,

God sent a host of angels to meet him on his way. Occasionally, God opens the eyes of His people to see His mighty power. The children of Israel caught a glimpse of it at the Red Sea. Elisha and his servant witnessed the armies of Angels surrounding the city. May God help us to visualize His complete sovereignty over everything, including the puny problems that are of immediate concern to us! It is this sort of a vision that brings things back into perspective. When a man sees tens of thousands of 100-foot tall angels surrounding the area, he would be hardly concerned about the band of 400 Edomites approaching the scene. Jacob called this place "Two Armies." By this designation, he testified to God's superior force over all who would be aggressors against God's people. For the remainder of human history, God's armies would always be near at hand and available to the people of God.

Verses 4–23. We may take a number of lessons from this passage relating to the important Christian duty of peacemaking. While God's armies are always ready to deliver His people, Jacob still understood his duty to address the present conflict. Usually, conflicts between humble believers ought to be resolved quickly, according to Jesus' instructions in Matthew 18. But this was not that kind of a conflict. What heightened the complexity of this particular situation was the fundamental disagreement between the two men. The first party was the son of the covenant and a servant of the living God. The second party was a man of the world. They shared different commitments in relation to God and to His covenant.

Long-standing rifts in families are nothing new, especially between Christians and their unsaved parents or siblings. Examples like this can be very instructive for those who find themselves in the midst of family feuds. Note, first of all, that Jacob took the matter to God in prayer. A prayer of faith is one of the first indications that a man is walking in relationship with the living and true God. With all his shortcomings and failings, Jacob was demonstrating himself to be that man of faith. In his prayer, he acknowledged God's goodness to him and his unworthiness as a recipient of His good gifts. Then, on the basis of the covenant promise made to him under heaven's ladder some twenty years earlier, he pleaded for God's protection on his family.

Having trusted everything to the sovereign hand of God in prayer, Jacob then prepared a substantial gift of 550 animals for Esau. "A gift in secret turneth away wrath," says the book of Proverbs. But what can we say about a gift amounting to upwards of $100,000 in value? When was the last time you have seen brothers exchange gifts of such value? The momentousness of the occasion cannot be underestimated here. Judging from the size of these men's households and holdings, any kind of animosity could have very well resulted in warfare between the two developing nations. That is what happened some four hundred years later between the Edomites and Israelites. But for now, Jacob wanted to establish a long-standing peace agreement between the two parties. Warfare is expensive and incredibly destructive. Peace is of immeasurable value, worth at least $100,000 to the families of Esau and Jacob.

After preparing the gift, Jacob sent messengers ahead to signal his interest in reconciliation with his brother Esau. The messages contained conciliatory signals. Most importantly, we should not ignore Jacob's humility. This is a characteristic that is essential in any peacemaking. In his message, Jacob referred to Esau as "my lord," and called himself "your servant."

Verses 24–29. On the evening before the critical meeting, Jacob sent his family ahead in two bands over the Jabbok river. There he wrestled with an angel for the remainder of the evening. Hosea 12:3–4 refers to this highly significant event in the life of Jacob:

"He took his brother by the heel in the womb, and by his strength he had power with God: Yea, he had power over the angel, and prevailed: he wept, and made supplication unto him: he found him in Bethel, and there he spake with us."

From his birth, Jacob had proven himself as a mighty wrestler. First, he grabbed the heal of Esau. He wrestled hard for the birthright and the blessing. Then for twenty-one years, he contended with his father-in-law for material wealth. Now here he was grappling with an angel for hours and hours on the north side of the river. In this strange interchange, God was testing Jacob's fortitude and commitment to the covenant. It was a test of faith. He had already challenged Jacob to return to the promised land and assume the covenant; but now it seemed as if He was "preventing" him from entering the land.

For hour upon hour, Jacob engaged in a strenuous, hand-to-hand wrestling match. His persistence is remarkable, as witnessed in his final desperate cry, "I will not let you go, unless you bless me!" Having already seen an army of angels surrounding the camp, Jacob probably sensed that this was no ordinary man opposing him. He must have realized that his dealings had to do with the living God. What right does a man have to wrestle with God, except on the basis of the covenant that God has already established with him? If God had not already promised the land to Jacob, he would have no right to "sue" Him for the blessing of protection and provision.

As the dawn broke and the wrestling ended, God changed Jacob's name to "Israel." This name is significant in its literal translation: "He will rule with God." Originally, man was created for dominion, to rule as God's vice-regent over His creation. But the fall of man severely crippled man's ability to think, to live, and to rule according to God's design. In this new covenant, man's ability to take dominion and to rule with God was restored. It is restored for us in Christ.

That Jacob was a man of high achievement, clarity of purpose, and indefatigable persistence, there should be no doubt. His passion, his energy, and his intense persistence was persuasive with God. But how does a man influence God when God Himself is the chief influencer of all things? Surely it is God who influences us both to will and to do of His good pleasure (Phil. 2:12–13). Yet the fervent prayers of a righteous man avail much (James 5:16). God influences us and we influence Him. But we influence Him, because He first influences us. We have to believe that fervency still matters. The more fervent and persistent the prayer, the more influence the prayers will bear upon the Almighty. But we have no influence apart from the covenant relationship He has already sovereignly ordained with us. If we were not His children, we would have no right to approach Him as a Father. A man cannot approach God apart from faith in the covenant promises that God has already made with him in Christ.

Verses 30–32. What a remarkable account of some of the most memorable events ever occurring in human history! In the end, Jacob recognized the source of all blessings. He finally understood that he was not wrestling with Esau or with Laban. He was in a wrestling match with God. Amazed that he survived a face-to-face confrontation with God Himself, he called the place "Peniel," meaning, "Face of God." Jacob walked away with a perpetual reminder of the wrestling match: a limp he would carry for the rest of his life. It was a monument to his weakness and his strength; both a sign of victory and a symbol of his dependence on God.

How does this passage teach us to walk with God in faith and obedience?

1. Jacob's persistence with God is a great lesson for us. Could it be that we might also bear influence upon God in our prayers? From time to time we may need to wrestle with God in prayer for hours, maybe even from evening to early morning. It is not in our own strength and pride that we may approach God. But there is a holy combination of humility, fear, bold confidence, and faith that enables us to engage effectual prayer. It is a gracious contract that God has made with us in Christ. It is only on this basis that we have the right to boldly approach the throne of grace.

2. God wrestled with Jacob in order to test and strengthen his faith. What father doesn't test his own son's physical strength from time to time by wrestling with him? He might push his son to his limits, but a wise father would never exceed those limits. In a similar sense, our all-wise heavenly Father may test the strength of His own children. He may delay an answer to prayer or extend a trial over many weeks and months. In so doing, He develops spiritual muscles and turns little boys into men. Are we willing to wrestle with God all the way until daybreak?

3. It is a good thing to desire the blessing of God. Far more important than a bowl of porridge or even a father's blessing is a blessing from God Himself. All other blessings pale in comparison. Jacob wrestled for God's blessing because he valued it. Do we value the blessing of God in this way? Or do we always seek blessings from earthly sources where all is fleeting and of no real eternal consequence?

4. Jacob serves well as a picture of the church in the wilderness, or even as the church in the present day. May God help us to see the church as it really is in history, that we may have no false confidence. The church limps along. The battle may leave a wound, but the wound is a reminder of our victory. Would you rather have a crushed head or a bruised heel? The

serpent's head is crushed in the battle, but the church is not without its constant weaknesses, tragedies, and trials. As the Christian church moves from generation to generation, it will always suffer persecution, church splits, heresies, schisms, the curses of false brothers, and other afflictions. But as we limp along, we remember that we are victors! Our Lord wrestled violently on the Cross in order that we would be blessed forevermore!

Questions:

1. What are the themes of Chapters 1 through 32?

2. What did Jacob meet on his way to Canaan that reminds us of his trip away from his home in Canaan twenty years earlier?

3. How did Jacob try to make peace with Esau?

4. What does the Bible tell us to do if we are anxious or fearful?

5. What is the literal translation of the name "Israel?"

6. Why would it be appropriate for believers to wrestle with God? Why does God wrestle with us?

Family Discussion Questions:

1. How have we addressed major conflicts in our own lives? Are there family feuds that need to be resolved?

2. Do we ever wrestle with God in prayer? Are we as persistent as Jacob was to hold God to the promise of His blessing? What kind of passion and persistence do we exhibit in prayer?

CHAPTER 33

Jacob Returns

And Jacob came to Shalem, a city of Shechem, which is in the land of Canaan, when he came from Padanaram; and pitched his tent before the city. And he bought a parcel of a field, where he had spread his tent, at the hand of the children of Hamor, Shechem's father, for an hundred pieces of money. Gen. 33:18–19

Events:

1. Jacob meets with Esau and they are reconciled.
2. Jacob settles in Canaan near the town of Shechem.
3. Jacob builds an altar to the Lord.

What does this passage teach us?

Verses 1–2. As he made final preparations for the dreaded meeting with Esau, Jacob divided his family into three groups. Apparently, he arranged the groups in the order of their dispensability to him. Zilpah and Bilhah with their children would go first, then Leah in the middle, and Rachel in the rear. The meaning behind the arrangement would not have been missed by the members of the family. Polygamy will always produce dysfunctional, contorted, and ugly effects upon family relationships. By his actions, Jacob was planting seeds that would bear sour fruit years later.

Verses 3–16. When Jacob finally met with Esau, the reunion was a good one. The God who commands the armies of heaven also works in the hearts of men! Esau's disposition towards Jacob had changed dramatically. Twenty years earlier, he had been muttering dark threats and contemplating his brother's murder. This change of heart could only be attributed to the work of God. If the hearts of kings are in the hands of God, who turns them "withersoever He will" (Prov. 21:1), then He can soften the heart of a murderous brother if He so desires. While Jacob's efforts to restore the relationship were not without some value, it was God who did the substance of the work in Esau's heart. God made all the difference in the reunion. If Jacob was to live peaceably and safely in the land, it was important that he be on good terms with Esau. This is not to say that Esau came into a right relationship with the God of the covenant. Esau's change of heart towards his brother does not necessarily imply a change of heart towards God. This distinction is important to remember in our own relationships with unbelieving friends and relatives.

Jacob's behavior towards Esau at their meeting was both conciliatory and humble. Seven times he bowed to his brother, and he even addressed him as "my lord." This respect appears odd to an informal, careless, and thoughtless age. But his concern to avoid the appearance of superiority towards Esau is commendable and worth emulating. How many children are caught up in sibling rivalry because one is trying to prove himself better than the other? The major root of all conflict between brothers and sisters is pride. Nothing stirs up conflict between siblings more than condescending treatment and proud attitudes in the home.

As you read the account, don't miss Jacob's constant reference to his faith in God. Three times in his conversation with Esau, he mentioned the name of God. He openly recognized God as the source of all of his blessings. What is also conspicuous about the interchange is Esau's failure to refer to God at all. Consequently, there was to be little unity between the Edomites in the Israelites in future generations, However, God did provide a land inheritance of sorts for the children of Esau because Esau was the son of His covenant man, Isaac. According to Deuteronomy 2:22, God gave Mount Seir to Esau by driving the wicked Horites out of the area.

Over his brother's protestations, Jacob insisted that Esau accept his gift of the animals. Jacob emphasized his commitment to avoid any conflict with his brother's family; then without further ado, the two brothers parted ways. As far as we know this was the last time the two brothers would see each other until their father's death. Apparently, Jacob felt the need to minimize future fellowship with Esau. This is a delicate balance. On the one hand, it is impossible to leave the world or separate ourselves entirely from unbelievers who disagree with our basic commitments. But there are still warnings against synthesis in Scripture. We are to avoid fellowship with the unfruitful works of darkness. How does one "come out from among them and be separate," while still fulfilling the mandate to be salt and light in the world? What God wants is maximum obedience to His laws, the fruits of the Spirit manifest, and an obliteration of pride and lust in all of our work. If we need to separate from certain influences in order to bring this about, so be it. If our contributions would only create more conflict, and less peace and joy and obedience to God's law with ourselves and others, it would be better that we pull away from these associations.

Verses 17–20. Jacob settled down near the town of Shechem, about eighty miles north of Mount Seir. He bought a parcel of ground where he pitched his tent. Then he built an altar to the Lord and called it El-elohe-Israel, translated as, "God, the God of Israel." In a polytheistic land where people served multiple gods, Jacob called upon the one true and living God. This was the God with whom his family had made a covenant. Appropriately, Jacob addressed his sacrifice to the "God of Israel." In a similar way, the Smith family might also make reference to the "God of the Smiths," and the Swanson family may refer to "the God of the Swansons." When we call upon God as our God, we are claiming Him for our own. We recognize His authority, and we commit ourselves to His worship.

How does this passage teach us to walk with God in faith and obedience?

1. Here we find the beginnings of what we call "family worship." The altar Jacob built was a means by which he and his family could worship God. After the sacrifice of Christ on the Cross, there is no longer any need for altars. But God will still be worshiped by His people. Today, godly families gather together and worship in the name of Jesus Christ who sacrificed Himself for us. Things haven't changed that much. Fundamentally, godly families still worship God in the same way that these patriarchs did. They gather the family together and call upon the name of the Lord. The New Testament people of God are known for singing psalms, giving daily exhortations, and engaging in unceasing prayer (Heb. 3:13, Eph. 5:19, 6:4, 1 Thess. 5:17, etc.). Does this characterize our lives? Is our family in regular fellowship with God?

2. God's people must also resolve to live at peace with all men. This includes efforts to resolve conflicts peaceably, and to otherwise govern all of our relationships with wisdom and care. Humility and deference to others is critical, especially in relationships between brothers and sisters. Sometimes communications between brothers and sisters devolve into informality, rudeness, and cutting insults. These rude communications will not sustain healthy relationships in the long term. What would happen if brothers referred to their brothers as "my lord?" Of course, such references come across as excessively formal and awkward in our culture. But still, a little more humility and respect would go a long way towards repairing and strengthening tenuous relationships.

Questions:

1. What are the themes of Chapters 1 through 33?
2. How is Jacob a good example to anyone who has a conflict with his brother or sister?
3. How did Esau demonstrate a change of heart towards Jacob?
4. What did Jacob build when he settled down in Shechem?
5. What does "El-elohe-Israel" mean?

Family Discussion Questions:

1. What are the best ways to cultivate peace with our unsaved friends and relatives? Is it wise to maintain some distance with extended family members that do not share our commitment to the Lord? Are we governing these relationships with wisdom?
2. How can we strengthen our relationships between family members? Are we humble enough? Do we use respectful language with each other, and prefer one another over ourselves?

CHAPTER 34

Jacob's Daughter

And it came to pass on the third day, when they were sore, that two of the sons of Jacob, Simeon and Levi, Dinah's brethren, took each man his sword, and came upon the city boldly, and slew all the males. And they slew Hamor and Shechem his son with the edge of the sword, and took Dinah out of Shechem's house, and went out. Gen. 34:25–26

Events:

1. Dinah visits with the women of the land.
2. Shechem, the son of the local ruler, commits fornication with Dinah.
3. Shechem announces his desire to marry Dinah.
4. Simeon and Levi trick Shechem and the men of the city into submitting to circumcision.
5. While they are still recovering from the circumcision, the sons of Jacob kill all the men in the city.
6. Jacob rebukes his sons for their actions.

What does this passage teach us?

Verses 1–7. Thoughtful readers who come upon the Bible for the first time are usually taken back by the brutal honesty of Scripture as it presents the lives of its protagonists in living color. These are flawed heroes operating in a broken world. But who are we to despise these men and women? We cannot help but see that their world is the same as ours. If we were to be honest with ourselves, we would find stories like this one surprisingly relevant and informative to our own situation.

This sad story begins with a young woman who left her father's house to associate with the pagans in the nearby city. These circumstances raise two issues of concern to Christian parents. In our present day, the emancipation and independence of young women from their father's home is considered normative. A family that desires to stay together until sons and daughters leave to cleave to their respective spouses is considered odd. But this was not the case for about 98% of world history. In the past, caring fathers felt a responsibility to look out for the well being of their daughters. They would carefully consider what social situations might be safe for their daughters. To this point, Jacob had avoided a synthesis with the Canaanites himself. The problem of synthesis would later become a major issue for Israel through the period of the Judges and the Kings.

Undoubtedly, the city of Shechem was just a small village with a population of 50-100 people. What occured here was tragic on several levels. It is true that these people were under God's sentence of judgment, but He was postponing this judgment for at least another 400 years.

Living in this world and having access to worldly people has its drawbacks. Jacob discovered this to be the case with his daughter Dinah. What happened to Dinah is no isolated event in human history. This sad circumstance has played out millions of times in every culture around the world. When a young Christian girl pulls away from the accountability of her home, she subjects herself to this kind of trouble. She can find it in the godless public schools and universities, or with the wrong crowd of teens at church. If she spends excessive amounts of time with unbelieving friends, she increases her risk of experiencing a life-altering tragedy. This is not to say that a young woman cannot or should not ever leave home. But the Apostle Paul does discourage excessive social interaction for women in 1 Tim. 5:13. He would rather they marry and manage the home (vs. 14). Also, a careful read of Titus 2:3-5 and Proverbs 31 reveals what the major focus of a wise young woman should be. She should be home-centered: taken up with managing the home. If she leaves the home, it is for the purpose of business, trade, and charitable endeavors. A Christian family's interaction with the world is limited mostly to evangelization and trade. Thoughtful Christian parents will carefully avoid sending their children into the world to be educated in a worldly manner of thinking. Why would we want our children socialized and trained in an unbiblical world and life view? The ultimate synthesis occurs when Christian children intermarry with the world. This was the situation Jacob confronted in this story. Tragically, in the case of Dinah, what began as social intercourse with the women in the land led to sinful intercourse with a man. The young son of the city leader took Dinah to bed—without making a marriage covenant. According to Exodus 22:16–17, the sin of fornication is serious and should be treated as a civil offense. The young man must either pay the dowry, or marry the young woman. Historically, this fine amounted to a 1-3 year salary, or at least $30,000. Whether Jacob's failure to protect his daughter contributed to this sad situation, or his daughter acted in rebellion to him, we do not know. It is clear that Jacob was passive, and seemed oddly disconnected, from everything that transpired. It was Dinah's brothers who took action. However, Scripture holds the father responsible and culpable before God for the protection and the paideia, the training and discipleship, of the children (Eph. 6:4; 1 Thess. 2:11; Neh. 4:14). Jesus Christ has hard words for the parent who causes a child to stumble. He says, "It would be better for him that a millstone be hung around his neck and he be drowned at the bottom of the sea" (Matt. 18:6). Yet, the Bible does not prescribe the specific measures or the extent to which that protection and paideia is to be employed. God commands a father to love his neighbor as himself. Therefore, the extent to which a father pours himself into the protection and paideia of his daughter depends on how much he loves his God and how much he loves his daughter. In a day where fornication is practically the norm and the average father is almost entirely disengaged from his daughter's dating relationships, it should go without saying that fathers do not love God or their daughters very much. It seems that fathers act like Lot or Jacob when parenting their daughters. However, with the coming of Jesus Christ, we begin to hope that the hearts of fathers will turn towards their daughters. We hope that there will be more loving fathers than either disengaged fathers or angry control-freaks who like to impose tyranny upon their homes. May God bring sharp conviction to the hearts of fathers everywhere! Only by an apprehension of the love of God in Jesus Christ will we begin to see the hearts of fathers warmed to love.

Verses 8–31. While Jacob could hardly be bothered with the news of Dinah's plight, her brothers reacted in vindictive rage. Family dynamics may have played a part in this. It is significant that Levi, Simeon, and Dinah were all Leah's children. From everything we have learned about Jacob thus far, we know that Jacob favored Rachel's children over Leah's. It may very well have been Jacob's favoritism that explains his apparent disinterest in the incident involving Dinah.

Dinah's brothers took Shechem's misdeed against their sister as an act of war and responded accordingly. Continuing in the old family tradition of deception, they deceived the men in the city on the pretense of a truce. They talked the men of the city into circumcising (cutting) the foreskin of every male in the city, and then put every one of them to the sword. The Bible does not justify their wrathful over-reaction to the Dinah affair. As James puts it, "The wrath of man does not work the righteousness of God" (James 1:20). Jacob later showed his displeasure for their actions, indicating that they had not consulted their father first, so we understand that they had clearly violated the fifth commandment when acted as they did. However, such harsh measures as that taken against the village hardly meets the standard of biblical justice. God's law would have only imposed a fine upon the young man who violated Dinah.

Under conditions where there is no established civil government to administer justice, small city states often take these prerogatives into their own hands. The situation here was similar to that found in the American "Wild West" during the latter part of the 19th century. Small town sheriffs, posses, and town militias would administer justice, sometimes getting into fights with nearby Indian tribes. Even under primitive conditions such as these, God's standards of righteousness must still be carefully applied in order to define a just war and the proper measures of justice.

It is worth pointing out that God did not correct, chastise, or punish Jacob and his family for this breach of justice. However, Jacob later remembered Simeon and Levi's actions when he pronounced his final blessings at the end of his life. The choices they made really mattered. The ripple-effect of their actions impacted future generations.

How does this passage teach us to walk with God in faith and obedience?

1. How many tragedies might be avoided if we lived according to the dictates of God's Word? Things come unravelled when we are outside of

the will of God. It is the will of God that fathers love their daughters and protect them, and that sons and daughters to honor their parents. This passage provides a good lesson to fathers and children.

2. Let us also cultivate among ourselves a strong sense of jurisdictional authority. God has delegated authority as He sees fit, and it is for us to recognize this authority. At the most basic level, this applies to children. In the home, our children should be careful not to usurp the authority of their parents. Oftentimes, older siblings will be bossy with their younger siblings and make decisions for them, even when that authority has not been properly delegated to them. The usurpation of jurisdictional authority is the root of all sorts of evil in the world. It contributes to both anarchy and tyranny, and disrupts family, church, and state. When children try to usurp parental authority and when parents abdicate their responsibilities, they sin against God. This is how things began to unravel in the story found in Genesis 34. Let us be careful not to assume authority that does not belong to us.

Questions:

1. What are the themes of Chapters 1 to 34?
2. How did Dinah fail to act wisely in this story?
3. How did Shechem fail to act rightly in this story?
4. How did Jacob fail in this story?
5. How did Simeon and Levi fail in this story?

Family Discussion Questions:

1. To what extent should a father intervene in his daughter's activities? If a father loved his daughter, how much interest would he take in her courtship and future marriage? How much should our daughters and sons interact with unbelievers in the surrounding neighborhoods and cities?

2. Does our family express honor for our parents? Do our children ever improperly usurp the authority of their parents? Is it clear when that authority is properly delegated?

CHAPTER 35

Jacob Worships

So Jacob came to Luz, which is in the land of Canaan, that is, Bethel,
he and all the people that were with him. And he built there an altar,
and called the place Elbethel: because there God appeared unto him,
when he fled from the face of his brother. Gen. 35:6–7

Events:

1. Jacob returns to Bethel and builds an altar to the Lord.
2. God blesses Jacob again.
3. Rachel dies while giving birth to Benjamin.

What does this passage teach us?

Verses 1–8. In the days of the Old Testament patriarchs and prophets, God selected certain locations where He wanted His people to worship Him. While in the desert, God met with His people in the tabernacle. Later, when they reached the Promised Land, the Tabernacle was set at Shiloh until David moved the Ark of the Covenant into Jerusalem. Yahweh insisted that His people worship Him at these specific locations. Because the earth itself was defiled by man's sin, God saw fit to set aside a special location where He would meet with His people. Ground zero for this place of worship was known as the "holy of holies."

You can see this pattern developing as God called Jacob back to Bethel. This was where He first revealed Himself to the young man in the dream of the heavenly ladder, and is where God's glory was first revealed to Jacob. Here was where God promised His presence and salvation. No doubt these memories were still fresh in Jacob's mind, probably producing strong sentiments of gratitude and reverent worship. It is important to understand that the word "Bethel" is the first reference to the "House of God" in Scripture. It was a term that would be used to designate the church of Christ that gathered for worship in the New Testament as well. Whenever God's people gathered to worship, God counted them as part of His family. He resided with His people as a human father lives with his children. In this primitive setting on the plains of Canaan, a fledging band of worshipers gathered to meet with the living God.

Before making the trip to the "House of God" for worship, Jacob cleaned the idols out of his house. True worshipers must come to God with "clean hands and a pure heart, who have not lifted up their souls unto vanity [or idols] and sworn deceitfully" (Ps. 24:4). Over time, idolatry may creep into the hearts and lives of any believing family. It is appropriate to clean the house of these idols from time to time. The idols mentioned here may have been the same Teraphim that Rachel took from her father's house when they left Haran. Whatever the case, Jacob took responsibility as the leader in his home by purifying his home of this idolatry. Such actions do not necessarily mean a complete rejection of sin and idolatry in the family, since Jacob's family seems to have carefully noted the place where the idols were buried. External actions are important, but the heart is of essence. Only time would tell whether this family's allegiance was to God or to vain idols and materialism. In the ensuing years, God would continue to test Jacob and his family's allegiance to Him.

The journey to Bethel was a major effort for this family. The journey may have taken a full week. This was no fifteen minute drive to church on a Sunday morning! In those days, the roads were undeveloped and the land was desolate. Roving bands of warriors, fierce tribes, and bandits ranged open country, unrestrained by law and order. It was very unlike the highly structured political states which most of us are familiar with today. But true to His promise, God protected Jacob's family on this journey. According to verse 5, the hearts of those in the area were struck with the terror of God.

On reaching Bethel, Jacob built an altar to God. He reviewed for his family his testimony of God's visitation so many years before. It is important for children to hear powerful testimonies like these from the mouths of their fathers.

Verses 9–15. God reiterated the Abrahamic blessing of land and posterity to Jacob. He promised a line of kings in his posterity—men who would rule as vice-regents of the King of heaven. This served as a preview for the Davidic covenant. All of the Old Testament covenants are fulfilled in Christ, and there is interconnection between all of them. About 1000 years before David and 3000 years before Christ, men were already looking forward to the righteous rule of the King! This prophecy was not fulfilled until the reign of Christ commenced at His resurrection and ascension into heaven. As the old Patriarchs wandered about the land of Canaan, the world continued to wait for the rule of a good and righteous King. The King to come would have a firm grasp on the true standard of justice.

The names whereby God is known are important to us. For the first time, God introduced Himself here as "El Shaddai." This was the God of the covenant, the God who revealed Himself to Abraham. He was God Almighty. Here was a subtle reminder that faith in the promise is always a faith in the One who is Almighty. Our God is absolutely sovereign and all-powerful, and we must believe that He has what it takes to make His promises come true.

Verses 16–29. God gave Jacob several major crises after Bethel. On the return trip, his favorite wife, Rachel, died in childbirth. Then his eldest son Reuben took his father's concubine, Bilhah, for inappropriate relations. Finally, Jacob's father, Isaac, died after a good long life of 180 years. Of all the horrible things that a man may experience in his life, none are more traumatic than the moral failure and rebellion of children, and the death of loved ones. But what can we say about the Christian life? This life is never void of trial. No one gets to heaven on "flowery beds of ease, while others fight to win the prize and sail through bloody seas!" Yet, as God sanctifies us through the fire of trials, we can be sure that He will comfort us with His presence and salvation.

How does this passage teach us to walk with God in faith and obedience?

1. In the Old Testament times, God would consecrate a particular geographic location for His worship. This changed in the New Testament. In His discussion with the woman at the well, Jesus announced a new era where God would meet any place, any time with His people (John 4:21-

24). Instead of consecrating a location, He consecrates His people as a temple for worship (1 Cor. 3:17, 6:19).

2. If anything, this chapter is a picture of a covenant family who is no stranger to idolatry, sin, and hard trials. How will our lives be any different from the pagan families who live about us? Hopefully, we are worshiping the true and living God. While others are consumed with serving these idols, we are busy eliminating these idols from our minds, our homes and lives. Before coming together to worship God on the Lord's Day, it is appropriate that we confess our sins, abandon our idols, and worship God with whole-hearted sincerity.

3. Idolatry is itself a trap that ever threatens the people of God. How soon we are drawn into idolatry, whether it be money, food, houses, or even some small trinket! When we become fixated on some trinket and displace the true worship of the living God, we have fallen into the sin of idolatry.

4. As Jacob took his entire family to worship God in Bethel, we should integrate our families into God's worship as well. Worship is a family affair, and practically every reference to public worship in the Bible includes children, even nursing babies! (Deut. 29:1, 31:12; Josh. 8:35; 2 Chron. 20:13; Neh. 12:43; Joel 2:16; Eph. 6:1)

Questions:

1. What are the themes of Chapters 1 through 35?
2. Where did Jacob take his family to worship God?
3. What does Bethel mean?
4. What does the family need to do first, before worshiping God?
5. What are some of the trials Jacob goes through after returning from Bethel?

Family Discussion Questions:

1. What sorts of idols must we purge from our hearts and homes before we worship God today?

2. What are the special lessons and comforting visitations from God that we have received as a family? It is good that fathers share with their families the things that God has taught them by His Word and Spirit.

CHAPTER 36

Esau's Line

Now these are the generations of Esau, who is Edom. Gen. 36:1

Events:

1. A list of Esau's wives, his sons, and grandsons is given.

What does this passage teach us?

Verses 1–8. This is the story of Esau. Although Esau was excluded from the covenant promises, God still blessed him with children, possessions, and land. Temporal reward does sometimes come through being related to men of the covenant like Abraham and Isaac. But there is more to the covenant than this. These temporal blessings should not be ignored, but they are not enough. Blood lines are important, but they do not guarantee eternal spiritual blessings. In one sense, the Edomites made up one nation proceeding from Abraham and Isaac and constituted a fulfillment of the Abrahamic blessings. Yet this was only a downpayment of what was to come. The motherlode blessings would come through Abraham's Seed, the Lord Jesus Christ. In Him, every tribe, nation, and tongue would find their place in the spiritual family of Abraham.

Actually, the spiritual blessings of God's covenant with Abraham did visit the line of Esau at points throughout Old Testament history. Of the two spies who returned from the land with the good report, Caleb the Kennizite was one of them. Kenaz was one of Esau's grandsons. It is also quite possible that Job and his friends were descendants of Esau, as Scripture places the land of Uz and Teman in the land of Edom (Job 1:1, 2:11; Lam. 4:21; Gen. 36:11).

All of this is in accord with God's promises. He promised a blessing to a thousand generations to those who love Him and keep His commandments

(Exod. 20:6). When the faith dies out in a family, very often it reappears within a generation or two. God remembers His covenant to a thousand generations! Sometimes unbelievers enjoy relative stability, wealth, peace, and strength of character in their communities. This is a result of what we call "common grace." Every nation and person across this globe enjoys common grace because of their generational and geographical connections with true men of faith. When unbelievers prosper, it is usually a result of their relationship with believers. Matthew 5:25 tells us that God sends rain on the just and on the unjust. Even though Esau rejected the covenant, the mercy of God was still extended to him as long as he and his sons lived on the earth.

Esau's children and grandchildren became kings and princes throughout the land of Edom, a mountainous area just southeast of the Dead Sea (also called the Salt Sea). God protected this land for Esau's future generations, and did not direct the Israelites to confiscate it as they had done with other Canaanite lands. In the succeeding centuries, though, the Edomites refused to provide any aid to the children of Israel as they journeyed through the wilderness. They proved to be an unfriendly and hostile neighbor to the people of God. As time progressed, the relationship between the two nations disintegrated, bringing God's wrath down upon the persecutor of His people. The prophets committed entire chapters and books to preaching God's judgment upon those wicked people (Is. 34; Jer. 49; Ezek. 35; Obadiah).

Verses 9–43. By divine inspiration, the biblical writers chose to include extended genealogies here and there throughout the Word. How are we to take these somewhat laborious readings? Before passing them off as boring and entirely irrelevant to our use, let us consider a few reasons why Moses would take the time to record these lists. At the most basic level, God wants us to know that children are a blessing. Children are not insignificant in God's reality. When a million descendants come about as the progeny of a single man, this should be taken as an amazing legacy and a blessing from God. A man's progeny is a true heritage of the Lord. Some families produce no posterity whatsoever, and others are blessed with millions. Consider two American preachers, for example. The generational legacy of Billy Sunday, the famed evangelist of the early 20th century America, completely disappeared. His last unbelieving grandson died, unmarried and childless, in the 1970s. Then there is the great legacy of Jonathan Edwards, the powerful preacher and American theologian of the 18th century. Several hundred years after his death, Edith A. Winship tracked down 1,400 descendants of Edwards. She found that this man's progeny included 13 college presidents, 65 professors, 100 lawyers and a dean of an outstanding law school, as well as 30 judges, 60 doctors and a dean of a medical school. Incredibly, Edwards' descendants included 80 holders of public office including three United States senators, three mayors of large cities, three state governors, a vice president of the United States, and a controller of the United States Treasury. Members of the family had written 135 books and edited 18 journals and periodicals. They entered the ministry in platoons and sent 100 missionaries overseas, as well as stocking many mission boards with lay trustees. They directed banks and insurance companies, and they owned coal mines, iron plants, and vast oil interests. Yet, this humble pastor, Jonathan Edwards, had been expelled from his own church of hardly 100 people and had spent the remaining years of his life working with the native American Indians. A man's descendants are his legacy.

Can one man make a difference in this world if God blesses him with children and a vision for the generations that follow? Yes! When we look at America, we see the imprint of Jonathan Edwards on millions of people. You can learn a lot about yourself if you know something about your heritage, the men from whose loins you came—to use biblical terminology.

Every generation is a testimony to God's faithfulness. If He will bring a covenant man like Caleb out of the line of Kenaz, then it makes sense to include Kenaz in the recorded history of the Edomites. Eventually, these written genealogies would include the names of more of God's covenant people—a church roll, so to speak. Every one of these names are important, because they stand for the people and the families with whom God establishes His covenant.

A short and seemingly insignificant biographical statement is included in verse 24. It is just a little record concerning one household economy, and how God blessed the family of Anah. Throughout Scripture, we find that children worked for the family economy. (We see the same thing with

Rebekah, Rachel, Joseph, David, John, and James in both the Old and New Testaments.) With the disintegration of the family in the modern nation states, it is hard for us to picture a family working together in a unified family economy. Nevertheless, we always find this pattern in a proper biblical society, where there are families producing a household income as families.

How does this passage teach us to walk with God in faith and obedience?

Consider the powerful influence of our godly founders upon this nation. There isn't a nation on earth which has sent more Christian missionaries to foreign nations. No other nation is more charitable. America still contributes twice as much to charitable endeavors as a percentage of the GNI (Gross National Income) than any other nation on earth. There isn't a nation which has provided as much economic and political freedom and wealth for as many people as America. This nation has more Christian schools, more Christian home schools, and more people who believe that God created man only 6000-10,000 years ago, than any other nation on earth. Does a heritage matter? Does it matter whether our grandfathers were loving God and keeping His commandments in 1765? Does it matter whether we are loving God and keeping His commandments in our day? Millions, if not billions, of people have enjoyed the godly heritage of the nation of the United States. Let us rejoice in the goodness of God, as He is gracious to us and causes the rain to fall on both the just and the unjust.

Questions:

1. What are the themes of Chapters 1 through 36?

2. What is common grace?

3. Why did God bless Esau?

4. Where was the land that was settled by the Edomites, with respect to the country of Israel?

5. What did the man Anah do for his father?

Family Discussion Questions:

1. Has God blessed the nation of America because of its Christian roots? How has God blessed us? What kind of blessing might God bring to our land 150 years from now if our family walks in God's ways and pursues His kingdom's interests with all that is in us?

2. What kind of heritage has God given our family? What will our legacy look like in a hundred years from now?

3. Have you seen the faith die out in certain families? Have you seen it reappear in succeeding generations?

CHAPTER 37

Joseph Sold

And it came to pass, when Joseph was come unto his brethren, that they stripped Joseph out of his coat, his coat of many colors that was on him; And they took him, and cast him into a pit: and the pit was empty, there was no water in it. Gen. 37:23–24

Events:

1. Joseph aggravates his brothers by giving a bad report about them to his father.
2. Joseph relates his dreams to his family, suggesting that he will sometime in the future hold a position of preeminence over his family.
3. Jacob sends Joseph to Shechem to find his brothers.
4. Joseph's brothers seize him and sell him into slavery.

What does this passage teach us?

Verses 1–11. This chapter relates a story of hatred, envy, and deceit. This sort of sin ruins families in all times and places. It is not unusual. There are sins that are corporate and systemic, which set the conditions for more sin. In this story, the conditions that served to foster sin and corruption among the sons of Jacob were polygamy, idolatry, and a fleshly rivalry rooted in pride. Should it be any surprise to us that the sons of Rachel and Leah took on the pride and jealousy of their mothers, or that the sons of Jacob gave way to deceptive ploys? Oftentimes, children will take on the sins of their fathers with increased consistency and greater passion. Such was the case with Jacob and his sons. Like the spreading of germs in a dirty hospital, sin is the leaven in the body of a family. It is impossible to entirely escape its effects in the lives of families, churches, and nations.

At this point, Jacob's failure to provide adequate spiritual leadership in his home should be fairly evident. A pattern emerges throughout the account of Jacob's life as we recall his hesitation to get involved in the Dinah affair, or his pursuit of more polygamy at Rachel's suggestion, or his apparent passivity towards Reuben's abominable behavior, or his angry response to Rachel in her barrenness. All of these sins of omission and commission served to create a "perfect storm" in the life of Jacob's family, as this story evidences. All in all, the fundamental problem was still the human heart. It was the corruption of their hearts that defiled these brothers and produced the dastardly, hateful deed.

Concerning the matter of favoritism, there is nothing essentially wrong with a father providing some special treatment for one child over another. Of course, a father should demonstrate true love for each and all of his children. But if a father should reward one child for responsible behavior, the others should take delight in this. Sadly, this is not usually the case. When hearts are already smoldering in bitter hatred, selfish pride, and sinful rivalry, favoritism will serve as gasoline on a pile of hot coals. In the case of Jacob, one would have a hard time making the case that he cared all that much for his older sons, especially in view of his treatment of Leah's sons on the day he had the encounter with his brother, Esau.

Before we start labeling this family as the worst possible example of family unity in the history of mankind, we should point out that Jacob's marriages stayed intact until the end, and the family still worked together as a unified household. These things could hardly be said of many Christian households in "developed" nations today. Families used to retain an integral solidarity as they formed their own economy, and as members of the family worked for that economic vision. In this case, however, it seems that Joseph was more honest and more dedicated to the success of his father's ventures than the rest of Jacob's sons. When he reported problems with his brothers in the field, this served only to sour their relationship. Relationships disintegrated even more when his father rewarded him with a coat of honor. In those days, a man's clothes communicated his wealth and his place in society, and Joseph's brothers did not miss the message.

To make matters even worse, Joseph told his family about some dreams he had, in which he assumed a position of preeminence over all of them, parents included. Does Joseph betray a lack of wisdom in his interactions with his brothers? Well, Proverbs warns us about the "wringing of the nose" and the provoking of strife among those who are already controlled by envy, hatred, and pride (Prov. 30:33). Yet even if this was a failure on Joseph's part, it is clear that Joseph was more righteous than all of them, and certainly far more deserving of his father's trust and honor.

Verses 12–36. Having appointed Joseph as supervisor over his brothers, Jacob sent him off to monitor his brothers who were tending the sheep at Shechem. Here Joseph again proved himself as the paradigm of a faithful servant and a responsible son as he followed his father's wishes and searched for his brothers. But it was just this moral quality about the young man that fueled the fire of envy in the hearts of his brothers. "Wrath is cruel, and anger is outrageous; but who is able to stand before envy?" (Prov. 27:4). When he finally came upon his brothers on the plains of Dothan, dark clouds were gathering. We can learn from this that if anger and envy are not addressed, these sins will eventually yield terrible, destructive effects, not even excluding the sin of murder. Remember that it was Cain who was warned about sin that crouched at the door like a tiger. If that sin is not mortified in the heart and in the tongue, it will often spring forward in violent, harmful actions. This is precisely what we see in this story, as the brothers made plans to kill Joseph. Thankfully, Reuben intervened and saved the boy's life. It is never too late to repent, and even the slightest shift in a man's heart is welcome. Repentance can avert a world of grief. In this case, however, their repentance was half-hearted and pusillanimous. The brothers proceeded to strip Joseph of his coat, breaking the Eighth Commandment. They threw him into a pit and sold him to Ishmaelite slave traders, breaking the Sixth Commandment. Afterward, they proceeded to concoct a false story for their father, breaking the Fifth and Nineth Commandments. This is a vivid picture of the sinful hearts of men involved in a whole series of sinful actions.

The story was not over. God was working. As the story unfolds, we will find that God was working through the evil actions of Joseph's brothers to accomplish His marvelous plans.

How does this passage teach us to walk with God in faith and obedience?

1. This is a good story for all children who possess the same sinful tendencies as Joseph's brothers. Let it be a warning to all of us! It reminds us of the dreadful evils of jealousy and hatred that lurk in every person's heart. If these sins are left to simmer in the hearts of boys and girls over many years, they will produce very bad fruit. Do you see how important it is that you repent of these sinful inclinations while they are still tiny, fleeting thoughts in the mind? Do not allow the sin of proud rivalry or hateful jealousy to grow in your heart. Confess these sins to Christ and receive His forgiveness today. It is very important that you deal with these sins when you are young. Plead for God's help now or your sin may cause terrible destruction in your family in the years to come.

2. What can we say about "tattling" or reporting the sins of others to parents and superiors? On the one hand, we want to be careful that we do not appear self-righteous to others. This happens sometimes when a child fails to acknowledge his own sins while at the same time being very up-front about everyone else's sins. Parents should watch for this sort of hypocrisy. Still, there is nothing wrong with a truthful witness. When a child truthfully reports sins happening in his home and confesses his own sins in the process, a parent ought to commend it. Of course, other rebellious hearts may hate that child for bringing their sin to light. According to Proverbs, the fool is defined as the one who hates reproof, but "he that regards reproof shall be honored" (Prov. 13:18). And "he that hears reproof gets understanding" (Prov. 15:32), but "he that hateth reproof shall die" (Prov. 15:10). God holds parents responsible for correcting sin, and we expect our children to be faithful in reporting sin to us. Our little ones should be careful not to despise the one who brings their sins to light, even if he "tattles." They should avoid playing the part of the lawyer who argues every little fact in the matter when they are clearly guilt of a sinful heart, sinful motivations, and sinful actions. If our children are in sin, then they should admit it, confess it, and receive forgiveness from those they have offended. People who instinctively recoil against every confrontation or accusation of sin, and those who argue with every reproof and rebuke, are playing the part of the scoffer and the fool.

Questions:

1. What are the themes of Chapters 1 through 37?
2. What did the coat of many colors symbolize?
3. How did Joseph's brothers react when Jacob favored Joseph with the coat of honor?
4. How did Joseph's behavior demonstrate his faithfulness and responsibility as Jacob's son?
5. How did Joseph's brothers show that their actions were motivated by hatred and envy?
6. How did Joseph's brothers deceive their father?
7. How did Reuben demonstrate his repentance towards his father in this story?

Family Discussion Questions:

1. What are the fundamental sinful heart inclinations in our family that might result in more sinful behavior?
2. Children, are you ever jealous of your brothers and sisters? Do you covet gifts that your parents give to any of your siblings? Is there any hate in your heart against a brother or sister today? How do we address sins like this?

CHAPTER 38

Judah's Sin

When she was brought forth, she sent to her father in law, saying, "By the man, whose these are, am I with child:" and she said, "Discern, I pray thee, whose are these, the signet, and bracelets, and staff." And Judah acknowledged them, and said, "She hath been more righteous than I; because that I gave her not to Shelah my son." And he knew her again no more. Gen. 38:25–26

Events:

1. God gives Judah three sons.
2. God kills the older two sons for their wicked behavior.
3. Judah fornicates with Tamar, his son's widow.
4. Tamar bears two sons.

What does this passage teach us?

Verses 1–10. If Jacob's sons were wicked, his grandsons were even worse. Immorality characterized the covenant people of God as they sank deeper into rebellion with each succeeding generation. This was the sad pattern that marked the people of God throughout the Old Testament. The world was hopelessly locked in the grips of sin before the coming of the Messiah and the outpouring of His Spirit. There were very few instances of generational faithfulness in 4,000 years of biblical historical record.

Judah was Jacob's fourth son. Thus far, Reuben, Simeon, and Levi had all been disappointments to their father. All three had succumbed to significant moral failure. Now, Judah joined his three elder brothers with his own sinful tryst. His troubles began at the same point where many other young men's troubles begin. He took a wife from among the ungodly Canaanites. How many times in Scripture do we find the breakdown of true faith happening when the children of believers marry into an unbelieving line? It wasn't that Judah was without any examples, both good and bad. His father had traveled four hundred miles for a bride. His uncle Esau had suffered from his poor choices for mates, and his grandfather and grandmother had openly expressed their disappointment in Esau.

Not surprisingly, Judah's two older sons followed the pattern of the Canaanites. We are not told the nature of Er's wicked lifestyle. But it was bad enough that God killed him. From earlier biblical revelation concerning the terrifying Nephilim, it is clear that covenant breakers are dangerous people. Syncretism in the godly line can be deadly! Undoubtedly, God would have been more patient with the average pagan family residing in the land of Canaan at that time. But He came down hard on this son of the covenant who turned against the covenant. Here is a stark reminder of God's intimate involvement in the affairs of men. Others may look at the death of a family member as a random accident. But there are no accidents in God's world. He is especially involved with His own people. During the early days of the New Testament Church, God killed Ananias and Saphira when they lied to the Spirit and to the church (Acts 5:1–10). Those who fail to understand the pure white holiness and infinitely precise justice of God quickly impugn God with irrational anger. They count God's actions against Er and Onan as arbitrary and impetuous. But, how could God act with anything but perfect justice? And, who are we to demand a reason for God's actions? He certainly does not need us to defend Him! Suffice it to say that God was concerned about this grandson of the covenant line who corrupted himself. At this seminal stage in the Old Testament church, such noxious weeds could corrupt the entire field. These examples of God's judgment are meant to strike fear into the hearts of those who hear about them.

What may seem unusual about this story is the involvement of the family in the death of a son and brother. The surviving brother was expected to take care of the widow of the deceased by taking her as his wife. Today, most "developed" countries are characterized by a socialist view of social relations. In these socialist countries, widows and single women are taught to be "independent" of the family and church. This means that they are dependent upon the civil government for their security and sustenance.

That is why single women are the largest demographic voting block that favors big government socialism in democratic elections. Of course, this new social system has destroyed the integrity of the family in most of these countries. Since the family as a viable social unit disappeared several generations ago, most modern readers will have a hard time understanding the practices found in this story. According to the biblical social pattern, a brother in a family (or the Christian church) will quickly marry a young widow upon the death of her spouse. This is Paul's injunction in 1 Timothy 5:14.

In spite of some of the dysfunctional and sinful aspects of Judah's family, at least there was some concept of the family as a viable institution. This family was still well ahead of the concept of family found in modern Western countries. They still felt a strong obligation to care for their own. Thus for Judah's family, it fell to the closest relatives (Judah's remaining sons, in this case) to look after the widow of the deceased. Therefore, Onan's sin is mainly seen in his refusal to love his deceased brother and to provide for his brother's widow. According to the text, he refused to "give seed to his brother." He went in to lie with his brother's widow, but evidently he was not committed to marry the woman or have children with her. For selfishness and the senseless violation of a woman, God killed the man. While this passage does not explicitly forbid birth control, it does provide a frightening condemnation of fornication and self-centered liaisons.

Verses 11–30. Sadly, the moral condition of the family continued to deteriorate when Judah's wife passed away. Instead of seeking another suitable bride, he sought the company of a prostitute. From the text, we learn that Judah had an unbelieving Canaanite friend named Hirah who supported him in this wicked tryst. Long term, ungodly friendships often lead to this kind of moral compromise. What was supposed to have been a simple, anonymous, and "harmless" act of sexual sin turned out to be far more complicated, embarrassing, and heinous in the end. When a man lies with his son's wife, it is clearly an abominable act and worthy of the death penalty (Leviticus 20:12). This may be the most scandalous story recorded in Scripture. How many times do men commit sin without intending to "harm" anybody? Their actions inevitably produce far more guilt, pain, and hurtful consequences than they would have expected!

Judah's reaction towards Tamar's pregnancy contains a powerful lesson as well. In an attempt to judge "righteously," he at first condemned her to death, which would have been appropriate in the case of adultery in Old Testament law. But this judge had already undermined his right to make a civil judgment, since he himself had committed the same sin (Matt. 7:1, 2). In the end, he confessed that she had been more righteous than he. Judah's humility is remarkable. Yes, the sin was scandalous. Yes, the woman was deceptive and somewhat to blame for the tryst. But Judah humbled himself and acknowledged his own responsibility in the affair. He felt guilt for neglecting the woman and his earlier promise to her (vs. 11), because upon the death of his two sons, he had promised Shelah to her for a husband (vs. 11).

This may be the most important chapter in the book of Genesis. It tells the true story of the unrestrained, wicked hearts of men. But it is also the story of God's mercy. Later, Judah becomes the favored son, the line from which comes the Lion of Judah and the Redeemer of Israel. But it all began with an embarrassing account of a wicked act, and a humbled man. God was ready and willing to pour out His mercy on a man who would humble himself and confess his sin. We live in an ugly, sinful world, but where men will just humble themselves, God shows His mercy in unbelievable ways!

How does this passage teach us to walk with God in faith and obedience?

1. The young men, Er and Onan probably died of what many today would call "natural causes." They may have been struck by lightning or perhaps they developed a case of intestinal cancer. Should a man of God walk into a forensics laboratory and declare that the dead man was killed by the living God Himself, he would be laughed out of the place. But that is because the mass of our population is discipled in a religion called "materialistic naturalism." For over a hundred years, our educated elite have received sixteen to eighteen years of education in the wrong worldview. It is a worldview that eliminates God from all of man's reality. But as Christians, we will look at a young man dead in the morgue and say without hesitation, "God killed him!"

2. One dead man provides us a startling reminder of the righteous judgment of Almighty God. Clearly, Onan despised his dead brother and his brother's wife, and he committed one of the most wicked, lascivious actions ever recorded in all of the long lists of sinful things done in this wicked world. But at the root of it all, Onan cared only for himself, and his selfishness eventually produced terrible fruit. Let us look after the interests of others, especially those of our own family and our own church. One of the ways that we look out for others is to look out for the widows in the church. As Paul reminds the church, the younger widows need to be married. If the unmarried brothers in the church ignore these widows year after year, do they also betray this self-centeredness? Could they also fail to love their neighbor or honor their dead brothers as well?

3. Tamar made a terrible mistake when she set out to solve her problems by sinning against God. If things are not going our way, we should never try to correct the problem by breaking the laws of God. We should instead turn to the Lord in prayer, and patiently wait upon Him.

4. "Be sure your sin will find you out" (Num. 32:23). It seems that Judah thought he could get away with sin when nobody was looking. But when everything was said and done, everyone found out about it, including those of us who just read the story again, thousands of years later. Do you ever commit sin in secret, counting on the fact that nobody will ever find out? Jesus promises that what you do in secret will be made manifest someday (Luke 8:17). Moreover, the eyes of the Lord are in every place, beholding the evil and the good. When you are tempted to sin in secret, ask yourself, "Am I willing for God and all my family, friends, and church members to see this?"

Questions:

1. What are the themes of Chapters 1 through 38?
2. How many sons did God give Judah?
3. What happened to the older two sons?
4. Why did God kill Onan?
5. How did Judah fail to take care of Tamar?

6. How does the Bible instruct us to take care of the young widows in the church?

7. How did Judah display humility in this story?

Family Discussion Questions:

1. How do we exhibit selfishness in our words and actions towards our family members?

2. Are there some hidden sins that we need to confess right now, and get out before God and our family?

3. Will we feel obligated to take care of our brother's wife, should something happen to our brother (both in the family and in the church)?

CHAPTER 39

Joseph Tempted

And it came to pass about this time, that Joseph went into the house to do his business; and there was none of the men of the house there within. And she caught him by his garment, saying, "Lie with me:" and he left his garment in her hand, and fled, and got him out.
Gen. 39:11–12

Events:

1. Potiphar buys Joseph as a slave.
2. Joseph is promoted to manager of Potiphar's entire household.
3. Potiphar's wife tempts Joseph and he resists her temptation.
4. The woman frames Joseph and he is put in an Egyptian prison.

What does this passage teach us?

Verses 1–2. This chapter returns to the story of Joseph, who had been sold into Egyptian slavery by his brothers. Through it all, Joseph remained the constant servant of the living God. He was a pattern for every Christian believer. But more importantly, he served as an Old Testament prototypical picture of Jesus Christ. Just as Christ lived out His days of humiliation and suffering, Joseph walked a similar path. He was a living picture of a suffering servant who must bear persecution with a glad and humble heart. All Christians are called to this life. It is our reasonable service (Rom. 12:1). Of all of the sons of Jacob, none was more undeserving of the treatment Joseph received, yet by God's ordination, the young man suffered grave injustices for year after painful year. Through all this he remained ever faithful, steadfast, courageous, and agreeable to these difficult providences in his life. While there is no reason to believe he was without sin entirely, the Bible sees fit to emphasize his upright character. It seems that Joseph was the most godly of all the patriarchs. Why did God subject the most faithful to the most severe injustices and persecutions at the hands of the Gentiles? There is only one possible answer to the question. It was His desire and delight. Several times in this chapter, we are told that God was with Joseph. This is a crucial element to the story. Of all the precious covenantal promises, the believer always holds to the promise of God's presence. "I will be with thee," He tells His people. God would never subject His faithful servant to such severe conditions without blessing him with His presence. Wherever Christians must stand alone in the world under the most miserable of conditions, they can count on the presence of God, and that is a sufficient comfort and strength. All the while His people suffer, we must believe that God is carefully monitoring the situation. And He will provide the resources necessary for the man of God to come out of it victorious.

Verses 3–6. Young Joseph in Potiphar's household is the prime example of grace under trial. Any man or woman who finds himself cut out of the family economy and enslaved to governments or to large corporate interests will find great encouragement here. There was not a hint of bitter resentment or angry vengefulness in Joseph. He was the picture of contentment. Committing himself to the place that God had brought him, he threw himself into his tasks. In accordance with Paul's admonition to servants in Ephesians 6, Joseph gave his utmost in obedient service to his master, "doing the will of God from the heart" (Eph. 6:6). No matter his condition, the man of faith knows that he is always in the employment of his heavenly Master. All rewards, paychecks, bonuses, congratulatory notes, honors, and promotions ultimately come from the Father of lights, "with whom there is no variableness neither shadow of turning" (Jam. 1:17).

Joseph set a godly example for every young man who must learn the lessons of diligence, respect, and obedience to their masters even during the most menial work. Although Joseph found himself in the employment of an unbeliever, good service and hard work was duly recognized and rewarded. By his conscientious, wise, and diligent labor, Joseph won the trust of his master, and Potiphar put all of his interests under Joseph's management.

Verses 7–19. From these verses we may glean another important insight concerning Joseph's sterling character. None of these temptations are unusual in the lives of men, and we have much to learn from this. The wife of Potiphar tempted Joseph to commit adultery with her, which was a clear violation of the 7th commandment. Over an extended period of time, he steadfastly resisted her repeated advances. Here is an example of a man standing with integrity against the wily temptress, and he did so by simply speaking the truth. One statement of truth will crush a thousand deceitful propositions. One small light bulb takes up only a cubic inch in spatial volume, but it can illuminate 1,000,000 square inches of darkness! If men and women would only speak the truth, those gigantic, evil dragons of deceit would melt on the spot. Mark the simple, straight-forward speech of this man, Joseph, as he says, "How can I violate my master's trust by stealing the one thing he has not given to me: his wife? How can I do this great wickedness and sin against God?" By invoking the law of God, he takes the argument to a higher level. What more can be said? How can a temptation retain its strength in the face of such powerful words? How many sins might be avoided if we were to break the silence with the truth, as Joseph did in this story?

While Joseph strongly resisted the temptation with these words, it wasn't enough to slow down this woman who was hell-bent in the path of wickedness. The woman falsely accused him of impropriety, and Joseph landed in an Egyptian jail.

Verses 20–23. Twice, Joseph had fallen victim to treacherous dealings. At this point he had even more reason to resort to self-pity, bitterness, and discouragement. His life had been one long series of ups and downs. After a promotion in his father's house, he suffered at the cruel hands of his brothers. Sold into slavery, he found himself in the household of an Egyptian. After a promotion to the chief position in the household, he was thrown into prison. After all of this ill treatment, did his courage flag? Did his outlook dim? Incredibly, in these dour conditions he proved himself the most responsible and diligent prisoner in the jail! Truly, Joseph had learned "to be abased and to abound." Whatever his conditions, he learned to be content therein (Phil. 4:11-12). Whatever life would deal him, he was determined to make the best of it! This is an example of true godly faith in action.

Both in verse 21 and 23, we are told in no uncertain terms that Yahweh God was with Joseph. This is the key phrase. When God is with a man, and the man knows that God is with him, that man will manifest the utmost strength, courage, uprightness, and steadfastness in the day of trouble! It was the Lord who visited Joseph in this no-account prison deep in the heart of Egypt, and it was the Lord who saw to it that Joseph was favored by the prison guard. It was the Lord who made him prosper in whatever he set his hand to in the miserable dungeon. Of course, God could have prevented any of this from happening to Joseph. But Joseph's whole life was part of God's story, and He would never allow Joseph to live the story alone.

How does this passage teach us to walk with God in faith and obedience?

1. Joseph provided an example of constant faith and steadfast obedience through many years of humiliation. Although his story benefited many of the children of God living in the Old Testament era, his life is just as instructive to those of us who live in the age of the New Testament Church. May God help us to be faithful in the hard days as we traverse the valleys of trial, especially as we contemplate the promise that He is with us, even to the end of the world.

2. Sin begins when we look at something that God has forbidden and we desire it. That was the sin of Potiphar's wife in this story. When a parent forbids a child from taking a cookie, the cookie jar becomes a source of temptation to the child. When a child continues to look longingly at the cookie while contemplating disobedience, he has already broken God's law, for God has commanded that children obey their parents. Flirting with temptation is to desire what God has forbidden. If God has said, "no," then let us not play with the idea of breaking God's law. We had better move along and get busy doing the things that God would have us to do.

3. This text teaches us a great deal about resisting temptation. The Christian must be prepared to resist temptation over and over again, even when it becomes increasingly more difficult. He must be willing to resist

temptation by speaking the truth, and by physically removing himself from the situation. Herein lies the difference between knowledge and wisdom. Knowledge is understanding that it is wrong to lie with somebody else's wife, but wisdom is actually leaving your coat in the hands of Potiphar's wife on your way out the door.

4. God gives us some situations in our lives that will either make us or break us. If Joseph had given in to the temptation, he would have undoubtedly suffered terrible consequences and his life would have been very different. May God give us the strength and the faith to pass the tests that He sends our way.

Questions:

1. What are the themes of Chapters 1 through 39?
2. How did Joseph's life represent a series of ups and downs?
3. How did Joseph react to the trying circumstances in his life?
4. How did Joseph resist the temptation of Potiphar's wife?
5. What happened to Joseph as a consequence of rejecting the woman's temptations?
6. What is the difference between wisdom and knowledge, as illustrated in this chapter?

Family Discussion Questions:

1. How equipped are we to resist temptation? What are the sorts of things that we can do right now to prepare ourselves for the more significant temptations and trials that might come our way?

CHAPTER 40

Joseph Imprisoned

And Joseph came in unto them in the morning, and looked upon them, and, behold, they were sad. And he asked Pharaoh's officers that were with him in the ward of his lord's house, saying, "Wherefore look ye so sadly to day?" And they said unto him, "We have dreamed a dream, and there is no interpreter of it." And Joseph said unto them, "Do not interpretations belong to God? tell me them, I pray you." Gen. 40:6–8

Events:

1. Pharaoh's chief butler and baker are placed in prison with Joseph.
2. Both the butler and baker have dreams.
3. Joseph interprets the dreams.
4. The baker is hanged and the butler returns to his service under Pharaoh.

What does this passage teach us?

Verses 1–22. Between 1800 and 1600 BC, Egypt's Middle Kingdom was in full swing, and Egypt was about to reach the zenith of its power and glory. This kingdom constituted the very heart of civilization in the ancient world. After the disintegration of Nimrod's kingdom, Egypt became an unequalled economic and technological powerhouse in the ancient world. It was a nation populated by millions of people and governed by an autocratic Pharaoh. We read very little about the kingdom of Egypt in this historical survey. Instead, we learn about a small jail cell and one solitary man incarcerated there in the middle of this gigantic empire.

Our God is not the disinterested god of the deists. He never leaves the empires of men entirely alone throughout the annals of world history. Before the Great Flood, human civilization centralized power through mighty men. These Nephalim unleashed unspeakable violence and unmitigated evil on the world, but it wasn't long before God intervened. After He destroyed the first world, powerful men again assembled a tower on the plains of Babel to make "a name for themselves." So God showed up on the scene once again and dispersed their little conspiracy. Since that time, He has never permitted another unified worldwide government to operate in competition with the Creator.

Throughout the rest of the biblical historical record, you will find God's people wandering into the very center of man's most important empires. Scripture tells of Joseph in Egypt, Jonah in Assyria, Daniel in Babylon, Esther in Persia, and Jesus' Apostles in Rome. God works His agenda quietly, doing what seems to the masses to be an inauspicious project. Few may be aware of what He is doing as He builds His own kingdom and works His own purposes within the kingdoms of men. But the kingdoms of men always rot and eventually collapse under their own weight. All the while, God's project continues to prosper from generation to generation, expanding from a narrow slice of territory on the eastern shores of the Mediterranean Sea to every continent across this wide globe.

But as Joseph lay in this ignoble prison deep in the heart of Egypt, we are told that Yahweh God was right there, chained beside him, as it were. As the story unfolds, we find that Joseph was promoted to the second highest position in the land. But how did he make it to that position? If history is God's story then you know it will be interesting. Each element of the story is nothing less than the providential outworking of His sovereign plan. This story is a living illustration of the sovereignty of God in action. Without question, He fully intended that both Pharaoh's butler and baker would end up in the same prison cell with Joseph. He planted the prophetic dreams in their minds and then provided Joseph with the right interpretation of the dreams. In order to foretell the future infallibly, one would have to infallibly control all future events. Thus, only the true and living God can issue any authoritative prophetic word, because only this one God is in sovereign control of the future. There is no man, no government, no power, and no other god who can possibly thwart His plans. If His prophecies will infallibly prove themselves true, no act of free will on the part of any one of the millions of people in the land of Egypt

CHAPTER 41

Joseph Promoted

And Pharaoh said unto Joseph, "See, I have set thee over all the land of Egypt." And Pharaoh took off his ring from his hand, and put it upon Joseph's hand, and arrayed him in vestures of fine linen, and put a gold chain about his neck; Gen. 41:41–42

Events:

1. Pharaoh has two dreams.

2. Joseph interprets the dreams.

3. Joseph is promoted to second in command over Egypt.

What does this passage teach us?

Verses 1–16. After Joseph spent two additional years in an Egyptian dungeon, God ordained another sequence of events that catapulted the young man to second in command in the land of Egypt. Truly, the heart of a king is in the hand of God, and He turns it whithersoever He will (Prov. 21:1). It should come as no surprise to us that God's hand was present here, interfering with the mind of the most powerful person in the world at that time. Such are God's prerogatives. First He ordained two dreams for the king. Then He jogged the memory of the king's butler concerning Joseph, the interpreter of dreams who was still in the prison.

Summoned to the court of Pharaoh, Joseph made himself ready for the meeting by changing his clothing and shaving himself in accord with the customs of the land. The Egyptians were known for their fastidious cleanliness and shaving. Thus far, nothing that Joseph did to fit into Egyptian society can be construed as a violation of the laws of God. It is at times important for us to take on the traditions of those around us as long as we are not endorsing sin represented by certain actions or symbols (such as eating food offered to idols).

When Pharaoh asked Joseph if he was capable of interpreting the dreams, the young man humbly pointed to God as his Wisdom. He understood that God was the Source of all wisdom and revelation of truth. As he stood before the most powerful monarch in the world with his life in the balance, his confidence was not in himself. Joseph trusted wholeheartedly in the Creator of heaven and earth. He knew that God was sovereign over all of the dreams and thoughts that occured to every single man who walked the earth.

Verses 17–33. Pharaoh carefully related his dreams in painstaking detail as Joseph listened. In his interpretation of the dream, Joseph stated in no uncertain terms that God was sovereign over the future of Egypt, and that now God was letting Pharaoh in on what He was about to do (v. 33). Such statements are worthy of some careful reflection. Weather patterns are clearly in the hands of our sovereign God. For the following fourteen years the clouds, the water temperature in the seas, the direction of the wind, and the birth rate of locusts and other pests would all serve the will of God. There would be no mistake and no error in the revelation. God absolutely assured seven years of good crops and seven years of famine. This was a clear testimony to the sovereignty of God.

Verses 34–37. Here Joseph acted as a true prophet of God by declaring the Word of God and telling people what to do about that Word. So Joseph advised the Pharaoh to prepare for this terrible famine that could potentially wipe out the whole country. The tribute program Joseph recommended was very unique, and is by no means the pattern by which God normally expects nations to govern. The biblical limit to governmental taxation is 10 percent (1 Sam. 8:15, 18) and anything more than that is a tyrannical imposition on the people. But Joseph spoke as one specially endowed with prophetic wisdom from God when he temporarily set the taxation rate at 20 percent. Of course, he was assuming that it would be even worse tyranny to impose any taxation whatsoever on the citizenry during the succeeding seven years of famine. This turned out to be extraordinarily wise counsel, and served to salvage the empire from destruction.

Joseph even recommended to Pharaoh that he install a "Federal Emergency Management Administrator" to oversee the major project of preparation for the famine. Whether or not this wisdom came by divine revelation is not clear. Nevertheless, Joseph again proved himself to be the consummate problem-solver and faithful manager. Whether it was his father's business, Potiphar's household, a prison operation, or an empire, Joseph was always looking after the well-being of whatever happened to be set under his purview. He was an excellent example for every home-manager (Titus 2:5; Prov. 31:10ff), and for any believer tasked with managing a business or department.

Verses 38–57. Pharaoh believed Joseph's words. It should be noted that the Egyptians were generally a religious people, worshiping many gods. Although they deified man in the state, they also retained a little humility to recognize powers beyond themselves. Even the most powerful Pharaoh felt the need for the approval of some other power beyond himself and the state. In one case, a Pharaoh named Amenhotep IV was a professed monotheist. Evidently, Joseph's Pharaoh registered a certain respect for Joseph's God (vs 38, 39), which impelled him to bring this man of God into that place of prestige. Occasionally, you will find a president, king, or Pharaoh who will still listen to some prophet or preacher of God, because he is not entirely confident in man's scientific, technological, and political power to save himself! He will pause to consider that wisdom for the simple reason that he still fears a higher power.

So Pharaoh promptly promoted Joseph to second in command over the entire land of Egypt. What a story of riches—to rags—to riches! God had been with Joseph through thirteen years of exile, oppression, and humiliation, preparing him for such a time as this. Like the Apostle Paul, Joseph had learned to be abased and to abound (Phil. 4:12). God had formed his character. He had prepared him to receive this promotion without falling prey to the destructive sin of pride. The God of the covenant richly rewarded this man with influence, property, and a family. God is good, and He does "restore the years the locusts have eaten" (Joel 2:25). One would have thought that Joseph had wasted the best years of his life in slavery and imprisonment. But no—not a minute of our lives is wasted as we take the experiences that God gives to us and make the most of them.

Finally, we need to remember that God was working His own sovereign will through all of this. He promoted Joseph to this position, because He had a plan to protect the covenant family of Jacob in the day of famine, and to bring His people into Egypt. And after that, He would deliver them by His mighty hand four hundred years later. This was all part of His glorious plan of redemption, sealed in eternity and forged through the centuries of human history.

How does this passage teach us to walk with God in faith and obedience?

1. Does this story remind us of another story of One who was humbled to the point where He hung on a cross with a couple of outlaws? His days of humiliation were quickly followed by a resurrection and an ascension to the right hand of the Father. We follow in these footsteps as we suffer for Christ in the short years of our tribulations, to commence in final glorification. This is the Christian story. We read it, we believe it, and then we live it ourselves.

2. The life of every Christian is carefully directed by God Himself. All of the difficulties in our lives prepare us for the wonderful things that God has laid out for us in this life and the life to come. We should never complain against God, as if His plan for our lives is some kind of a mistake. Rather, let us receive our circumstances with joyful and hopeful expectation, knowing that a loving Father directs the paths of our lives.

3. Even the disasters that happen in this world are planned and directed by our sovereign God. When we hear about airplane disasters, floods, tornados, famines, and wars, let us always remember that these things are under God's control. He planned these things for some purpose which we do not and will not fully understand. Still, we are responsible to obey Him and praise Him for His sovereign power, His justice, and His preserving grace to us in all of the disasters of life.

4. God preserved the land of Egypt during this terrible famine for His own purposes. He is a merciful God. He wants to protect His covenant people.

Questions:

1. What are the themes of Chapters 1 through 41?

2. How many more years did Joseph spend in prison after the butler left him?

3. How does God know what is going to happen in the future? How can He be certain about it?

4. What are prophets supposed to do?

5. What percentage of the people's crops did Joseph recommend the Pharaoh take for the first seven years? Why? What is God's normal limit on civil government's power to tax (according to 1 Samuel 8)? How much does our governments tax our income (at federal, state, and local levels)?

6. How did God prepare Joseph for this great promotion?

7. Why did God bring the famine to Egypt?

Family Discussion Questions:

1. What happens when you ask a person running for political office if he fears God? Have you ever asked someone this question? How many of our civil leaders fear God? Do they fear God more or less than the Pharaoh feared God?

2. Are there any customs of the culture around us to which we may conform without breaking God's laws? What are these customs? Also, provide examples of where it might be sinful to borrow from the customs of the heathen around us.

CHAPTER 42

Joseph's Brothers

And Joseph was the governor over the land, and he it was that sold to all the people of the land: and Joseph's brethren came, and bowed down themselves before him with their faces to the earth. Gen. 42:6

Events:

1. Joseph's brothers come to Egypt to buy grain.
2. Joseph sends them all to prison for three days.
3. Joseph keeps Simeon, and sends the others back to Canaan to retrieve Benjamin.
4. The nine brothers return to their father with the grain.

What does this passage teach us?

Verses 1–3. For a story to convey meaning, the story has to go somewhere. There must be unity of thought that will give it purpose. But what about the story that unfolds in our reality? Is there any meaning to our lives, or is everything disconnected from a larger plan? As those who believe in God, we defend the meaning of life by pointing to the God who is behind it all. As the aphorism says, "What goes around, comes around!" Some attribute these "going-around-coming-around" patterns to impersonal fates, but true believers know that there is a personal God behind these things. He is always involved. He fully intends to teach lessons, exercise justice, and capture the attention of the characters involved in the story. Certainly this is what we see in the story of Joseph. If you were reading this story for the first time, you would no doubt expect that one day Joseph's brothers would encounter with Joseph again under the sort of circumstances we find in the story, that Joseph's brothers would one day get their due, and that his brothers would face the consequences of their sins, even if they had to wait twenty long years for that to happen. We expect this because there is a God orchestrating the details of history. The ironies, the coincidences, and the comeuppances of history show God's fingerprints upon the stories of our lives. In these stories, we pick up on God's design, God's will, and God's nature. The enslavement, the dreams, the famine, and Joseph's ascension to power are each essential elements of God's grand purpose. As the famine in the land worsened, God saw to it that Jacob sent his ten sinful, guilt-ridden sons down to Egypt for food.

Verses 4–24. The brothers failed to recognize Joseph upon their first meeting with him. As they rendered him obeisance, they did not know that they were fulfilling Joseph's prophetic dream from many years earlier. These were the ten sheaves bowing before Joseph's sheaf!

But what can be said about Joseph's initial reticence to betray his identity to his brothers? Is it ever ethically right to assume a false identity for a time, without correcting it? Throughout the biblical record, you will find multiple instances of this prophetic method. For example, the prophet Nathan lead David to believe his story concerning the theft of a lamb. Later on he clarified the true meaning of the parable to David. Also, David purposely deceived an enemy by pretending to be a lunatic. Scripture does not require kings and prophets to completely reveal their strategies, identity, intentions, and perspectives to everyone at all times. Wisdom dictates. People believe incorrect things all the time, and it is not always wise to correct their misconceptions all at once. From the perspective of these brothers, Joseph was a powerful Egyptian leader. At this stage, his relationship with them was in shambles because of their ill treatment of him twenty years earlier. So he set out to restore their relationship by first testing their hearts through several interesting scenarios. He was wondering if there was any change of heart in these men or if they would still seek to endanger his life as in the past. As a representative of Pharaoh's government, he wanted an assurance that his brothers would not behave maliciously towards himself or to the Egyptian interests he represented. We have no reason to think that this course of action was unwise or harmful. In his heart, Joseph was seeking restoration and reconciliation with his brothers. From the account provided in Genesis, there is not a trace of any vengeful bitterness in the man.

This story demonstrates the power of guilt over the thoughts and actions of men. Twenty years earlier, these men had committed that shameful act towards their brother Joseph. When things began to turn sour in Egypt, their minds immediately reverted back to that wicked act committed on the plains of Dothan (vs. 21,22). Despite all the efforts that men put into denying sin, minimizing it, hiding from it, or blaming it on others, that sin still dogs their heels. In relentless, nauseating, forceful repetition, the guilt of their sin torments their minds. When a man commits a dreadful sin, he cannot escape the guilt of it. If he is too ashamed or too proud to confess it, then it is that sin that will be the one memory that will persist in his mind, even after every other memory has faded. The memory of his sin appears again and again in his thoughts and dreams. It may even drive him to irrationality and insanity. It is impossible to escape it; denial is futile. This is the most undeniable fact in all of human existence—there is a God and men sin against Him. For man, there is nothing more real than the reality of God. Any attempt to suppress the knowledge of God is futile. There is nothing more horrifying than the knowledge that they have offended the God of heaven.

Verses 25–38. Joseph chose to incarcerate Simeon while the others returned to Canaan. But why would he choose Simeon? From Genesis 34:25 and 49:5, we know that Simeon was among the most violent and cruel of the brothers. Also, we know from the account that Joseph kept Simeon to assure the safekeeping of Benjamin and his safe transport to Egypt later. There is no question that Joseph distrusted his brothers. Given the jealousy they had demonstrated towards him, Rachel's firstborn, what might they do to Rachel's second son? This was the reason for the test. Amazingly, Joseph's heart was still filled with love and compassion towards his brothers as he put them through this test. There is not a hint of a vengeful spirit in any of his interactions with them. Rather, he wept over them and even returned their money to their food sacks. Joseph applied wisdom and caution in his dealings; at the same time, his heart was yearning to forgive and restore relationship with his estranged brothers. This is a beautiful picture of the Christian heart.

How does this passage teach us to walk with God in faith and obedience?

1. You cannot sweep your sin under the carpet and forget about it. The proper way to deal with the terrible sins that you commit is to confess them and repent of them. Be very honest with yourself, and be very open with the Lord about that sin. Ask forgiveness of those you have offended and ask forgiveness of God. Then, with faith, engage the ongoing battle with sin. This is the life of repentance.

2. This passage gives us insight into a forgiving heart. Let us emulate Joseph and cultivate a soft heart of forgiveness towards those who offend us. Of course, we should encourage their repentance. Before they come to us with an apology, we should be eager, willing, and waiting to forgive them. We are in the forgiveness business, because we have been forgiven by God! May God release us from a cold and bitter attitude towards those who have offended us! We must never hold on to the "right" to punish others for hurting us. Vengeance belongs to God (Rom. 12:19). Let us always recall the Lord's merciful frame of mind at the very moment of His death at the hands of murderous men. He prayed, "Father forgive them, for they know not what they do."

3. There are times when it is wise to withhold the whole truth from others. Should you meet a bank robber just released from prison, it may not be wise to inform him that you have $50 in your wallet. At the same time, you must also be careful not to mislead somebody and take them down the wrong path. Joseph would eventually reveal his identity when the timing was right. When the truth is helpful and needful for others with whom you are communicating, it is wrong to conceal it.

Questions:

1. What are the themes of Chapters 1 through 42?

2. Why didn't Joseph reveal his identity immediately to his brothers? Did Joseph tell a lie by not revealing his identity?

3. What was the first thing the brothers thought about when they met with trouble in Egypt?

4. Why did Joseph keep Simeon in prison while the others returned home?

5. How do we know that Joseph had a tender heart, ready and willing to forgive his brothers?

Family Discussion Questions:

1. What should we do when we sin against others and against God? Are there sins that we may have committed years ago that we should be confessing now? To whom should we confess our sins?

2. Under what circumstances might we wisely avoid telling the whole truth to somebody?

CHAPTER 43

Joseph's Feast

And they sat before him, the firstborn according to his birthright, and the youngest according to his youth: and the men marveled one at another. And he took and sent messes unto them from before him: but Benjamin's mess was five times so much as any of theirs. And they drank, and were merry with him. Gen. 43:33–34

Events:

1. Jacob finally agrees to send Benjamin with the other brothers to Egypt.
2. When they arrive in Egypt, they are sent to Joseph's house.
3. Joseph prepares a feast for them.

What does this passage teach us?

Verses 1–16. By this time, Jacob's household had grown to 70+ persons. If our count includes servants, his household may well have numbered in the hundreds. Therefore, it is doubtful that the first load of corn from Egypt lasted Jacob's household more than six or seven months. As the famine continued, the family was left with no other option than to return to Egypt for more food.

What best describes the Christian life in both the Old and New Testaments are the characteristics of humility and repentance. We get this from the stories about God's people in the book of Genesis, and we should not miss this point as we reach the final chapters of the book. Notice that repentance is evident in Judah's interaction with his father in this text. Where self-centered jealousy once led to kidnapping and forced servitude, Judah now was pledging his own life to protect the others. This change of heart was not a consequence of any change on Jacob's part. His favoritism towards Rachel's sons had not subsided in the least. Yet, the brothers were now less controlled by envy because of this favoritism. Now they were definitely more interested in looking out for the well-being of others. This radical change of heart perspective is called "repentance."

So at this time, Judah took full responsibility to care for the favorite son. Previously, Reuben pledged the lives of his own two sons on the safe return of Benjamin. But it was Judah who was persuasive in convincing the old patriarch. Finally, Jacob agreed to send Benjamin with the others to Egypt, though not before he did two important things. He prepared a gift for the man who held his son Simeon, and he prayed for God's sovereign protection over his family. This is how a good Christian lives his life. He takes full responsibility to make wise provision for his family. He does everything in his power to keep peace with the civil magistrate and others surrounding him. At the same time, he refuses to compromise his own faith, and leaves the outcome in the hands of a sovereign God. It is plain that Jacob was trusting the all-controlling sovereignty of God over the hearts of the most powerful rulers on earth. We have to believe that our God holds absolute control over the hearts of men! "The king's heart is in the hand of the LORD, as the rivers of water: he turneth it whithersoever he will" (Prov. 21:1).

Verses 17–34. Unquestionably, the brothers were fearful of what could happen to them at the hands of this powerful ruler in the land of Egypt. They were still apprehensive as they sat for a meal at Joseph's house. Several interesting exchanges occurred while they were visiting Joseph's home. Initially, his steward put the brothers at ease, insisting that the money returned to them in their sacks was an act of divine providence. Here is some insight into the household of a righteous man in a pagan state. Joseph's servant had some respect for the God of the Hebrews! As a believer in the true God, Joseph must have spoken of God and His over-arching sovereignty with the men in his household. Yet there were still cultural differences between Joseph's people and the Egyptians. We learn from verse 32 that the Egyptians refused to eat with the Hebrews. Evidently, the City of Man was proud of their ritual cleanliness and cultural standards of morality.

Throughout, Joseph was a true, paradigmatic peacemaker and reconciler. He invited to his table the men who had kidnapped him and subjected him to slavery and potential death—and fed them sumptuously. What magnanimity! We also read that Joseph's bowels yearned for his brother, Benjamin, a term that describes the kind of love, compassion, and appreciation that we all need to feel towards our natural and spiritual brothers.

Finally, they sat down to the feast and Joseph placed them in their birth order. There is something about eating together that lightens the heart and fosters companionship. Eating with brothers and communing around a table is a vital part of human life. It renews and restores relationships. While the Bible forbids drunkenness and gluttony, there is a proper role for enjoying food in company with others, for God intends food to provide more than just physical energy. We enjoy food and we enjoy each other, but most importantly, we enjoy God's provision of these things.

How does this passage teach us to walk with God in faith and obedience?

1. "Trust in God, but keep your powder dry," is an adage that dates back to America's War for Independence. The godly man is equally convinced of God's sovereignty and his own responsibility. He doesn't use one of these truths to weaken the other. To believe in God's sovereignty is to know that He has absolute control over the outcome. But to believe in human responsibility is to submit ourselves to God's revealed will. So we will protect and provide for our families and we will keep God's commandments. If we handle ourselves foolishly, we may lose our lives and the lives of others, and we will be at fault for making foolish decisions. As we embrace our responsibilities, we must trust in the sovereign hand of God who retains complete control over the outcome of every situation. These two obligations stir up in us the courage and confidence to take action. They also give us hope and confidence in the outcome of those actions.

2. We ought to love our brothers as Joseph loved his brothers. Even before his brothers acknowledged their sin and begged for his forgiveness, he

treated them with kindness. His love for Benjamin is seen in his bursting into tears when he saw him. Relationships today are often too cold and distant. We do not want cold relationships between those in our family. Let's work on cultivating affectionate, loving relationships.

Questions:

1. What are the themes of Chapters 1 through 43?
2. Who tried to convince Jacob to allow Benjamin to go with the brothers to Egypt?
3. What two things did Jacob do before sending Benjamin with the other brothers to Egypt?
4. How did Joseph manifest his love for his brothers?
5. Why didn't the Egyptians eat with the Hebrews?

Family Discussion Questions:

1. How much love is there between brothers and sisters in our family?
2. Does our family take action with courage and confidence, while at the same time trusting God's sovereign control of the outcome? Do we err more in the area of taking responsibility or in the area of trusting in God's sovereignty?

CHAPTER 44

Joseph's Cup

And he searched, and began at the eldest, and left at the youngest: and the cup was found in Benjamin's sack. Then they rent their clothes, and loaded every man his ass, and returned to the city. Gen. 44:12–13

Events:

1. Joseph's steward fills the sacks and puts Joseph's cup in Benjamin's sack.
2. The brothers leave but are soon overtaken by Joseph's servants.
3. The servants search the sacks and find Joseph's cup in Benjamin's sack.
4. The brothers return to Joseph's house and plead for mercy.

What does this passage teach us?

Verses 1–12. Unlike other religious writings, the Bible presents realistic stories of sinful men doing sinful things. This is bothersome to the unbelieving mind. Natural man does not want to face his sinful condition. But these stories should humble us, because our lives are also filled with gross mistakes, unwise decisions, and sinful actions. Therefore, we need to be careful not to justify every action taken by the characters in the stories. Nor should we rush to judgment concerning their standing with God. Every man's life is a journey. If you judge a man by his most sinful moment, when a proud and envious spirit has taken the upper hand in his life, you would make a poor judgment of him. But how does the rest of his life go? Does the man humble himself and seek mercy? Before you draw the verdict on the characters represented in the story, you need to read the whole story! Often, you will find reconciliation, humble repentance, and true faith in God. This is the case with Joseph and his brothers.

In this chapter, Joseph prepared an elaborate test for his brothers so that he could determine once and for all if their hearts had changed towards the sons of Rachel (Benjamin and himself). Had their hearts really and truly softened since they had thrown Joseph into a pit on the plains of Dothan and sold him to slave traders? The brothers had come into his house, already disturbed about the money found in their sacks. Now, Joseph upped the ante by placing his own special cup in Benjamin's sack. He wanted to test their love for Benjamin. Previously, they had no regard whatsoever for Joseph's life. Now, to what measures would they go to protect Benjamin from imminent harm?

In order to make the test look real, the servants referred to Joseph's use of a silver cup in "divining." Apparently, magicians would fill the divining cup with water and try to "see" into some future event. This is a difficult passage. There is not enough evidence here to convict Joseph of the sin of witchcraft. It is possible that Joseph lied concerning the divining in order to seem like an Egyptian to his brothers. Or, he may have used the cup as the Urim and Thummim were used by the priests in the Mosaic era to receive God's revelation. We do know that, from his earlier testimony (Gen. 41:6), Joseph attributed all prophetic insight to the only true God, the covenant God of Abraham.

Verses 13–34. The servants caught up with the brothers and searched the bags. When the cup was found, the brothers immediately displayed heartfelt repentance in their love for Benjamin. They tore their clothes in an expression of sadness and horror. They begged for Benjamin's life in front of Joseph, and Judah offered to substitute his life for Benjamin's. All of this was exactly what Joseph was hoping to see—a complete change of heart regarding the sons of Rachel. Beyond any doubt, their reactions demonstrated true love and sincere concern for their brother Benjamin.

Throughout these proceedings, Judah acted as the head of the family. There are reasons for this. First, it was Reuben the eldest who had previously dishonored his father by taking his father's concubine. Also, Simeon and Levi dishonored their father by their unwarranted mass execution of the men of Shechem. By their actions, the first three sons had forfeited their right to serve as representative head for the family.

The exchange between Joseph and Judah is instructive. First, Joseph presented himself as one who "knows," or one who can "divine." All knowledge concerning future, past, and present events resided with God Himself. There was truth to this claim. Clearly, Joseph had received from the Lord a special gift of knowledge concerning future events. He may have been able to discern when others would steal "divining cups." But this was of little concern to Judah. He was far more concerned with the all-seeing, all-determining counsels of Almighty God. It is impossible to miss the humility and faith in Judah's testimony to Joseph. He says, "God hath found out the iniquity of your servants." Of course, he speaks of another sin committed twenty years earlier. This was preeminent on his mind. His concern was not that he had offended this high official in the Egyptian empire. He had offended the God of heaven! And this was much more serious. While maintaining their innocence in the matter of the cup, Judah took the opportunity to recognize the real issue, the glaring problem in the lives of Judah and his brothers. In the midst of this dramatic confrontation, Judah recognized the hand of God in all of it. God was getting their attention, and Judah discerned the message. God preached by these acts of providence in his life. It is most astonishing to find that Judah took this moment to bring this up in the presence of an "Egyptian" prince! But what else could he do? He finally understood the real issues at stake. It wasn't about the cup and the money in the bags. It was about a dreadful sin committed twenty years earlier. Now Judah could clearly see the hand of God working. This was the time to acknowledge God's hand and submit to it in humble confession. It was time to address the "elephant in the room" and come clean about what had happened when they sold their brother into slavery.

How does this passage teach us to walk with God in faith and obedience?

1. God is always at work in our lives. He may use civil trials, illnesses, and tragedy to send a message. He speaks to us through His Word and by His many acts of providence. But are we listening? Can we discern what He is saying to us, and will we respond with true confession and repentance? The Scriptures provide the standard by which we interpret all

of our experiences, dreams, and thoughts. But our hearts must be in the right place to rightly receive what God is teaching us.

2. While it is important to seek reconciliation for broken relationships, we must rely on God to humble the hearts of those involved. We should root out all bitterness in our own hearts and be always willing to grant forgiveness. Yet it may still be difficult to restore trust in the relationship. If a friend has broken confidence and proven himself malicious and untrustworthy, it may take some time to restore that trust. Just like Joseph, we should be willing and eager to see this trust restored. That is why Joseph put his brothers to the test.

We may wish to test the waters of our relationships in various ways. Generally, it would not be prudent or appropriate for us to repeat the same elaborate test that Joseph used. Joseph was a civil magistrate and had more leeway in how he dealt with his brothers. Moreover, Joseph's brothers had previously committed the capitol offense of kidnapping, and they had even contemplated murder.

If we truly desire to restore relationship, we will do our utmost to confess our own faults, offer forgiveness, and restore trust. Usually, peacemaking is a process that takes concerted time and effort. But peacemaking is worth it! "Blessed are the peacemakers, for they shall be called the children of God" (Matt. 5:8).

Questions:

1. What are the themes of Chapters 1 through 44?
2. How did Joseph test his brothers in this story? Why did Joseph submit his brothers to this test?
3. Why did Judah speak for his brothers?
4. What were the Urim and Thummim? What evidence do we have that Joseph would not have been involved in witchcraft?
5. How can you tell that the brothers were repentant of their evil treatment of Joseph?

Family Discussion Questions:

1. What are some good ways to restore trust in a broken relationship? How much time can it take to restore a relationship?

2. Are you willing to lay down your life for your brother(s) or sister(s) as Jacob's sons were willing to sacrifice themselves for Benjamin? Or does self-centeredness and pride create bitter feelings towards your siblings? If your father gave your brother a beautiful new bicycle (but somehow didn't give a gift to you), could you rejoice with your brother? When there are two slices of cake available, do you let your sister have the bigger piece?

3. Has God ever brought something to your attention by creating a unique circumstance in your life? What sorts of things does He teach you through His providences?

CHAPTER 45

Joseph Revealed

And Joseph said unto his brethren, "I am Joseph; doth my father yet live?" And his brethren could not answer him; for they were troubled at his presence. And Joseph said unto his brethren, "Come near to me, I pray you." And they came near. And he said, "I am Joseph your brother, whom ye sold into Egypt." Gen. 45:3–4

Events:

1. Joseph reveals himself to his brothers.
2. Joseph sends his brothers back to Canaan to retrieve their father and the rest of the family.

What does this passage teach us?

Verses 1–8. The most dramatic stories are real-life stories! These are always the best stories, because God is the great architect of history. His stories will always turn out to be the most creative and the most meaningful. While unbelieving skeptics will look at coincidental meetings as random events in an impersonal, chance universe, the godly will see the hand of an all-determining, personal God behind it all. That is the message of Genesis chapter 45.

Everything came out in this chapter. The pretenses dissolved. The brothers were reunited. Forgiveness flowed. Unquestionably, the leading figure in this story, the man who brought the pieces back together, was Joseph. As he heard his brothers plead for the life of young Benjamin, his heart burst with genuine love and compassion for his brothers. Possessing a heart that was aching to forgive and to reconcile, Joseph broke into a wailing cry as he revealed himself to his brothers.

The brothers were petrified. To their horror, they realized that the second most powerful man in Egypt was their brother whom they had persecuted twenty years earlier! They knew he was capable of executing them all then and there. But Joseph turned the whole situation on its ear. What was shaping up to be the worst day in their lives became the best day. Joseph was nothing but magnanimous and gracious in his grand revelation. He was honest and forthright with them concerning their sin, but he was also quick to comfort them. "Now therefore be not grieved, nor angry with yourselves, that ye sold me hither: for God did send me before you to preserve life." Three times in his explanation, Joseph insisted that it was God who sent him to Egypt. Now how did God do that? As you may recall, the story began with Jacob sending his son to search for his brothers. A stranger wandering through Shechem directed Joseph to the plains of Dothan, where he found his brothers. But then it was his brothers who sold him into slavery, and Reuben was the one who assuaged their murderous intent. Then there were the traveling Ishmaelites who happened to come upon the scene. So, how exactly did God send Joseph into Egypt? We must conclude that God was working through Jacob, Joseph, the stranger at Shechem, the brothers, Reuben, and the Ishmaelites in order that He might bring this grand scheme about. Of course, this is something that we cannot do. How could any of us have made sure that the brothers would have followed through with the act or that the Ishmaelites would meet them at exactly the right time and place to make the exchange? We could have coerced Jacob to send his son to the brothers, and we could have forced the brothers to sell Joseph into slavery under threat of imminent harm. But God is able to coordinate all of these decisions and actions without violating the free choices made by the men involved. This is only something that a sovereign God can execute. None of us can predestine the free actions of men. We can hardly comprehend the idea itself!

God's intentions in these events are also revealed here. Joseph told his brothers that God intended to preserve life, to redeem a posterity, and to save lives by a great deliverance. Now, these intentions of Yahweh were much different than the intentions of the dark, evil hearts of ten brothers consumed by jealousy. This marks the difference between God's will and the human will which work simultaneously in these events. God did not commit the sin because His intentions and purposes are always pure and holy, just and good. While the brothers acted out of hatred, God acted out of a desire to see His people preserved and His promises held sacrosanct. So you see, God is sovereign even over the sinful acts of men. At the same time, He is immune from the sinfulness of those acts.

In verse 8, Joseph intensified the point concerning God's sovereignty even more when he said, "So now it was not you that sent me hither, but God." Of course, if we had been standing by that pit twenty years earlier, we would have been pretty sure that it was the ten brothers who sent this young man down to Egypt in the care of the Ishmaelite slave traders. But Joseph insisted that God's cause was primary and preeminent, so much so that the brother's intentions were negligible. Moreover, in the following verses, he acknowledged that it was God who made him a father-like figure to Pharaoh and promoted him to his powerful position in the Egyptian empire. Above all, Joseph understood God to be central and sovereign in man's reality.

Verses 9–24. Joseph invited the family to live in Egypt for protection and provision during the remaining years of the severe famine. In those days, raiding bands of warriors and would-be empire builders were wiping small tribes like Jacob's little family off the map, or they were absorbing them into their own kingdoms. By the careful, all-wise providence of Almighty God, the large empire of Egypt provided sufficient protection for this insignificant little group of people who bore the mark of His covenant. Throughout the history of this world's empires, God raised up important figures like Joseph, Daniel, and Esther, who wandered into the middle of these powerful states. The grand purpose of history is hardly about these great empires that come and go. What really matters is the people of God who are covenanted to Him through Abraham and his seed by faith.

Before his brothers left to retrieve the rest of the family, Joseph showered them with more gifts, further sealing his commitment to reconciliation. Always the consummate peacemaker, he encouraged them not to fall into strife on the way home. This was no time for further contention. It was a time of forgiveness, reconciliation, and family unity.

Verses 25–28. These final verses contain the best part of the story. It would be hard to imagine the effect this stunning news had on Jacob, the old Patriarch! God was good to the aged father. Over the years, Jacob's family had been hurt repeatedly by polygamy, strife, jealousy, treachery, and sin. Tragedy marked practically every chapter in his life. In a single moment, all of this changed as God brought His grand purpose to fruition. What joy must have swept through Jacob's entire being to hear that Joseph was alive! Finally, God brought about reconciliation to a divided family. This is a good Old Testament representation of God's work of reconciliation. As He restores His relationship with us in the vertical sense, he restores our relationships with brothers and sisters in the horizontal sense. This story also makes for a great illustration of Romans 8:28: "All things work together for good to those who love Him, to those who are called according to His purpose."

How does this passage teach us to walk with God in faith and obedience?

1. What was shaping up to be the worst day of these brothers' lives, turned out to be the best day. But everything hinged on Joseph's willingness to show mercy. This Old Testament picture reminds us of the mercy shown to us through Jesus Christ. It is at our lowest moments that God turns to us in mercy. At the final judgment, many sinners will experience the worst day in all of human existence. But for those of us who are in Christ, the very worst day will turn into our best day! After casting the lawless into the lake of fire, the Judge will turn to us, and say, "Enter thou into the presence of thy Lord!"

2. Everything that happens to us, whether it be good or evil, is all part of God's plan. We must believe that everything that happens to us is for our good and His glory! This does not excuse our sin, or relieve us of the responsibility to obey Him in all the situations into which He puts us. We will still suffer consequences for our sins. But rather than fretting over the bad things that happen to us, we should spend our time far more profitably by repenting of our rebellion, trusting in His sovereignty, and praising God for weaving a beautiful fabric out of the broken threads of our lives. Instead of focusing on the evil things that men are doing to you or to others, think on the things that God is doing through all of it. This was Joseph's perspective.

3. This passage also teaches us to maintain a forgiving heart towards those that have offended us. Even if they have yet to apologize, we should follow the example of Joseph. His heart was fairly bursting with readiness to forgive and reconcile with his brothers who had sinned against him.

Questions:

1. What are the themes of Chapters 1 through 45?

2. How do we see Joseph's big heart in this story?

3. Who was responsible for Joseph being sold to slave traders and who made sure that he had a free ride to Egypt?

4. What did God intend to happen when He ordained the evil actions that were taken against Joseph 20 years earlier?

5. What were the brothers' motives and intentions in selling Joseph to the slave traders? Contrast their motives and intentions with God's motives and intentions.

Family Discussion Questions:

1. What are some of the most difficult trials that we have faced as a family? Can we say that God will work these out for good? Can we be sure that our story will end as well as it did for Jacob and his sons?

2. What do we consider to be the chief causes in the events that occur in our lives? What do we generally think of as the most important cause—man, God, or chance? Do we acknowledge the all-controlling sovereignty of God in all the events of our lives, or do we refer more to chance and luck?

CHAPTER 46

Jacob's Line

All the souls that came with Jacob into Egypt, which came out of his loins, besides Jacob's sons' wives, all the souls were threescore and six. Gen. 46:26

Events:

1. Jacob worships the Lord in Beersheba before leaving Canaan for the last time.
2. God promises to bring his family back to Canaan.
3. Jacob's line of descendants is listed.
4. Jacob is finally reunited with his son Joseph.

What does this passage teach us?

Verse 1. It is important that families keep their priorities straight. Before taking his family to Egypt for the grand reunion, Jacob made a point to visit Beersheba, where his grandfather had built an altar years earlier. There he conducted "family worship," rendering his allegiance to the God of his father Isaac. This identification with his father's faith showed Jacob's fundamental commitment. Here was the mark of a godly man. Jacob's first allegiance was to God. Before rushing to Egypt he did not forget to render his sacrifices to Him. How often do families embark on their vacations and enjoy their holidays while neglecting family worship? God is shoved to the side while they enjoy His good gifts. But when God is in the center of the life of a godly family, He is worshiped first.

This testifies to Jacob's faith in the Lord. Jacob had not forgotten the God of his fathers. He had not adopted the gods of the Canaanites, nor was he going to adopt the gods of the Egyptians. In all of the land of Canaan, one man stood alone in covenant with the true and living God. It should go without saying that we need to worship the right God. To specifically name the true and living God in our worship is important. He should be correctly identified, in order that He might be distinguished from all of the other gods of man's inventions. When Jacob offered a sacrifice to the God of his father Isaac, he identified the correct God with whom he was still in covenant. In our own worship, it is appropriate to refer to God as the Creator, the God of Abraham, Isaac, and Jacob, and the God of our own fathers (if we have a godly heritage). We also have the New Testament renderings of Father, Son, and Holy Spirit. We need to worship the right God. This places our object of worship in proper context as we commence our prayer and praise.

Verses 2–4. But what would become of the covenant promises made to Abraham and reaffirmed to Isaac and Jacob? What would happen to the children of Israel in Egypt? Would they intermarry with pagan tribes and synthesize into the worship of false gods? How would they inherit the land of Canaan if they were living in Egypt? Surely, these questions crossed Jacob's mind as he prepared for the trip down into Egypt. At this critical juncture in the life of this family, the Lord God spoke to Jacob in Beersheba. He assured him that one day He would bring the family back out of Egypt, and that He would be true to the covenant, come what may. He repeated to Jacob a theme that had been part of almost every revelation since Bethel: "I will be with you in Egypt." Jacob's family may have been of little account in Egypt. In fact, not one contemporary Egyptian history records the sojourn of this family there. Yet Jacob's family was an important family to God—and they enjoyed His special presence.

Verses 5–27. As the entire family moved to Egypt, a list of the names of the family, including sons and grandsons, is given. The family numbered sixty-six (seventy, including Joseph's family). These included forty-eight grandsons, one granddaughter, four great grandsons, one great granddaughter, eleven sons, and one father. Mention is only made of one daughter and one granddaughter, presumably because they were not married. In a biblical social order, a daughter is included under the headship of the father. Upon marriage, she would join herself to a new family as she came under another head.

Reference to Simeon's marriages is made because he married a Canaanite. The choice of spouse was important for God's people, both then and now! Until this point, Isaac and Jacob's family had placed a high priority on avoiding the Canaanites for prospective marriage partners. The fact that Simeon married a Canaanite is particularly ironic, since Simeon and Levi had reacted so strongly against their sister's relationship with a Canaanite. Nevertheless, the book of Genesis is especially concerned with the godly's synthesis with the ungodly. This sort of treachery towards the covenant is to be eschewed by the people of God. Marriages matter, and the families into which our children marry, matters—because it concerns the spiritual heritage of our families.

Verses 28–34. Finally, Joseph was reunited with his father in the land of Goshen. It was a deeply emotional meeting, and the two hugged each other for an extended length of time, and wept. What a terrific example of a son who honored and loved his father!

In keeping with the Lord's direction, Joseph provided for his father by taking care of the whole tribe during this time of severe famine. He arranged for Jacob's family to settle in the fruitful land of Goshen, a place where the family would grow from a population of seventy to at least one million in several hundred years. Joseph respected the covenant God had made with his fathers by arranging for them to live in a land that was distant from the Egyptian culture. He introduced his family to the Egyptians as cattle and sheep herders, a line of work the Egyptians despised. This prejudice served to lay down a healthy boundary, preventing the Israelites from intermarrying with Egyptians throughout the years. Inevitably, intermarriage would have tainted the Israelites' covenantal heritage and religious distinctive.

How does this passage teach us to walk with God in faith and obedience?

1. God the Father loves the Son, and the Son loves the Father. From biblical records, we know that God goes to great lengths to bring us into His family and reconcile us to Himself. A microcosm of this grand story is found in the account of Jacob's family. Joseph loved his father, and despite

ill treatment at the hands of his brothers, he worked to bring about a joyful family reunion in the end. Not only does this story serve as a wonderful pattern for human families, but it also speaks to what God is doing with his own household in Jesus Christ (His Son).

2. With each new revelation of Himself, God always remembers His previous revelations and often refers back to them in subsequent revelations. The God of Jacob is the God of Isaac, and the God of Isaac is the God of Abraham. We, too, would do well to root our faith in the full revelation of God in His Word. Our God is the God of Adam, Seth, Noah, Abraham, Isaac, Jacob, Moses, Joshua, David, Daniel, Jesus, and Paul. Our covenant with God is the covenant of Adam, Noah, Abraham, David, and Jesus. God did not introduce a new religion with Jacob and neither did He introduce a new religion with Jesus. You can identify false religions and false interpretations of Scripture when there is strong discontinuity between new revelations and old revelations. This is the legacy of false teachers like Joseph Smith and Mohammed.

3. Often unbelievers will despise true believers who serve the living and true God. Sometimes this brings persecution and sometimes it means a categorical rejection of a Christian evangelistic message. But looked at another way, this antagonism can also enforce a healthy boundary between the world and God's people. It can protect the church from mixing into the world and taking on its sinful inclinations. We still need to influence the world for Christ and take down false ideas that deceive the world around us (2 Cor. 10:4, 5), but God also calls us to separate from the world—"Come out from among them and be separate" (2 Cor. 6:14–18). He insists that His children remain "unspotted from the world" (Jam. 1:30). Let us be careful not to sit in the seat of the scornful or walk in the way of sinners (Psalm 1:1). Young people sit in the seat of the scornful when they passively accept a godless worldview through powerful movies, popular music, and classic literature written by humanists. When we turn our children over to humanists who refuse to teach the fear of God in history and science, we are doing the most destructive thing possible to the worldview of our children. We are turning them over to the Egyptians to form their minds and erode their faith in the true and living God. Believers must always live in the land of Goshen.

Questions:

1. What are the themes of Chapters 1 through 46?

2. What did Jacob do in Beersheba before leaving the Promised Land?

3. How many people came down to Egypt with Jacob? How many grandchildren did Jacob have? How does this compare with the average family today?

4. How did Simeon's marriage differ from that of Jacob and Isaac?

5. What was special about the land of Goshen that made it a good place for the children of Israel?

Family Discussion Questions:

1. Does our family put God first in all that we do? Do we seek God's will and engage in family worship even when we're on vacation or traveling in some far country?

2. Are we living in the land of Goshen? How do Christian families retain healthy separation from the pagan tribes around them? Is it possible to separate ourselves too much from our culture?

CHAPTER 47

Jacob's Request

And the time drew nigh that Israel must die: and he called his son Joseph, and said unto him, "If now I have found grace in thy sight, put, I pray thee, thy hand under my thigh, and deal kindly and truly with me; bury me not, I pray thee, in Egypt: But I will lie with my fathers, and thou shalt carry me out of Egypt, and bury me in their burying place." And he said, "I will do as thou hast said." Gen. 47:29–30

Events:

1. Joseph introduces five of his brothers to the Pharaoh.
2. Joseph takes his father to visit the Pharaoh.
3. Joseph wisely manages Egyptian affairs through the famine years.
4. Jacob makes Joseph swear that he will bury him in the land of Canaan.

What does this passage teach us?

Verses 1–6. Shall God's people separate from worldly people, or integrate into the businesses and politics of this world? There is no easy answer to this question. While separation from the world of lust and pride is the Christian's constant obligation, this does not mean we are to separate from all of the people who operate by lust and pride (1 Cor. 5:11). Most of us will run into unbelievers every day in classrooms, stores, governments, companies, and neighborhoods. In these casual meetings and business interactions, we are still to maintain adherence to God's laws. We cannot count on unbelievers playing by God's laws. It is for us to be sure that we are obeying God on our side of the conversation, in our side of the business transaction, and in the decisions we make when we engage the political sphere.

Joseph is a good example for believers today. He was virtually surrounded by unbelieving pagans, while intimately involved in the affairs of the government of the great Egyptian empire. As part of his duties, he provided the pagan priests with grain for food. If he disagreed with the religious cult of Egypt, did he compromise his relationship with the true God by his public work? Of course, there is nothing inherently wrong with selling or giving food to unbelievers, even to those who may engage in immoral activities. Moreover, Joseph was working under the authority of the Pharaoh. It must have been the established policy of Egypt that the religious cult be supported by the state. He was in no position to reverse this policy. To exceed his authority as a civil magistrate would be to exercise rebellion against God's established order. A God-fearing man would not do this. Joseph's respect for Egypt's established policies did not constitute an implicit endorsement of their false gods. Given that Joseph was unable to use his political position to "impact" pagan Egypt and its state-endorsed idolatry, why did God put this godly man in this country? Without question, Joseph's wise administration of resources preserved the Egyptian people from complete annihilation. But this is not why God brought him to Egypt. Joseph's first priority was to protect and preserve God's people. This is always the first priority for every true believer who works in the socio-economic systems of this world (Gal. 6:10; Luke 16:8–9).

After their meeting with Pharaoh, the family solidified an economic plan that would provide them with sustenance while they sojourned in the land of Egypt. The men made it clear that they were "just visiting." They would live apart from the Egyptians as they assumed the despised occupation of shepherds, content to live lives that were separate from this pagan civilization. Later, we find Moses leaving his position in the courts of the Pharaoh to become a shepherd and lead the people of God out of Egypt. The life of faith seldom values those things that the world values.

Verses 7–10. In these verses, Jacob meets the Pharaoh and blesses him. These blessings given by godly men like Jacob, are appropriate and often have long-lasting effects on the civil society that is blessed.

Jacob's brief statement hardly provided any sort of wise counsel to the Pharaoh, but it does lend some insight into his assessment of his own life. As he approached death, Jacob looked upon his life as a pilgrimage, or a long visit to some foreign country. In the words of the writer to the Hebrews, he looked for "a better country, that is, an heavenly: wherefore God is not ashamed to be called their God: for He hath prepared for them a city." Jacob also spoke of his years on earth as few and evil, an accurate view of life in a sinful world that perpetually lies in the throes of wickedness, suffering, and death. This is a painful, evil life, and only hope in a resurrection and final glorification can possibly mitigate the pain and make life worth living.

Verses 11–26. Typically, human empires always become slave-based economies, where people rely more on the state than they do on their families and local churches. This is the nature of empires. Instead of taking responsibility for themselves and saving for the years of economic downturn (which are inevitable), people live for the moment. Similar to the character named Passion in Bunyan's *Pilgrim's Progress*, they insist on enjoying all of the good things now. Over time, they sink deep in debt as they seek to satisfy their immediate desires. Consequently, they consume all their present capital and leave their children bankrupt. As the character of their nation continues to degrade, especially during economic downturns, they instinctively turn to the civil government for womb-to-tomb security. This is the fate of most western nations and of all other nations who have followed the West. Therefore, it is hard to blame the growth of the power of the state and increased centralized control on anybody but the citizens themselves. This is especially true in Western democracies or constitutional republics where the people have some access to the vote.

This seven-year famine was terribly devastating to the lands of Canaan and Egypt, producing a severe economic downturn. Had it not been for Joseph's keen foresight, careful planning, and management skills, millions of people would have starved to death. What we find in Egypt is still a far cry from the redistribution of the wealth schemes operating in modern western nations. For those who did not have the foresight to save for a rainy day or a drought, their only resort was to appeal to the Pharaoh. But Joseph's food distribution was not a government welfare program, which always destroys the character, the work ethic, and the productivity of a nation. Welfare programs serve only to create more dependence upon the socialist slave state, and this was something that Joseph refused to do. Although the old Egyptian state was well-known for its frequent use of chattel slavery, Joseph refused to place the entire population into bond slavery. He suggested an approach that was better than total subjection to a family-disintegrating, absolutely-tyrannical slave state. Far more preferable was what we call "feudalism," or a rent-based economy. Since the people had exchanged their property for food, the Pharaoh retained ownership of a great deal of property. But the people could still rent the farm land and obtain seeds in exchange for 20 percent of the harvest. This, therefore, was not a tax, but a business trade between individual families and the Pharaoh. In the end, the result was still an expansion of the Pharaoh's wealth and ownership of the land. Joseph made the best out of a bad situation. This is what all righteous men must do when they work with fallen men in a fallen world.

Verses 27–31. Jacob was still a man of the covenant. Though he was about to die in a foreign land, his commitment was still to God and to the promises God had made to Abraham, Isaac, and to himself. It had been over 250 years since God first revealed the promise to Abraham and now Jacob still clung to it.

The place where a man is buried is highly significant to himself and to his heirs. It bears a testimony to his legacy and his roots. Therefore, when Jacob made Joseph swear that he would bury him in the promised land, this became a testimony to all his heirs. This burial would work strongly on Moses' mind four hundred years later as he prepared to return God's people to the land of promise. Jacob's final request was a tremendous act of faith.

How does this passage teach us to walk with God in faith and obedience?

1. We should not become overly attached to the things of this earth. Of course, we can own houses, work our businesses, get good Christians elected to government, and take every thought captive to the obedience of Christ. Our work on earth is important, but we work on earth in anticipation of a heavenly inheritance.

2. Unbelievers ignore God's laws in business and politics. The only difference between political parties that are controlled by unbelievers is found in the particular laws of God they choose to break. Party A may choose to ignore some aspect of the 8th commandment. Meanwhile, Party B is ignoring some aspect of the 6th or the 7th commandment. Thus, Christians cannot very well align themselves with any political party governed by unbelievers.

3. The highest priority for a Christian in politics is to protect God's people from the tyranny of the state. This means that they should protect the family's freedom to worship and to raise their children in the fear of the true God. They should also protect the church from state controls on the pulpit. Secondarily, the Christian in politics preserves society from destroying itself. Thus, laws against cannibalism, murder, abortion, infanticide, and homosexuality help to preserve a society from self-annihilation (Gen. 9:4-6, Lev. 18:22,27).

4. Regrettably, some level of slavery is inevitable for humans living in this sin-drenched world. It is not a preferred condition. Without strong character and self-control, it is impossible to be free. Nevertheless, godly leaders must still work hard to minimize slavery as best as they can. But we are always limited by the character of the nation that we lead. Certainly, Christians ought to oppose all efforts to enslave people by civil government. Above all people, we should stand against the constant pressure to increase taxation, government expenditures, government debt, and redistribution of the wealth. These are all paths to slavery. Policies which increase the people's dependence on government through welfare and "social security," as well as those programs that erode family responsibilities, produce this slave state. "Where the Spirit of the Lord is, there is liberty," and righteous men would never support these slave state policies. In fact, the biblical limit to taxation is 10 percent (1 Sam. 8:15).

Questions:

1. What are the themes of Chapters 1 through 47?

2. Was it wrong for Joseph to provide sustenance for pagan priests? Explain.

3. What arrangements did Jacob's family make with Pharaoh?

4. Why did Jacob call his years on earth a "pilgrimage?"

5. How were Joseph's policies on grain distribution different from those of the modern welfare state?

6. How did Jacob's request to be buried in Canaan serve as a testimony to his faith?

Family Discussion Questions:

1. Do we believe God's promises?

   The Bible says, "Believe on the Lord Jesus Christ, and you will be saved." Do we believe this?

   Jesus says, "I go to prepare a place for you." Do we believe that Jesus is preparing a place for us?

   The Bible says, "Honor your father and your mother, that it may be well with you, and that you may live long on the earth." Do we really believe that promise?

   If we really believed God's promises, how would this affect the way we live our lives?

2. How much of our money is taxed on all levels (by federal, state, and local governments)? How much slavery do we contend with in our situation today? To what extent are we enslaved to banks through debt? To what extent are we enslaved to powerful governments? Would you call America a slave state?

CHAPTER 48

Jacob's Adoptions

And now thy two sons, Ephraim and Manasseh, which were born unto thee in the land of Egypt before I came unto thee into Egypt, are mine; as Reuben and Simeon, they shall be mine. Gen. 48:5

Events:

1. Joseph hears that his father is sick and takes his two sons to visit him.
2. Jacob counts Joseph's two sons as his own and blesses them.

What does this passage teach us?

Verses 1–7. After seventeen years in Egypt, Jacob was approaching his final hours. One crucial matter played prominently in his mind. He refused to forget the promise God made to his fathers and to him in Luz—the promise of the land. One day, Jacob's family would inherit the land of Canaan. Jacob believed this with all of his heart. Of all of Jacob's sons, none were as integrated into Egyptian politics and culture as Joseph. If anyone would have immersed himself into the culture and abandoned the covenant, it would have been Joseph or his sons. Therefore, Jacob took it upon himself to claim Joseph's two sons for his own. He wanted these young men and their posterity included in the inheritance of Canaan. It was the covenant that was of essence to this man. In his dying moments, he wanted to do everything in his power to ensure that his sons, Joseph included, would play a part in this covenant. Granted, he had little control over what would happen ten generations hence, but he took significant steps to influence the minds and hearts of his sons and grandsons. In this final encounter with his family, Jacob again certified his commitment to the covenant and handed the baton to his sons and grandsons. Since Jacob had adopted these two grandsons and included them in his inheritance, any attempt on Joseph's part to incorporate them into the Egyptian socio-economic system would have directly violated his father's last pronouncements. It would have been the ultimate treasonous act against his own father—something that Joseph would never do. Thus, you can see how the dying words of an old patriarch really do carry binding authority. Jacob certified his commitment to the covenant that would resonate for generations.

What may have played in Jacob's mind was as he prepared to die—the covenant promises of God and his precious wife, Rachel, who had passed away over a century earlier. WWhen a man marries a woman, they become one flesh, and when she dies, he looses a part of himself.

Verses 8–20. Joseph was still the favorite son, the oldest son of Jacob's primary wife. It was fitting, therefore, for Jacob to bless Joseph first and provide him with the double portion of the inheritance. Typically, the oldest son received a double portion of the inheritance in a biblical economy. Before pronouncing his blessing on the two young men, Jacob gave God the glory for reuniting his family in Egypt. As a true prophet of God, he crossed his arms in order that he might confer the blessing for the oldest son upon the younger. No reason is given for this break in normal procedure. What may have played in Jacob's mind was God's own sovereign working in his life. Before he was born, the Lord informed his mother that "The elder shall serve the younger." God's ways are not our ways. Although we may grow accustomed to "normal" practices where the rich are served first and the elder children are the privileged ones, God always reserves the right to turn this system on its head. In another place, our Lord Jesus says, "The first shall be last and the last shall be first" (Matt. 20:16). This leaves no room for presumption on the part of the privileged, but it allows room for hope and mercy for the least privileged, the humble, and the poor in spirit.

In a highly significant, prophetic statement, Jacob issued the blessing from God and the Angel "who redeemed him from all evil" (Verse 16). He could never have claimed this blessing with authority, had God not first conveyed it to him. He was speaking the words that he had already received and believed. But who was this mysterious Angel? The text provides an important clue. While acknowledging God as the source of his physical protection and provision, he also referred to the Angel as the One who redeemed him from all evil. This salvation includes physical protection, but it cannot be limited to that, for Jacob saw this Angel as the One who saved him from the evil of sin and its consequences. As God's revelation unfolds in the New Covenant, we learn that the only Redeemer of God's elect is the Lord Jesus Christ. This Angel must be God's Messenger, the Messiah, the Christ of God.

Verses 21–22. Jacob closed his address with a blessing for Joseph. Of all of the promises God provided His people, there was hardly one so comforting as the Bethel promise: "I will be with you." As Jacob took this old promise and placed it in the hands of his son, we know that it was precious to him. He had carried this old promise with him and clung to it for over 100 years! What is more comforting to a man of true faith than the assurance that he has God's special attention and presence? He was fully confident that God would bring Joseph safely back to the land promised to his family.

In his closing words, Jacob attributed the source of his material wealth, at least in part, to the battles he waged against the Amorites. Warfare is a legitimate activity on the part of God's people, and God will often bless His people with the substance of the wicked (Ps. 37; Ex. 12:35,36).

How does this passage teach us to walk with God in faith and obedience?

1. The last-shall-be-first principle commends a constant humility and gratefulness for those of us who do enjoy God's sweet blessings. Whether you happen to be an older child in your family or a member of a Christian family, a Christian church, or a Christian nation, you have every reason to remain humble and grateful for your position. Often, those who expect these blessings as if they are owed them will soon find themselves the last—who used to be the first.

2. The world offers many temptations and delights that would draw us away from our love for the Lord and His kingdom. When there is a choice between seeking God's kingdom and receiving the rewards of power or wealth, we should always choose the former. The world's offerings may look good to us. But in the long run, we will be ruined if we do not seek the Lord and His Kingdom. Seek His kingdom first and you will find

that God always rewards the meek with a rich inheritance. The meek shall inherit the earth.

3. Do we look to the Lord for His salvation? It is our prayer that our own families be blessed even as Jacob desired that his children be blessed by the Angel Redeemer of God. We know that this Angel Redeemer is the very Son of God—the Lord Jesus Christ. Let us take a moment to pray God's blessing of salvation on each of our children.

Questions:

1. What are the themes of Chapters 1 through 48?
2. Why did Joseph bring his two sons to his father's death bed?
3. How do we know that Jacob was a prophet in this passage?
4. Did Jacob believe in Jesus Christ?
5. What is the old promise that God gave to Jacob many times in his life?

Family Discussion Questions:

1. What are the promises of God's Word that we will cling to with tenacity all the way to our dying day?
2. What are the special privileges that we enjoy as a Christian family? Have we ever lost sight of "the last shall be first" principle?

CHAPTER 49

Jacob's Prophecy

And Jacob called unto his sons, and said, Gather yourselves together, that I may tell you that which shall befall you in the last days. Gen. 49:1

Events:

1. Jacob gathers his sons together and prophesies over each of them.
2. Jacob dies.

What does this passage teach us?

Verses 1–2. As Jacob prepared to die, he gathered his sons for a round of prophetic declarations. In our day, we cannot expect that any godly father would speak under similar divine inspiration as Jacob did with his sons. Nevertheless, every father should speak with prophetic force over his children. He may employ what he knows from Scripture and from his own experience with his children to craft prescriptive exhortations and blessings for them.

Verses 3–27. Future generations were affected both by Jacob's prophetic declarations and by the character of each progenitor of the twelve tribes. The life of a father really matters. That one life will profoundly influence the lives of many in succeeding generations. Therefore, the decisions that fathers make are extremely important. Not only do they affect their own lives for better or for worse, but these decisions may impact the lives of millions who come after them.

Reuben: Reuben's wicked decision to take his father's wife to his bed produced disastrous consequences. Though he was the oldest son in the family and would have claimed the primary position, he forfeited this place of honor by his own actions. Fundamentally, Reuben lacked moral integrity and loyalty. This is not to say that he was incapable of making right decisions occasionally, but he was not one upon whom anyone could rely over the long haul. Noting this fundamental weakness of character in his son, Jacob forecasted an ignominious future for the family of Reuben. As it turned out, the tribe of Reuben became one of the smallest tribes in Israel, never producing a leader of any note. It was the progeny of Reuben: Dathan and Abiram, who led the rebellion in the wilderness. And they were swallowed up in the earth for their treachery.

Simeon and Levi: However, neither did Jacob speak any blessing over the next two oldest sons, Simeon and Levi. He recalled the violent action these two men took against the city of Shechem after the affair involving their sister Dinah, against the wishes of their father. They would be scattered and dispersed in Israel. Later, in true fulfillment of this prophecy, we find Simeon's inheritance mixed with Judah's; and, of course, the Levites were scattered over the cities throughout the land. While this passage illustrates the terrible, long term consequences of sin, God still may turn a curse into a blessing by His mercy. This is what He chose to do with the Levites, as they became the ministers and teachers of the Word of God to the people. This tribe was blessed with the priesthood until another Priest of a different order took their place.

Judah: After passing over his first three sons, Jacob turned the mother-lode of blessings to Judah. This included great material blessing: wine so plentiful that he would wash his clothes in a tub of it! Judah was likened to a lion, the great beast universally recognized as the dominant force in the jungle. This was the part Judah played in the nation of Israel. His tribe was given the authority to rule over the entire nation, a prophecy which was fulfilled in David and his kingly line.

"The king's scepter will never depart from Judah" was the clearest reference to the Messiah since the proto evangelium revealed to Adam and Eve in Genesis 3:15. Jacob spoke of the eternal reign of the Son of David and the Son of Judah, in the person of the Lord Jesus Christ. But what can we make of this semi-veiled statement that the scepter shall not depart from Judah "until Shiloh come?" Many believe the word Shiloh refers to "his Son," and both Jewish and Christian commentators almost universally agree that this must refer to the Messiah. Ezekiel 21:26–27 refers to the removal of the diadem during the exile, which did happen. For many years there was no king, no descendant of Judah sitting on the throne of David. In true fulfillment of this prophetic word, the scepter remained with Judah upon the ascension of Christ to the right hand of the Father (Acts 2:25–32). It would be more appropriate to translate this text as, "The scepter shall not depart from Judah when Shiloh comes."

Zebulun: Jacob's word for Zebulun was exactly in accord with historical record. As it turned out, Zebulun inherited the land on the Mediterranean sea in the northwest corner of Canaan. Whether or not Joshua and the leaders took these ancient prophetic words into account when distributing the land many years later is unknown. Undoubtedly, Jacob spoke under the influence of the Holy Spirit of God.

Issachar: Jacob described Issachar as a tribe as strong as a mule, yet unwilling to fight for freedom from the nations that would enslave him. What a shame that those who claim the name of the true God can so easily capitulate to slavery! The fight for liberty is an uphill battle all the way, and must include a constant struggle with our own fleshly temptations.

Dan: This prophecy could very well refer to Samson, who was himself a judge from the tribe of Dan. Never a particularly powerful tribe, Dan was still an enemy with which to contend. Just as a snake that bites the heal of a horse, he would inflict a deadly wound on the enemy.

In an interlude of sorts to this soliloquy of prophecy, Jacob broke out in a prayer, "I have waited for thy salvation, O LORD." Here is the heart-cry of every Old Testament saint who felt a deep and abiding need for God's salvation. In this sinful world filled with evil, temptation, and guilt, one can only look above for true and eternal salvation. And these saints waited patiently for that salvation in faith for another 1,600 years. Upon the coming of Christ, old Simeon held that little Child in the temple and prophetically declared the consummation of these desires.

"Lord, now let your servant depart in peace, according to your word, for mine eyes have seen your salvation which you have prepared before the face of all people; a light to lighten the Gentiles, and the glory of your people Israel!" (Luke 2:29.)

Gad: The obscure tribe of Gad would come under oppression. But in the end, this tribe was persistent and it overcame. This is a picture of the church throughout Old Testament and New Testament times. The church is always under oppression, but it overcomes again and again throughout history, and will overcome in the end.

Asher: Jacob spoke of a rich material inheritance for the tribe of Asher in the land of Canaan.

Naphtali: This tribe was gifted with the ability to speak and negotiate. As that blessed family referred to in Psalm 127, they were to speak with the enemy in the gates—and prevail.

Joseph: When Jacob spoke of Joseph escaping the arrows of the archers, he was most likely referring to the persecution Joseph received from his brothers, Potiphar's household, and others. Yet God strengthened Joseph through it all, and rewarded him with victory in the end.

In yet another prophetic pronouncement concerning a Messiah Savior, Jacob spoke of the Shepherd and the Stone of Israel who must proceed from God Himself. These men of faith in the Old Testament certainly knew that they could never save themselves. From the earliest days of the church, the saints referred to the Rock, the Shepherd, and the Salvation of Israel—a role that can only be filled by the Lord God. These men could not see what we see now—the fulfillment of these prophecies in the final Prophet, Priest, and King of God, in the Person of our Lord Jesus Christ. But they spoke in great faith and hopeful expectation.

Benjamin: Benjamin was mentioned as a ferocious fighter. Apparently, the tribe would become a people that would live more off of plunder than cultivation and production. This may be a reference to King Saul and the military power he developed as the first king of Israel. With all of Saul's faults, David gave credit to Saul's military accomplishments against the enemies of Israel upon his death, as recorded in 2 Samuel 1.

In one final act of faith on the part of the old patriarch, Jacob provided instructions to his sons to bury him in Canaan. Then he pulled his feet up on his bed and surrendered his life. He was "gathered to his people," an ancient and veiled reference to the surety of life and fellowship somewhere beyond the grave.

How does this passage teach us to walk with God in faith and obedience?

1. We must believe that it is God who provides our salvation. This is fundamental to the Christian faith—the true faith. Before the coming of Christ, the Old Testament saints waited in hope and faith for their salvation. Now, the New Testament saints (including us) receive salvation provided by the death and resurrection of Jesus the Messiah with the very same hope and faith. Let us look to God for salvation with the same faith old Jacob had as he breathed his last breath on his death bed so many years ago.

2. What can we learn from the lives of the elder brothers in this family? A failure to honor fathers and a weak moral character will result in spiritually weak families. In later generations, the children of Israel were marked by spiritual compromise and weakness. May God pour out His Spirit upon us and our children, that we might be men and women of character, and that our future generations will be blessed with strength of faith and character. Let us pray that each of us will be strong in our convictions, and stand in the hour of temptation.

3. It takes hard work and a real struggle to be free. Our nation is under severe tribute today because we have given up the struggle for freedom. Since the 19th century, tyrants have imposed huge taxation and massive regulations over the citizens of nations throughout North America, Europe, and Asia. For our lack of character and courage, we have become nations under tribute, as Issachar of old. Without hard work, a love for liberty, and a courageous struggle, we will never enjoy true freedom.

Questions:

1. What are the themes of Chapters 1 through 49?
2. Why did Reuben lose a blessing?
3. Why did Simeon and Levi lose a blessing?
4. What happened later to Simeon and Levi in the inheritance of the land?
5. What great prophecy was given concerning the tribe of Judah?

6. What famous judge came from the tribe of Dan?

7. What was the final act of faith on the part of Jacob before he died?

8. How did the Old Testament speak of heaven?

Family Discussion Questions:

1. What can we say about our own children? What gifts and opportunities lie ahead for each of our children? What sort of warnings and blessings might we present to our children?

2. How do we rely on the salvation of God? What will be the final prayer on our lips as we pass from this earth?

CHAPTER 50

Jacob's Burial

For his sons carried him into the land of Canaan, and buried him in the cave of the field of Machpelah, which Abraham bought with the field for a possession of a burying place of Ephron the Hittite, before Mamre. Gen. 50:13

Events:

1. Jacob dies and the Egyptians mourn over him for seventy days.
2. Joseph requests Pharaoh's approval to bury his father in the Cave of Machpelah in Canaan.
3. The family buries Jacob in the Cave of Machpelah.
4. Joseph's brothers once again ask for his forgiveness for their evil actions against him.
5. Joseph dies.

What does this passage teach us?

Verses 1–3. The love that a son has for his father will express itself in many ways. It will certainly reveal itself upon the father's death. Our chapter begins with Joseph weeping over his deceased father, while his friends grieve with him out of a common sympathy. You would hardly weep over the death of a stranger if you read of it in the obituary column of a large city newspaper. But when a loved one dies, everything that person has meant to you comes rushing back all at once. The emotional impact of the memories will bring you to tears. You weep in gratitude for his love, in sadness that you will never again be able to express your love to him, and in grief that the relationship is for the time being interrupted by death. No record is made of whether the other brothers expressed their love for their father, but it is clear that Joseph was devoted to him until the very end.

The Egyptians were greatly concerned with the burial of the dead. In the case of Jacob's burial, they took a full forty days for the embalming of the body. This involved the application of certain chemicals that would preserve it. Very likely, the Egyptians employed the same methods used for the preservation of the bodies of their Pharaohs. Their 70-day period of mourning was excessive, as later in the chapter we read that Joseph limited it to seven days. When it comes to the tragedies of life, "There is a time to weep and a time to laugh" (Eccl. 3:4). Wisdom dictates, but those without hope in the resurrection will inevitably fail to strike the right balance in these circumstances. Men and women of true faith have no business soaking in hopeless grief indefinitely. As in the case of David upon the death of his child, we must hope in the resurrection. At some point, we wash our face and return to God's worship and our daily responsibilities (2 Sam. 12:23-25). The way a Christian handles the death of a loved one is a true test of his faith.

Verses 4–13. Before taking Jacob back to Canaan for the burial, Joseph requested permission for a leave of absence from his employer—the Pharaoh. The burial made for quite a procession, as all of the family and a number of Egyptians (including some of the distinguished elders in the land) made the journey to the Cave of Machpelah.

Let us learn something from the story of Jacob's death, the care for his body, the weeping, and the burial in the Cave of Machpelah. These are important details, for what people believe always reveals itself in the way they live and die. People will profess to believe certain things, but the way they live will often prove that they believe something else. Eventually, what people believe will be revealed in what they wear, how they educate their children, and how they bury their dead.

While there are a few exceptions in Scripture, the godly usually bury their dead in the ground. Many of the pagan tribes, including the Greeks and Romans, preferred cremation. But Christians bury their dead because they expect imminent resurrection. Throughout Scripture, we find at least eight resurrections (or temporary resuscitations). Then, there is the ultimate resurrection of our Lord Jesus Christ. As believers in the resurrection of Christ, we fully expect that there will be somebody walking in that body once again, and it may happen tomorrow! About 2,000 years ago, the bodies of the saints, "which were only sleeping," came out of their graves and appeared to many in the city of Jerusalem (Matt. 27:52). Such records come across as ridiculous to people who, for the last two hundred years, have been told that they are nothing but cosmic dust floating around in a material universe. They don't believe that anything supernatural could ever happen because they have inculcated a purely naturalistic, materialistic worldview. Of course, this is why we have seen a huge increase in the number of cremations since 1880.

Verses 14–21. With their father gone, Joseph's brothers were concerned that Joseph might take revenge on them for their wicked treatment of him years earlier. They sent a mediator, and then approached him themselves with their concerns. In true form of the greatest Forgiver of all—our Lord Jesus Christ—Joseph graciously offered his forgiveness to his brothers again.

Even as Joseph forgave his brothers, he refused to take the place of God, the only one to whom vengeance belongs. Whether God forgave them or not was outside of Joseph's purview, and those brothers still had to personally deal with God against whom they had sinned. At the most basic level, forgiveness is releasing the right to revenge. But within the family and the church, true forgiveness must also include the reconstruction of relationships. This is an ongoing process and it usually takes time. Clearly, Joseph was willing to engage this process of forgiveness by expressing willingness to nourish his brothers and their little ones. Yet, rebuilding relationships is a two-way street, and it is possible that his brothers had not done much to restore the relationship that had been so terribly damaged when they had sold Joseph into slavery.

Joseph also responds in verse 20 with a beautiful formulation of the doctrine of the sovereignty of God:

> *"But as for you, ye thought evil against me; but God meant it unto good, to bring to pass, as it is this day, to save much people alive."*

Did God fully intend for Joseph to be sold to slave traders and journey to Egypt? That is the plain meaning of Joseph's words here. In all of the actions taken by men, whether by individuals or human governments, Christians must always affirm double causality. That is, there are always at least two wills acting and two hearts engaged in any particular situation. There are also two motivations and two ends in view. The brothers wanted to get rid of their brother once and for all, but God wanted to save His people from the devastation of famine. The hearts of these brothers, overwhelmed by envy and sin, effected an action that enslaved their brother.. But there was another heart acting in this situation. God's motives played a part in the event in order to bring about something good. Thus, you should see that the problem of evil is answered when we can say that "God has a morally sufficient reason for the evil that exists in the world." In this case, He glorified Himself by saving His people from a severe famine. You may wonder why God brought a famine to the land, but of course, He had His reasons for this too. In humility, we must acknowledge that God has many reasons for what He purposes, and we are not privy to all of them. We must simply trust that God knows what He is doing.

Here is an Old Testament profession of Romans 8:28: "All things work together for good." In the final analysis, Christians should be the most hopeful, even as they must slog through the most difficult days of their lives. We may be subject to the most cruel tortures at the hands of men, but we can still receive these trials with hope and optimism, knowing that it is all still under the sovereign purposes of a God who makes all things work together for good.

Verses 22–26. Joseph himself died at 110 years of age. In his final words, he certified his own commitment to the covenant promises of God by requiring that his family promise to bury him in Canaan. In this way, Joseph carried on the heritage of the faith of his fathers, Abraham, Isaac, and Jacob. He died believing in the promises of God.

How does this passage teach us to walk with God in faith and obedience?

1. We honor our loved ones and demonstrate love and appreciation for them when we weep over their death. In the New Testament, we find Jesus weeping over the death of Lazarus, in love for His friend and in sympathy with the others weeping (John 11:35). Yet at the same time, we must be

careful not to give want to excessive sorrow. For if we cry too much over a death or other disappointment, we give way to hopelessness, and it may cross over to complaining against God.

2. Does life ever seem as if it is spinning out of control? Suppose that something terrible was to happen to you tomorrow afternoon. What if your mother or father was to die, or suppose that you were hit by a car. Would you be gripped by fear in such a situation, as if everything was spinning out of control? Joseph had a firm sense that God was in absolute control of everything that happened. Everything. It is safe to say that nothing will happen to you today that God does not fully intend to happen. If you love God, you must believe Romans 8:28. "All things work together for good to them that love God, to them who are the called according to His purpose."

Questions:

1. What are the themes of Chapters 1 through 50?

2. What are the biblical principles regarding the death and burial of a loved one?

3. Why is Joseph one of the best examples in the Bible of one who forgave others?

4. Both Joseph's brothers and God Himself were involved in the sale of Joseph to the slave traders. How did their heart motivations differ in this act? Did Joseph's brothers get what they wanted? Did God get what He wanted?

5. Why should we not be afraid when terrible things happen to us?

6. How did Joseph express his faith in God's promises before he died?

Family Discussion Questions:

1. How do we handle it when people sin against us? What if they repeatedly sin against us? Do we feel as if we must take vengeance against them? Are we willing to rebuild relationships as Joseph did with his brothers?

2. Do you believe that everything that will happen to you will happen for your good? As this only applies to those who love God, perhaps the more important question is—are you among those who love God and are called according to His purpose?

Appendix A

1 – *The Creation*

2 – *Man Created*

3 – *Man's Fall*

4 – *Cain's Line*

5 – *Seth's Line*

6 – *Flood Plans*

7 – *The Flood*

8 – *The Dove*

9 – *The Rainbow*

10 – *Noah's Line*

11 – *Shem's Line*

12 – *Abram Called*

13 – *Lot Chooses*

14 – *Lot Captured*

15 – *Covenant Confirmed*

16 – *Hagar's Son*

17 – *Covenant Sign*

18 – *Sarah Laughs*

19 – *Sodom Destroyed*

20 – *Abraham's Sister*

21 – *Isaac Born*

22 – *Isaac Sacrificed*

23 – *Sarah Buried*

24 – *Isaac's Wife*

25 – *Abraham's Line*

26 – *Isaac Blessed*

27 – *Jacob Blessed*

28 – *Jacob's Ladder*

29 – *Jacob Tricked*

30 – *Laban Tricked*

31 – *Jacob Flees*

32 – *Jacob Wrestles*

33 – *Jacob Returns*

34 – *Jacob's Daughter*

35 – *Jacob Worships*

36 – *Esau's Line*

37 – *Joseph Sold*

38 – *Judah's Sin*

39 – *Joseph Tempted*

40 – *Joseph Imprisoned*

41 – *Joseph Promoted*

42 – *Joseph's Brothers*

43 – *Joseph's Feast*

44 – *Joseph's Cup*

45 – *Joseph Revealed*

46 – *Jacob's Line*

47 – *Jacob's Request*

48 – *Jacob's Adoptions*

49 – *Jacob's Prophecy*

50 – *Jacob's Burial*

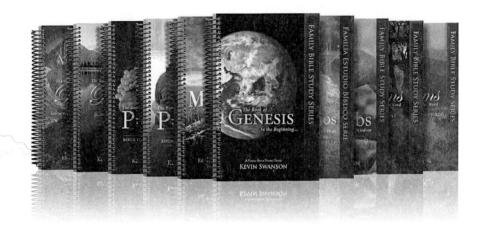

To order other Family Bible Study Guides:
Order online at: *generations.org*
Send us an email at: *mail@generations.org*
Or give us a call at: *888-389-9080*

....

The Bible is the Core Curriculum in the education of a child. If we provide our children excellent academic instruction in mathematics, science, and grammar, but neglect to teach them Genesis, Psalms, Proverbs, and the Gospels, we have failed in the education of our children.